PSYCHOLOGY LIBRARY EDITIONS:
MEMORY

Volume 16

RETRIEVAL AND ORGANIZATIONAL STRATEGIES IN CONCEPTUAL MEMORY

RETRIEVAL AND ORGANIZATIONAL STRATEGIES IN CONCEPTUAL MEMORY

A Computer Model

JANET L. KOLODNER

Psychology Press
Taylor & Francis Group
LONDON AND NEW YORK

First published in 1984

This edition first published in 2014
by Psychology Press
27 Church Road, Hove BN3 2FA

and by Psychology Press
711 Third Avenue, New York, NY 10017

Psychology Press is an imprint of the Taylor & Francis Group, an informa business

British Library Cataloguing in Publication Data
A catalogue record for this book is available from the British Library

ISBN: 978-1-84872-321-4 (Set)
eISBN: 978-1-315-77503-6 (Set)
ISBN: 978-1-84872-411-2 (Volume 16)
eISBN: 978-1-315-77493-0 (Volume 16)

Publisher's Note
The publisher has gone to great lengths to ensure the quality of this book but points out that some imperfections from the original may be apparent.

Disclaimer
The publisher has made every effort to trace copyright holders and would welcome correspondence from those they have been unable to trace.

Retrieval and Organizational Strategies in Conceptual Memory: A Computer Model

Janet L. Kolodner
School of Information and Computer Science
Georgia Institute of Technology

1984
LAWRENCE ERLBAUM ASSOCIATES, PUBLISHERS
Hillsdale, New Jersey London

Lawrence Erlbaum Associates, Inc., Publishers
365 Broadway
Hillsdale, New Jersey 07642

Library of Congress Cataloging in Publication Data

Kolodner, Janet L.
Retrieval and organizational strategies in conceptual memory.

(Artificial intelligence series)
Bibliography: p.
Includes index.
1. Memory—Data processing. 2. Recollection (Psychology)—Data processing. I. Title. II. Series: Artificial intelligence series (Hillsdale, N.J.)
BF371.K65 1984 001.53′5 83-25387
ISBN 0-89859-365-4
Printed in the United States of America
10 9 8 7 6 5 4 3 2 1

To Mike

CONTENTS

PREFACE xi

PART I: INTRODUCTION

1. **The Nature of a Long-Term Memory for Events** 3
   - Getting Started 3
   - The Reconstructive Nature of Human Memory 5
   - Memory Organization for Reconstructive Retrieval 6
   - Constraining Memory Search 12
   - Maintaining Memory Organization 18
   - CYRUS 19
   - Our Goals 22
   - Using People as a Model 23
   - Cyrus as a Psychological Model 25
   - Summary 27

2. **Background and Motivation** 28
   - Memory and Understanding 28
   - Conceptual Memory 29
   - Conceptual Dependency 33
   - Relating Events to Events 36
   - Situational Context 37
   - E-MOPs and Memory Organization 37
   - Episodic Versus Semantic Memory 47
   - Question Answering 48
   - Summary 50

PART II: RETRIEVAL STRATEGIES

3. **Traversal and Elaboration** 55
Retrieving an Event from an E-MOP 55
The Need for Elaboration 59
Elaboration in Human Protocols 67
Implications of Traversal/Elaboration 68
Summary 74

4. **Instantiation Strategies** 75
Introduction 75
Elaborating Components of Events 76
Enumeration Strategies and Maps 83
Instantiating Events from Events 85
Summary 94

5. **Choosing a Context for Search** 95
Introduction 95
Context Construction 95
Component-to-Context Instantiation Strategies 97
Memory Organization for Context Construction 103
Human Protocols and Context Construction 107
Implications of Context Construction 108
Summary 109

6. **Alternate-Context Search** 110
Introduction 110
Alternate-Context Search 111
When is Alternate-Context Search Useful? 130
Human Protocols and Alternate Context Search 131
Implications of Executive Strategies 132
Summary 135

PART III: MAINTAINING MEMORY ORGANIZATION

7. **Automatic Index Selection** 141
Introduction 141
Why Index by Differences? 142
What is a Difference from a Norm? 144
What Makes a Good Index? 146
Choosing Indices 150
Classifying E-MOPs to Guide Indexing 153
Summary of Indexing 163

8. **Generalization and Memory Reorganization** 165
Introduction 165
Adding a New Event to an E-MOP 165
Generalization 172
How CYRUS' Memory Grows 182
Further Implications of Memory Reorganization—Forgetting 189
Summary 190

PART IV: STATE OF THE PROGRAM, STATE OF THE ART

9. **How CYRUS Works** 194
Introduction 194
CYRUS' E-MOPS 194
Retrieval in CYRUS 198
Memory Update in CYRUS 207
A Vance Example 213
A Muskie Example 218
Differences Between the Vance and Muskie Memories 221
Summary 226

10. **Discussion, Perspective, Conclusions** 227
Introduction 227
How CYRUS Fits in With Other Research 227
Conclusions 237
Where Do We Go from Here? 247
Summary 250

REFERENCES 251

AUTHOR INDEX 255

SUBJECT INDEX 257

PREFACE

Someday we expect that computers will be able to keep us informed about the news. People have imagined being able to ask their home computers questions such as "What's going on in the world?" or "How long has the Arab Israeli conflict been going on?" or "Where is the President today?" In order to answer questions such as these, computers must have the capability of remembering events. Remembering involves finding requested information in memory. Thus, it requires processes both for memory search and for organizing information in memory so that it can be found easily. This book presents a theory of remembering that begins to address many of the hard problems implicated in the quest to make computers remember. It also presents a computer program called CYRUS which stores day-to-day events from the lives of former U.S. Secretaries of State Cyrus Vance and Edmund Muskie, and answers questions posed in English about the two men. Many of the events it answers questions about were extracted automatically (i.e., by computer) from English-language news stores. Thus, we present a first step toward the development of computer systems that can keep us informed.

In developing the computer system, it was necessary to first derive a theory of remembering to base it on. This was a hard problem, since there was no theory that could be taken off the shelf and implemented on the computer. Computer scientists have been working on means of storing and retrieving information from the computer. Psychologists have long been interested in how people remember. Yet neither of these disciplines provides a theory comprehensive enough to deal with organization and retrieval of day-to-day events.

So where did we begin? Our starting point was to derive a theory of remembering based on the way people do it. People remember past experiences many times in the course of a normal day. How do they do it? Again, we were faced with a hard problem, since people are largely unaware of the processes they use to remember. We therefore asked people questions that required them to search their memories extensively. We asked them to report what they thought about in deriving their answers. It was not the answers that we cared about, but rather the train of thought that produced the answers. Based on what we observed people doing, we began to derive a theory of reconstructive retrieval. Our next step was to implement that theory on the computer. Using the computer as an experimental tool, and taking new protocols from people as new questions arose, we both expanded the initial theory and refined it to produce a comprehensive theory of reconstructive memory. What makes it comprehensive is that it considers memory organization (storage), retrieval, and integration of new items into memory (encoding) as problems that cannot be separated from each other, and explains all three taking the others into account.

Thus, the theory of remembering that we present is a theory of human information processing. Using the computer as a tool, we have been able to produce a theory that provides novel answers to many of the questions psychologists traditionally ask. It can be differentiated from psychological theories in two ways. First, it is a process model: a process of remembering is presented. Second, it provides detail and rigor that psychological models do not usually have. Particular strategies for organization and retrieval, particular structures for organizing memory and storing knowledge and events, and particular knowledge necessary for remembering are presented. Using the computer as an experimental tool has not only allowed such detail and rigor, but has also required it.

We thus have two purposes in presenting our theory of remembering. First, it can be used in implementing intelligent computer systems. This includes fact retrieval systems, but also includes intelligent systems in general. Any intelligent program needs to store and use a great deal of knowledge. The strategies and structures presented here were designed to be used for that purpose. Second, the theory attempts to explain how people's memories work, and makes predictions about the organization of human memory.

We expect, then, that this book will be read by three different groups of people—computer scientists interested in making computers store and retrieve relatively unconstrained information, AI researchers interested in defining large memories for their intelligent programs, and psychologists interested in human memory. Since the interests of the three groups may be divergent, we provide a guide to the book that may make it easier for readers to find their way around in it.

This book is divided into four major parts—introduction, retrieval, memory organization and maintenance, and summary. Chapters 1 and 2 are the introductory chapters. Chapter 1 introduces the problems involved in constructing a theory of remembering and gives the flavor of the solutions. Chapter 2 gives a short history of Natural Language Processing and the background about question answering, memory representations, and memory organization necessary to understand the technical details of this report.

The retrieval section includes chapters 3 through 6. The introduction to that section summarizes the problems that are involved in retrieval. Some of those include choosing a context or category for search, elaborating on a given retrieval specification, and guiding search for items different than but related to the one originally requested. The chapters in the section address those problems in detail. In each of the chapters, conclusions are drawn concerning the kinds of knowledge that must be resident in memory.

The third section of the book concerns memory update, or the integration of new items into memory. Such integration requires the assimilation of new items into the already-existing memory structures along with accommodation of the existing structures to include the new item. Accommodation of the existing structures includes generation of the knowledge needed by retrieval strategies to search the structures. Chapters 7 and 8 address those issues.

The last section is a summary of the state of the art and frontiers of research. Chapter 9 presents CYRUS in detail, describing where the retrieval and organizational strategies presented fit into the implementation. That chapter also presents aspects of CYRUS' implementation that have not been explained in previous chapters. Chapter 10 presents a literature review, comparing this work to related research in the fields of psychology, artificial intelligence, data base management, and information retrieval. It also presents conclusions about memory organization and retrieval processes, from the point of view of intelligent information retrieval, and from a psychological point of view. In that chapter, limitations of this theory and areas for future related research are also explained.

At the end of each chapter is a summary of the major points made in the chapter. Readers trying to decide whether or not to read a particular chapter may want to read its introduction and summary first. Chapters 1 and 2 provide background for reading other chapters of the book. Chapter 9 explains the implementation of the memory processes and how they are integrated into the computer program. It will be useful to readers interested in the program itself.

The research presented in this book was done while I was a graduate student in the Department of Computer Science at Yale University and a member of the Yale Artificial Intelligence Project. Like most research endeavors, the work presented in this book was not done in a vacuum. My thesis advisor, Roger Schank, taught me what I know about doing AI research. He was and remains a great source of inspiration. Drew McDermott and Chris Riesbeck read earlier forms of this manuscript and made invaluable comments concerning its content and style. Bob Abelson and John Black provided pointers to the relevant psychological literature. I am also grateful to Wendy Lehnert, Michael Dyer, Mike Lebowitz, Larry Birnbaum, and Ann Drinan for many stimulating discussions while I was a student. Special thanks to all of the other members of the Yale AI Project who made it an exciting and friendly place to be.

Since finishing the initial version of this book (i.e., my thesis), my understanding of the relevance of this work to psychology has increased immeasurably, largely due to the input of Gordon Bower, Mike Williams, and Larry Barsalou. Jean Early has provided considerable help in preparing the manuscript.

Though almost all of the programming of CYRUS' memory and strategies was done by me, a number of people at the Yale AI Project worked on programming many of CYRUS' auxiliary parts. Those people include Martin Korsin, Rod McGuire, CJ Yang, Alan Cypher, Tim Scerba, Warren Odom, Natalie Dehn, Steve Lytinen, Nat Mishkin, and John McCreery. The interface between CYRUS and FRUMP could not have been done without Jerry DeJong's help as a consultant, nor could the question parser have been done without Larry Birnbaum's expert advice.

Michael Klein, my husband, has provided considerable moral support, putting up with all of my doubts and frustrations, and making my life a pleasant one to live.

This work was supported in part by the Advanced Research Projects Agency of the Department of Defense and monitored under the Office of Naval Research under contract N00014–75-C-1111, and in part by the National Science Foundation under contract IST-7918463 while I was a graduate student at Yale. Since leaving Yale, it has been supported in part by the National Science Foundation under contract IST-8116892. Figures were prepared on a Xerox STAR.

I INTRODUCTION

1 The Nature of a Long-Term Memory for Events

1. GETTING STARTED

There are many manifestations of memory use in our everyday life. When someone asks us a question, and we attempt to answer it, it is quite obvious that we are remembering something. When we are "reminded" of something that happened previously, it is also obvious that memory is involved. But in many of the other tasks we do each day, we are not cognizant of the fact that memory is necessary to the task. In order to perform even the simplest task, such as mailing a letter, for example, it is necessary to remember the procedure for doing the task. When we empathize with another person's problems because we have had similar problems, we are remembering our own previous experiences. When we understand more of a story than is told to us, we are using our memories to fill in the details. When we walk to the right place at the end of the day to get into the car, we are remembering, whether consciously or unconsciously, where the car was parked in the morning.

One prerequisite to achieving intelligence in computer systems is to give them memories with many of the capabilities people have. For intelligent fact retrieval, memory is especially important. Consider, for example, the following hypothetical situation involving the computer:

****

You haven't been keeping up with the news lately, and you are concerned about developments in the Middle East. You know that the secretary of state went on a trip to the Middle East recently. You want to find out what he discussed during that trip and what was accomplished. Instead of leafing through two weeks worth of newspapers, you walk up to the computer terminal at the library and have the following conversation:

>When did Cyrus Vance return from the Middle East?

LAST NIGHT.

>Which heads of state did he talk to there?

MENACHIM BEGIN OF ISRAEL, ANWAR SADAT OF EGYPT, KING HUSSEIN OF JORDAN, AND KING KHALAD OF SAUDI ARABIA.

>Did he talk to President Assad of Syria?

NO.

>...

****

Although the situation above is hypothetical, the computer program illustrated and the dialog with that program are real. The dialog is with CYRUS (Computerized Yale Retrieval and Updating System), a computer program that stores episodes from the lives of former Secretaries of State Cyrus Vance and Edmund Muskie, and later retrieves those episodes to answer questions posed to it in English. Although CYRUS itself was designed to store information about important people, we can imagine CYRUS embedded in a larger system capable of storing a wide range of current events. Such a system would be useful to people who haven't been keeping up with the news and want to catch up quickly or learn about some event in detail, to reporters who need to find background information for a new story, or to school children as interactive encyclopedias. On a very practical level, it would be useful to newspapers, which already maintain huge files containing biographies of famous people. One can easily imagine other uses for computer memories capable of natural language interaction.

Any system that keeps track of even a subset of current events will be very large, maintaining data bases of many hundreds of thousands or millions of events. In a system that large, it is important to organize the data so that only relevant records are searched, and so that the number of relevant records to be examined at any time is as small as possible. In a system that keeps track of current events, the memory will constantly be changing. As new events happen, they must be added to the memory. As memory grows, it is imperative that good organization be maintained: otherwise, the initially well-organized system will be useless after many additions.

How can we achieve such results? The algorithms and structures a memory must have are not at all obvious. While we want the computer to perform like a person, it is difficult to discover the way people remember. People effortlessly recall past events and episodes, yet they are largely unaware of the cognitive processes they use in remembering. Since it is usually an unconscious process, it is hard to monitor the human retrieval process to see how it is actually done. We do know, however, that in people memory is a cognitive process that operates on concepts present in memory. We must therefore describe memory in terms of processes that work on conceptual information.

This book reports the results of research aimed at constructing a theory of long-term event memory. A process model of long-term memory is presented as a theory of conceptual information processing. Because people are good conceptual information processors, we turn to people as an available example of the intelligent processes we are trying to explain.

There are three questions that must be answered in addressing this problem:

1. What processes are implicated in retrieving events from memory?
2. What kind of memory organization do the retrieval processes imply?
3. What are the processes for adding new events to memory—how can good memory organization be maintained and how does memory organization change as new events are added?

These questions cannot be answered independently of each other. The organization of memory places constraints on the types of retrieval and updating processes memory must use. On the other hand, memory organization, and therefore procedures for adding information to memory, must be designed with retrieval requirements in mind.

The remainder of this chapter presents an overview of some of the problems involved in retrieving events from memory and some of the requirements the retrieval process places on memory's organization. We do that by looking at examples. We also discover some of the capabilities and limitations of human memory. In so doing, we discover the requirements of a computer program that "remembers" and motivate many of our design decisions. An overview of CYRUS, a computer program that implements the theory, is also presented.

2. THE RECONSTRUCTIVE NATURE OF HUMAN MEMORY

For the most part, people are expert at recalling information about their pasts. When people try to retrieve information about a particular episode in their lives, however, they often find they don't have the entire episode immediately available. In that case, they attempt to *reconstruct* the rest of the episode. When asked to recall a recent trip, one person started his reconstruction as follows:

> Let me see. When we got there, we must have had to find a hotel. Yes, I remember, we had a guidebook with a lot of hotels in it, and we called a few of them until we found one with a vacancy. It was late afternoon, so we must have gone out to eat soon after that.[1]

[1]Unless stated otherwise, all protocols are real and were collected from colleagues and acquaintances at the time this study was taking place.

Clearly, the trip was not stored in memory in one large chunk. Instead, it must have been stored in bits and pieces requiring reconstruction to put them back together. Such reconstruction can happen through application of generalized knowledge. In the protocol above, the knowledge that "one must have a hotel to stay in during a trip" and "usually after arrival, the next step of a trip is to check in at the hotel" allowed "finding a hotel" to be recalled.

The process seems to involve building a description of "what must have happened" and then filling it out with "actual" details. We can thus conclude the following about human memory for events:

Memory Principle #1
Human remembering is often a process of reconstructing what must have happened rather than directly retrieving what did happen.

This process of *reconstruction* is almost always used by people trying to remember episodes, as evidenced by the fact that people tend to "remember" details incorrectly so often. In fact, retrieval confusions and false recall must be inherent to a process that produces probable rather than actual explanations. We see later why we might want to give this capability to the computer despite the fact that it often produces errors in details.

3. MEMORY ORGANIZATION FOR RECONSTRUCTIVE RETRIEVAL

In discovering a memory organization for reconstructive memory, we must find one that not only supports such retrieval, but also *requires* it. To begin addressing that issue, consider the following hypothetical dialog:

Q: Have you been to Saudi Arabia recently?

A: Yes, most recently last month, to discuss the Camp David Accords with King Khaled and Prince Fahd.

Q: Where did you go afterwards?

A: To Syria. I was touring the Middle East talking to each of the Arab leaders about the Accords.

The answers given in this dialog would have been reasonable ones for Cyrus Vance to give while he was secretary of state. During the 4 years he was in office, however, he went on hundreds of trips, among many other memorable activities. How could he choose the correct ones from memory to answer specific questions? If memory were arranged in lists, then we could imagine a process that searched down an appropriate list until the correct episode was found. This seems unreasonable, however, for a memory with hundreds or thousands of events of the same type: Searching down a long list is a slow process that becomes slower as additional items are added to the list. People's memories do not slow down as they learn more.

Furthermore, if people searched down long lists in their memories to retrieve events, then it would be easy for them to enumerate experiences of particular types. For instance, a question such as the following would be easy to answer:

(Q1): Recall all the times you have been to museums.

This question, however, is not easy for people to answer, as suggested by the following protocol:

> I know I've been to a lot of museums in Europe. I've been to England, and I went to a number of museums there—some in London—the British Museum, the National Gallery, and a few smaller galleries. . . . I was at a museum in Brighton—the Royal Pavilion. I've been to museums in Paris—the Louvre and some smaller ones. In Rome, I've been to. . . . In Naples, to. . . . In Florence, to. . . .

The lists of experiences people enumerate are constructed on the fly as they are answering a question. In the protocol above, the person tried to recall "experiences in museums," "experiences in museums in Europe," "experiences in museums in England," "experiences in museums in London," and so on, filling in (or reconstructing) additional details with each iteration. Generalizing from that, we can make the following hypothesis:

Memory Principle #2
Remembering requires progressive narrowing in on a description of the event to be remembered.

We can describe that process as a process of specifying details that can differentiate the targeted event from other events in memory.

The protocol above and others like it suggest that narrowing the description of a sought event, or focusing in on an event by providing more detail, is a *necessary* part of remembering (Williams, 1978). Thus, we can state the following principle of memory retrieval:

Memory Principle #3
In a reconstructive memory, memories are not directly enumerable. Instead, the features that describe individual memories must be reconstructed.[2]

---

[2]Of course, there must be a capability for doing some types of enumeration. People remember short lists, for example, such as the 12 months of the year. Our thesis is that these lists are either committed to memory or derived from a well-structured concept which serves as a map or chart. People report generating the list of 50 states, for example, by mentally walking around a map of the United States. Such enumeration is discussed in chapter 4, section 3.

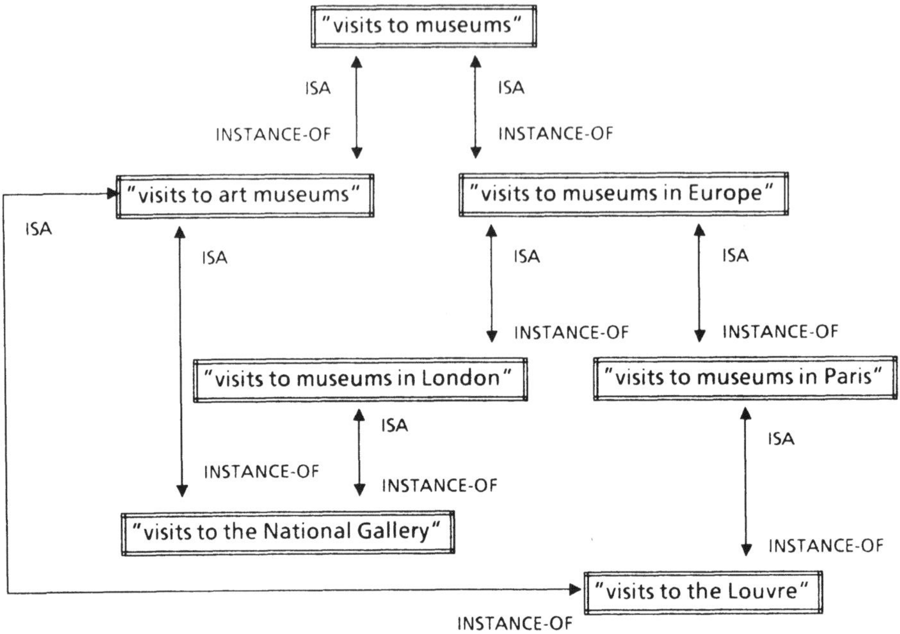

FIG. 1.1. A Conceptual Hierarchy.

What kind of memory organization would make such a retrieval process necessary? One thing we know about human memory is that it is organized around concepts. Since a "visit to the National Gallery" and a "visit to the Louvre" are closely related concepts, we can imagine that they are organized in memory in close proximity to each other. Since both are "visits to museums," both must be intimately related to that concept. We would expect the memory organization to reflect this proximity in a way similar to that illustrated in Fig. 1.1.

In this organizational structure, similar concepts are placed in close proximity to each other in a semantic network. The links are bi-directional and form an inheritance or ISA hierarchy. Each concept points back to the concepts it is an instance of (through ISA links) and forward to all of its example concepts (through INSTANCE-OF links). Nodes in the network can be described in terms of the more general concepts they are instances of. Using this network, we can describe the "visit to the Louvre" as a "visit to a museum in Paris" and a "visit to an art museum." The graph can also be traversed downward by following INSTANCE-OF links. Starting from "visits to museums in Europe," "visits to museums in London" and "visits to museums in Paris" can be retrieved.

Although this network both organizes similar concepts in proximity to each other and allows traversal from more general to more specific concepts, it has a major flaw: it allows too much. In an organization such as this, there would never be any possibility of forgetting, a phenomenon frequently observed in humans. Nor does it explain false starts such as the following:

> Was I in a museum in Oxford? No, I was only there for a couple hours, and I only had time to see the outsides of the buildings.

In this fragment, the answerer has attempted a reconstruction of a possible museum visit by considering a "museum visit in Oxford." However, after further reasoning, he decides that this event never happened. In a fully enumerable memory, this phenomenon would not occur. Reconstructive specification of details would not be necessary if arcs were all labeled by ISA and INSTANCE-OF. All examples could be retrieved and checked without guessing at details. No contrafactual episodes would be considered, and no false starts would be observed.[3]

While we do see false starts and forgetting in people, it may seem strange to require such behavior from a computer memory. Computers, after all, have large memories and never need to forget. Or do they? The major problem in a computer program with a memory organization like the one in Fig. 1.1 is control of memory search. If all instances of a concept were related through INSTANCE-OF links, then all examples of any concept could always be enumerated. While this would not be a problem if a concept had only a few instances, consider the implications of this organization in a memory where each concept had hundreds or thousands of instances. To find any particular instance, all instances would have to be enumerated and the correct one chosen from those. This, in fact, is equivalent to sequential search of a list, which we have already said is undesirable: memory slows down with each new addition.

The major reason for problems in the structure illustrated above is that the relations represented by its arcs are inadequate. In order to control search, the relationships in a conceptual network must be more sophisticated than INSTANCE-OF and ISA links. We can figure out what the relations represented by the arcs should be by looking again at the observed retrieval process. Reconstructive retrieval is a process of building up a plausible description of the target item. One step of the process involves narrowing a broad concept that describes too many similar items by specifying additional features. After the concept is narrowed to describe only one item, that item can be found in memory. The arcs,

---

[3]Note that if we had a strength associated with each arc in the network above, and thresholds for cut-off or output interference, then we would get a memory that forgets and that cannot enumerate. While reconstructive retrieval strategies could be laid on top of such a structure, the structure itself would not provide enough information to guide and control reconstruction. We shall see that the memory structure to be proposed can actually aid the reconstructive process.

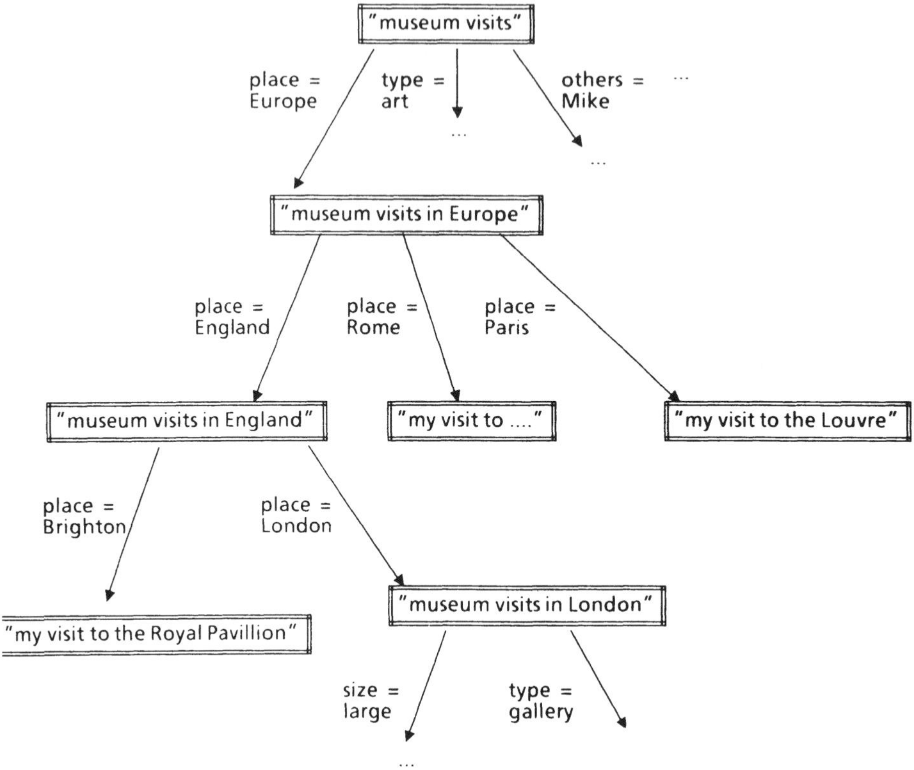

FIG. 1.2. Museum Visits.

then, should represent features of items organized by a particular concept. Specification of one of these features will allow traversal of the corresponding arc, arriving in memory at a more specific concept. Part of the memory structure implied by the protocols above is exhibited in Fig. 1.2.

The arcs are labeled by features of the concepts they point to, and thereby serve to *differentiate* those items from other similar items. Thus, the observed retrieval process implies a memory organization with the following feature:

Memory Principle #4

Similar items in memory are organized around the same concept according to their differentiating features.

We must put two additional restrictions on this organization. First, its arcs must not be enumerable. If they were, then so would all of the associated nodes. This restriction also explains the false-start fragment above where the person was wondering if he had been to a museum in Oxford. If arcs are not enumerable, then their labels must be reconstructed during retrieval. Reconstruction can produce descriptions of events that are not in memory.

The second restriction follows from the first. Arcs may be traversed only if their labels have been specified. Such an organization will prohibit enumeration, but will allow directed traversal through memory. Intuitively, we can think of these structures as "locked conceptual networks." The arcs can be thought of as locks that can only be opened (and thus traversed) if the correct key is available to open them (i.e., if the label on the arc can be specified). In this way, each concept organizes all of the concepts related to it, but obtaining any of these related concepts requires specifying the feature designated as its path "lock" or key.

Such an organization accounts for some of the reconstructive memory phenomena we observe in people. But why use such a restrictive memory organization in a computer system? While it may seem that a locked network requires more work for retrieval, the alternatives require enumerating, and therefore examining, many more items. In a large memory, directed retrieval is preferable to enumeration. A locked memory structure is oriented toward a directed retrieval process involving incremental specification of possible features of items to be retrieved. Instead of examining a large number of items, extra effort is made to direct search to a small number of the most relevant items. Reconstruction is a method of directing search to only relevant items in memory.

3.1. E-MOPs

We are now ready to introduce the basic structures organizing events in our memory model. We refer to these structures as Episodic Memory Organization Packets (E-MOPs). E-MOPs correspond to concepts in memory that index or organize other concepts and events in a manner consistent with the memory principles introduced above. Labels of arcs in an E-MOP are called its *indices* and are said to *index* the items organized by an E-MOP (i.e., events). When an event is entered into one of these structures, the features that differentiate it from other items in the E-MOP are extracted and used to index it in the E-MOP. To retrieve events from an E-MOP, features of a targeted event are specified, the corresponding arcs are traversed, and the concepts indexed by the specified features are retrieved.

The E-MOPs implicitly and explicitly referred to in the examples above were "museum visits," "trips," "finding a hotel," "diplomatic trips," and "diplomatic meetings." In general, we can expect an event memory to have E-MOPs for each major type of event it knows about. Thus, E-MOPs for day-to-day events might include "getting up in the morning," "eating in a restaurant," "going to the movies," "driving to the office," and so forth. Memory for a diplomat will also include E-MOPs for "diplomatic trips," "diplomatic meetings," "negotiations," "speeches," and other diplomatic activities. The E-

MOPs necessary to organize events in the life of a particular person will depend on that person's activities and experiences. No matter what type of experiences it is organizing, however, each E-MOP will organize its events according to their differentiating features.

E-MOPs can be thought of as conceptual categories and will often be referred to in that way. It must be pointed out, however, that they are not categories in the conventional sense of the word. Although they organize similar concepts, their members cannot be enumerated. E-MOPs are introduced in more detail in the next chapter and are further explained throughout this report.

4. CONSTRAINING MEMORY SEARCH

In a memory with the organization just described, retrieval consists of choosing an E-MOP for retrieval, specifying features of the event to be retrieved from the E-MOP, and traversing indices corresponding to those features. There are a number of issues relevant to directed retrieval, which are manifested in this retrieval method. In the next sections, we present some of those problems, along with some examples of the way people deal with them, and suggestions about how we can make computers cope with them.

4.1. Choosing a Category for Search

In order to search a memory organized around conceptual categories, the category or categories to be searched must first be specified. Consider, for example, the following question:

(Q2): Mr. Vance, when was the last time you saw an oil field in the Middle East?

If "seeing oil fields" were one of memory's categories or E-MOPs, then this question would be fairly easy to answer. "Seeing oil fields" would be selected for search. If it indexed an episode in the Middle East, that episode could be retrieved from it. Similarly, if "seeing objects" were a memory category, it could be selected as a category for retrieval, and events in the Middle East and at oil fields could be retrieved from it.

Suppose, however, that neither of these categories existed in the memory being searched. In that case, an E-MOP for search would have to be chosen. We can imagine that the following reasoning process might take place during the process of answering (Q2):

A1: An oil field is a large site. Perhaps I saw an oil field during a *sightseeing* episode in the Middle East.

If one used information about episodic contexts associated with "large sites," a "sightseeing" category could be chosen for retrieval. Its contents could be searched for an episode at oil fields in the Middle East. If episodes in the sightseeing category were organized by the type of site and part of the world where they took place, and if there had been an episode in the Middle East at an oil field, then "a sightseeing episode at an oil field in the Middle East" could be retrieved.

The need to choose a category for search is common to both artificially constructed data bases and human memory. In a complex data base, such as one that stores many different kinds of events, we cannot expect a user to know all of memory's categories. Nor can we expect that every natural language query asked of a data base will specify a category or record type for search. The retrieval processes must therefore be prepared to generate categories for retrieval. To see that this process also occurs in human memory access, consider this question and a typical response:

(Q3): Who is the most famous person you have ever met?

The following protocol is typical of the answers to this question:

> First I thought how somebody could be famous, and politics was the first thing I thought of. Then I thought about circumstances where I could have met a famous politician. I searched for political experiences I have had—mostly political rallies I participated in and experiences campaigning for candidates. I remembered that I had met McGovern. But since you said "most famous," I went on to think of other famous people I might have met. Next I thought of entertainers, and how I could have met them. I remembered going backstage a few times after seeing shows, but I couldn't remember who I had met. I started going through TV programs and the entertainers on those programs. I couldn't think of meeting any of those. Then I thought of famous scientists, and where I could have met them.

The diverse kinds of situations recalled in answering this question suggest that this person had no conceptual category (E-MOP) for "meeting famous people." Rather, he seemed to use knowledge about "famous people" to choose types of situations in which he could have met one. Using that information, he was able to direct search for episodes where he might have met politicians, entertainers, and scientists. His knowledge about politicians directed his search toward political rallies and campaigns where he could have met politicians. His knowledge about actors directed the search toward times he had been backstage after a show.

To find out how search can be directed toward the right kinds of situations, consider the inferential knowledge that must be present in memory to direct search in the protocol above:

1. Politicians take part in political rallies.
2. Politicians take part in political campaigns.

3. Actors perform in theaters.
4. After shows, actors are backstage at theaters.
5. Actors perform in TV shows.

Each of these statements associates a class of people (e.g., politicians, actors) with a type of situation (e.g., political rallies, going to the theater). If each item in memory describes the event contexts in which it normally occurs, then appropriate categories for search can be chosen by selecting from the concepts associated with event components specified in or inferred from a question.

Memory Principle #5
Retrieval from memory requires knowledge about the contexts associated with target items.

If this is so, then memory search can be constrained and directed only to relevant categories. A conceptual category chosen for retrieval provides a context for search. ''Political rallies'' can be chosen as a context for search because they are associated with ''politicians,'' one kind of famous person. ''Sightseeing'' can be chosen as a context for ''seeing oil fields'' if ''oil fields'' are defined as a ''large site'' and if ''large sites'' are associated with ''sightseeing.'' The strategies for choosing contexts for retrieval are called *component-to-context instantiation strategies*. They are discussed in chapter 5.

4.2. Choosing Category Indices During Retrieval

Searching for an event in a conceptual category requires specifying its features. Indices corresponding to those features become ''unlocked,'' and corresponding events can be found. Features specified in a question, however, might not correspond to features indexed in memory. Just as we cannot expect a user of a computer system to know all of the categories represented in the computer memory, neither can we expect him to know another memory's indexing scheme, whether it is an artificial computer memory or a natural human memory. We must therefore look for some means of automatically deriving features that are indexed in memory from others a question might specify.

Consider again, the question above:

(Q4): Mr. Vance, when was the last time you saw an oil field in the Middle East?

We mentioned earlier that if a ''sightseeing'' E-MOP organized its episodes according to their geographical location or the type of site, then this question would be easy to answer. Suppose, however, that our ''sightseeing'' category does not organize its episodes by either of those features. In that case, the following *elaboration* of the event sought in the question might be appropriate to answer the question:

A2: Which countries in the Middle East have oil fields? Iran and Iraq have oil fields, and so does Saudi Arabia. Have I seen an oil field in any of those places?

If sightseeing episodes are organized by country, then elaborating on "the Middle East" and specifying particular countries in that area of the world would enable retrieval of sightseeing episodes that took place in each of those places. Instead of searching for "sightseeing at an oil field in the Middle East," one could search for each of the more specific episodes, i.e., "sightseeing at an oil field in Iran" or "sightseeing at an oil field in Iraq." This process of transforming given features into features that might be indexed is called *index fitting*. Since the values of indices are not enumerable, this process is actually one of elaborating plausible features of sought items in the hope that one of these will be an index and "unlock" the network. Index fitting allows *downward traversal* in memory's networks to find nodes representing more specific concepts.

Elaboration is also necessary when a target concept describes too many items in memory. In that case, plausible features of the targeted concept can be generated, differentiating different instances of it and allowing further downward traversal of memory's networks. This elaboration process is called *plausible-index generation*. Consider, for example, a previous example (repeated below) of a person recalling museums he had visited:

> I know I've been to a lot of museums in Europe. I've been to England, and I went to a number of museums there—some in London—the British Museum, the National Gallery, and a few smaller galleries. . . . I was at a museum in Brighton—the Royal Pavilion. I've been to museums in Paris—the Louvre and some smaller ones. In Rome, I've been to. . . . In Naples, to. . . . In Florence, to. . . .

We observed that this person was trying to better specify or elaborate his descriptions of museum visits so that he could remember them one at a time. We can now further explain that phenomenon as a process of generating the keys for downward traversal of the memory structures. Elaboration through index fitting and plausible-index generation is discussed in more detail in chapters 3 and 4. The retrieval strategies used for elaboration are called *instantiation strategies*.

4.3. Searching for Something Other Than What Was Asked for

One of the observations we can make from the protocols above is the following:

Memory Principle #6

Retrieval often requires search for something other than what was requested.

Two reasons why it is often necessary to search for something other than what was requested are that (1) a category for search might not be specified in a question, and (2) a given specification might be insufficient for retrieval. In the second case, the given context is elaborated and a better specified context is searched for. Elaboration of plausible features is not always successful, however. Unsuccessful elaboration is a third reason for searching for something other than what was requested.

Consider, again, our sightseeing example from the previous section. Suppose that there were not enough information available to choose indices for traversal. In a memory where contextually related records refer to each other, another way to find a sought event is to search for events it might have been related to. Another related event might be more easily retrieved and, if found, might refer to the targeted event. Since any sightseeing episode in the Middle East must have happened during a trip to the Middle East, the following reasoning would also be appropriate to recall "sightseeing episodes in the Middle East."

A3: In order to go sightseeing in the Middle East, I would have had to have been on a trip there. On a vacation trip, I wouldn't go to see oil fields, so I must have been taken to oil fields during a diplomatic trip to the Middle East. Which countries might have taken me to see their oil fields? Saudi Arabia has the largest fields, perhaps they took me to see them. Yes, they did when I was there last year.

Search of this kind is quite often done by people, as shown in the following example of a person naming the museums he had been to:

> Let me see. . . . What other museums have I been to? The last time I was in England, I went to a bunch of museums in London—the British Museum, some gallery whose name I can't remember, and Mme. Taussaud's Wax Museum. And I also went to some palaces there that were museums—the Royal Pavilion in Brighton and some other palace in London, um, . . . it was called Hampton Court. When I went on my first trip to France. . . . I once went on a trip around New York State, and I went to the photography museum in Rochester and the Corning Glass Museum. During my trip to California, . . .

In each of these examples, we see search for a different kind of event than the one originally asked for. To find sightseeing experiences in A3, we see search for diplomatic trips during which the sightseeing might have taken place. In the human protocol, we see the person recalling trips to remember museum visits. Searching for a different type of event than the one targeted for retrieval is called *alternate context search*. Once a related event is retrieved, it can provide cues to use in reconstructing the originally targeted event. Features of a trip to England, for example, can be useful in filling in details of museum visits experienced

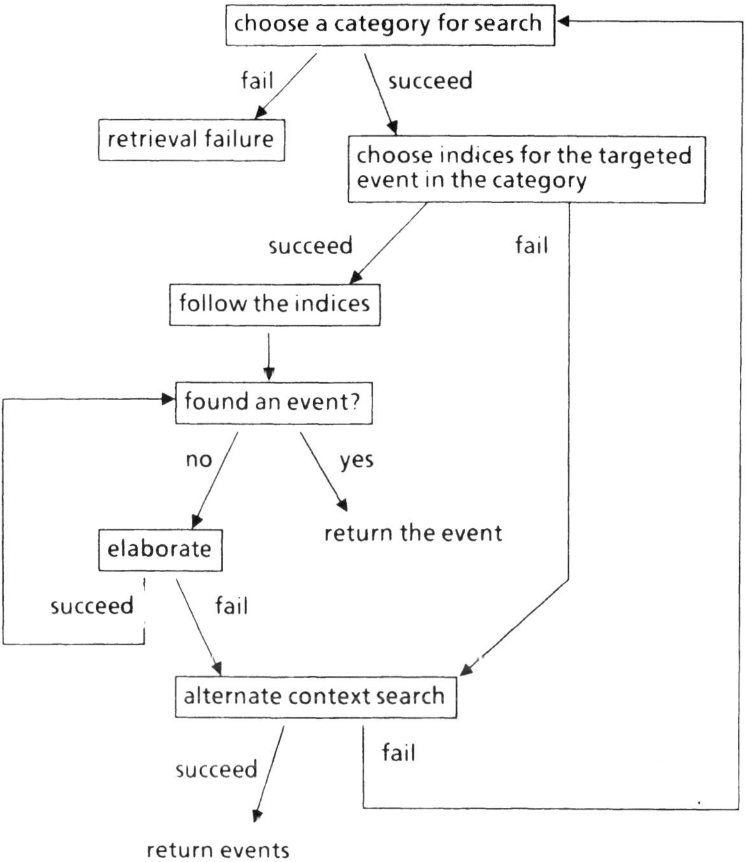

FIG. 1.3. Memory Search.

during the trip. The strategies that guide search for alternate contexts are called *executive search strategies.*[4] These strategies are presented and explained in detail in chapter 6.

While index fitting and elaboration direct depthwise search within memory, executive strategies direct *lateral traversal* of memory, i.e., search within different E-MOPs, or contexts, than the one originally selected for retrieval. One problem associated with searching for alternate contexts is constraining the search. Search should be constrained to contexts that have a possibility of being related to an item targeted for retrieval. In general, for search to be constrained to relevant contexts, memory categories must hold *generalized information* con-

[4]In previous papers, these strategies were called search strategies.

cerning the relationships of their items to items in other memory categories. If "museum visit" holds the information that its items are often parts of "trips" or "visits from out of town friends" or "visits to New York," then search can be constrained to only those three alternate contexts. This suggests the following feature of reconstructive memory:

Memory Principle #7
Conceptual categories organize generalized information describing their items.

The generalized information E-MOPs hold will be discussed as its use in the retrieval process is examined. Acquisition of some of that generalized knowledge is discussed in chapter 7.

4.4. Summary of Memory Search

Search, then is a process of specifying and elaborating on contexts for retrieval. To search memory for a particular targeted event, a memory category (i.e., E-MOP) to be searched must first be chosen. Within that E-MOP, searching for a particular event involves specifying which of the MOP's indices should be traversed. That often requires elaboration of the information given in a question. If an event targeted for retrieval cannot be retrieved from the selected E-MOP, it is often useful to search for an alternate related context that might refer to the target event. Figure 1.3 summarizes that search process.

5. MAINTAINING MEMORY ORGANIZATION

Another constraint in designing a memory for events is maintaining the memory organization as new items are added to memory. People learn new things every day, but they do not get slower at remembering as new events are added to their memories (Smith, Adams, & Schorr, 1978). In a computer system, too, retrieval should not slow down significantly as new events are added to the memory.[5] Since time consumed by any algorithm that examines each input item must grow linearly with the number of items in a category, this puts the following constraint on memory:

[5]In fact, there is some debate about this among psychologists. Anderson (1974, 1976) cites the "fan effect" as evidence that retrieval slows down with the addition of new items about a particular concept. Smith, Adams & Schorr (1978), on the other hand, has shown that retrieval does not slow down with the addition of new items when context is guiding the retrieval. Reder and Anderson (1980) conclude that when people make consistency judgements, rather than retrieving actual facts from memory, there is no interference to slow down the retrieval process.

Memory Principle #8
Retrieval from memory categories happens without enumeration of the items in the category.

Both the memory organization and the retrieval processes proposed thus far are designed with this constraint in mind. The retrieval processes will be of little value, however, if the memory organization is not maintained as new items are added to memory. As a first step, maintaining the memory organization requires that new items be indexed appropriately in conceptual categories as they are added to memory. This process will result in new conceptual categories being created. Since retrieval strategies use generalized information associated with conceptual categories, maintaining memory organization also requires formulating generalized information for new categories as they are created.

Memory, then, must be able to grow and change as new items are added. Control of that growth is a major problem. If memory categories are heavily indexed by salient features, retrieval processes will have a large selection of features to specify, any of which might point to the target event. The retrieval process will be made easier since easier elaborations can be attempted first. Thus, rich indexing will make retrieval easy.

The richer the indexing, however, the more space is needed for storage. Indexing must be constrained so that memory does not grow uncontrollably. Similarities between events can be used to control indexing. If memory keeps track of the similarities between events within a category, then indexing can be limited to the differences between events. Thus, if almost all the events in a "diplomatic meetings" category are with foreign diplomats, indexing meetings according to the occupations of the participants would add no distinction between events. If, however, one of those meetings was with someone other than a foreign diplomat, indexing that meeting by the occupation of its participant (i.e., a feature which differentiates it from all other meetings) would differentiate it from other events in the category.

Similarities between items in a conceptual category also play another role in memory processing. They comprise the generalized information retrieval strategies need. Chapters 7 and 8 discuss integration of new events into memory, and present a generalization process as a control on indexing.

6. CYRUS

CYRUS (Computerized Yale Retrieval and Updating System) (Kolodner, 1978, 1981; Schank & Kolodner, 1979) is a computer program that implements the theory of long-term memory presented here. CYRUS is meant to be both an intelligent fact retrieval system and a model of human long-term memory for events. CYRUS has been designed to keep track of events in the lives of important people. It answers questions posed to it in English pertaining to that information. Thus, it both organizes events in its memory and searches memory reconstructively to retrieve them.

CYRUS can be used with either of two data bases—one each for the experiences of former Secretaries of State Cyrus Vance and Edmund Muskie. Cyrus Vance was initially chosen as the subject for the memory for two reasons: (1) as secretary of state, he was in the news often enough to make a self-updating data base interesting, and (2) news articles about a secretary of state report few enough of the types of activities he does to make initial organization of the system's memory feasible. When Vance resigned from office, a separate data base for Muskie, who succeeded Vance, was started. No changes had to be made to the program.

Events in CYRUS' memory are organized in E-MOPs according to their differences. CYRUS' E-MOPs include "diplomatic trips," "diplomatic meetings," "negotiations," "speeches," and "state dinners"—all examples of normal activities of a diplomat.

When CYRUS adds new events to its memory, it automatically organizes them so that they can be easily retrieved using reconstructive memory techniques. As it adds a new event to memory, CYRUS indexes the event in the appropriate categories, reorganizing those categories as necessary, and creating category/subcategory hierarchies specific to the experiences it is given. Although the Vance and Muskie data bases started out with the same categories, because of the differing experiences of the two men, the evolving organization of the two memories as events were added is quite different.

Because CYRUS does not have the capability to understand stories expressed in Natural Language, stories must be read and conceptual representations for them produced before CYRUS can add them to its memory. The information in CYRUS' memory has been collected from news stories in two different ways. Most of the representations for events concerning Vance were hand-coded from newspaper stories. The Muskie data base, on the other hand, has had all of its information collected by FRUMP (DeJong, 1979a, 1979b), a computer program that reads stories from the UPI wire and produces summaries. When FRUMP produces a summary of a story about Muskie or Vance, it sends the conceptual representation underlying the summary to CYRUS. CYRUS then adds the new events to its memory and can later be queried about them.

CYRUS answers questions posed to it in English and gives English answers. The following are actual question/answer (QA) dialogs with CYRUS. The first is a dialog with the Vance memory, the second with the Muskie data base. Questions were typed in English to the system. Some of CYRUS' intermediate processing is given. Its answers are capitalized.

****

@CYRUS

Are you interested in Muskie or Vance? (M or V) : *VANCE

*(DIALOG2)

>When was the last time you were in Egypt?

inferring a diplomatic trip
answering question using time context

ON DEC 10 1978.

>Why did you go there?

answering question using previous context

TO NEGOTIATE THE CAMP DAVID ACCORDS.

>Who did you talk to there?

inferring undifferentiated political meeting
answering question using previous context

WITH ANWAR SADAT.

>Has your wife ever met Mrs. Begin?

inferring a social political occasion

YES, MOST RECENTLY AT A STATE DINNER IN ISRAEL IN JAN 1980.

>What heads of state have you met?

inferring a diplomatic meeting
searching directly for diplomatic meetings
...
applying strategies to search memory
...
searching for conferences
...
searching for diplomatic trips
searching diplomatic trip instance for diplomatic meetings
...
searching for negotiations
...

KING HASSAN, MENACHIM BEGIN, MUSTAFA KHALIL, IAN SMITH, PRESIDENT ASSAD, KING HUSSEIN, AND ANWAR SADAT.

>Last time you went to Saudi Arabia, where did you stay?

inferring a diplomatic trip
answering question using time context

IN A PALACE IN SAUDI ARABIA ON SEP 23 1978.

>Did you go sightseeing there?

answering question using time context

YES, AT AN OILFIELD IN DHARAN ON SEP23 1978.

****

```
@CYRUS

Are you interested in Muskie or Vance? (M or V) : *MUSKIE

*(DIALOG2)

>Where are you today?

   inferring a diplomatic trip

  PROBABLY IN THE UNITED STATES ON JUN 14 1980.

>Where were you three weeks ago?

   inferring a diplomatic trip

  IN EUROPE.

>Why did you go?

   answering question using previous context

  TO TALK TO ANDREI GROMYKO.

>Who did you talk to?

   inferring undifferentiated political meeting
   answering question using previous context

  TO NATO IN BRUSSELS ON MAY 14 AND TO ANDREI GROMYKO IN VIENNA.

>Did you give a speech?

   answering question using previous context

  YES, ONE TO A GROUP OF REPORTERS AND ONE TO NATO.

>Are you going to Asia?

   inferring a diplomatic trip

  YES, THIS MONTH.

>Who will you talk to?

   inferring undifferentiated political meeting
   answering question using previous context

  TO NATO IN ANKARA, TURKEY.

****************************
```

7. OUR GOALS

In working on CYRUS, we had two objectives. One was to enable the computer to do the kinds of intelligent memory tasks that people can do—remembering. The other objective was to use the computer as a tool to investigate human reconstructive memory. This study emphasizes reconstructive memory for day-to-day events. Our bias in this direction stems from observations that it is day-to-day events, and the generalizations that can be made from them, that form the core of our ability to understand language. Episodic structures such as scripts, goals, and themes (Schank & Abelson, 1977) have already been shown to play a major role both in understanding and in getting around the world. Such episodic structures can only arise by keeping track of the events they are derived from in an episodic memory. In keeping track of events, we must figure out how to organize them. The reconstructive abilities of people give us pointers into such an organization. We thus study reconstructive memory rather than rote memory, and episodic memory rather than semantic or factual memory.

In implementing our model, we are most interested in those parts of memory that directly contribute to reconstruction. Our model of Cyrus Vance thus does not model all of Vance's memory, but only those things necessary for reconstruction of day-to-day events during his tenure as secretary of state. Thus, we do not store what he knows about Egyptian history or about international relations before he became secretary of state, though in a more complete memory, those things might be relevant and useful to have. Nor do we store childhood memories. The Vance memories we store are strictly those parts relevant to a very restricted interpretation of his secretary of state role.

Another restriction on our model is that we are not dealing with recency or frequency data. While some questions we use as examples seem to depend on such knowledge, it is only in CYRUS in the most rudimentary way. What we are really interested in, in those questions, is the capability of finding anything at all in a large store of events. Thus, in answering "how many," our intention is to show how CYRUS can find a large number of events without enumeration, rather than show that it makes frequency judgments.

8. USING PEOPLE AS A MODEL

Earlier we stated that we would look to people as motivation and as a starting point in developing principles of memory organization and access and for designing intelligent fact retrieval systems. There are two good reasons for this. We have already seen that there are many problems in common between human memory and computer data base access. In addition, the things we want our intelligent retrieval system to do are exactly the things people find easy. Human memory is very large and complex. People constantly learn new things and add new information to their memories and just as often attempt to remember or retrieve old information. People cannot anticipate all questions that will ever be posed to them, yet they are able to answer questions they have not encountered before. People understand natural language utterances and are able to access their memories and provide appropriate responses. If we want to build computer systems with human capabilities, then it seems logical to turn to people as a model.

Furthermore, people are the only intelligent systems we know that have these capabilities, and thus the only system available for modeling. Although there may be other ways of simulating intelligence, perhaps the only way to construct an extensive and extensible intelligent system is to model human beings. Certainly it is an approach worth trying.

Human long-term memory, then, is relevant to this endeavor as a model of an existing intelligent system on which to base our computer systems. Using human memory as a basis, our first step in building an intelligent retrieval system is to develop a theory of human long-term memory. We can then apply its organizational constraints and algorithms to computer systems to build more intelligent information retrieval and data base systems.

One place one might look for general principles of memory organization is in the psychological literature. Unfortunately, this is not sufficient for our purposes. In working with the computer, all processes and algorithms must be well defined, as must the memory structures these processes work on. This "process model" approach to memory has not been emphasized by psychologists. Thus, for the most part, psychological models and theories are inadequate for computer implementation. We have therefore had to augment psychological findings with judgments of our own. Based on protocols we have taken, we have attempted to discover what processes people use in remembering. We then implemented those theories on the computer and observed the way the program behaved. We have produced and tested our theory of memory by an iterative procedure that involves observing people, implementing inferred algorithms on the computer, testing the computer program under a variety of circumstances and observing its behavior, then going back and observing people again, and so forth.

We have also looked at the relevant psychological literature to make sure our predictions and observations are consonant with previous results. In terms of psychology, the process model produced has two contributions to make. First, it puts forth a process that helps explain previous psychological observations. Second, the resulting model of memory and its implications and predictions are amenable to psychological testing (e.g., Kolodner & Barsalou, 1982, Reiser, Black, & Abelson, 1982).

This research is thus addressing two problems. One is the very practical computer science problem of developing a means of storing and retrieving large amounts of complex interrelated experiential information in the computer. Because we believe the solution to that problem is deeply rooted in a human model of memory, we have also been interested in how people remember. Thus, the second purpose of this research is to explore and discover how human long-term memory is organized, and how its retrieval processes work. Using the computer as an experimental and developmental tool, we can add to the current knowledge of how human memory might work.

Clearly, a model of people will behave differently from traditional computerized data bases. A memory based on a human model will make the same kinds of mistakes that people make. If the correct memory category for an event cannot be inferred, or if a relevant feature of an event cannot be elaborated, the event will not be retrievable from memory, that is, forgotten. Thus, a system based on a human-oriented scheme will be good at making the inferences necessary to reconstruct events and generalized information from memory, but it will be bad at enumerating lists of episodes. Details of episodes will not always be remembered correctly.

When people ask traditional data bases for information, they often ask to have lists enumerated for them. There are two reasons for this. First, the information in traditional data bases is information that people find hard to remember and would keep on paper if the computer were not available. Second, data base systems usually do not make inferences about their contents, so people must retrieve lists to make those inferences themselves.

We can all observe, however, that when people ask experts for information, or when they talk among themselves about past experiences, they rarely ask for lists of items, but tolerate (perhaps prefer) generalizations and presumptions, interspersed with examples confirming those generalizations. Thus, it is not always necessary for a memory to be able to enumerate lists accurately. Generalized knowledge is often sufficient and preferred. Retrieval failures are acceptable if the processes that allow those failures also give added inferential and retrieval power to the memory. A false or missing datum is considered a flaw in traditional data bases, rendering all information retrieved suspect; a phantom event constructed by a memory can actually enhance its performance.

9. CYRUS AS A PSYCHOLOGICAL MODEL

There are a number of features that make this approach to long-term memory novel in the field of psychology, and before going on, it may be helpful to point them out. First, we are examining the system as a whole. Rather than looking at encoding, storage, and retrieval as separate entities, we define and examine them in relationship to each other. Integration of new items into memory (our analog to encoding), for example, both reflects retrieval capabilities we've observed in people and takes the underlying memory organization into account. Similarly, in considering memory organization (our analog to storage), we've examined the constraints implied by human retrieval—its successes, failures, and the strategies used. The model presented is an integrated approach to memory's processes and stores. What we know about understanding has also been taken into account in devising the model.

Second, and related to this, we are looking at memory as both a process and a store. Thus, we have put forth specific algorithms and memory structures that define a *process model*. Those algorithms are defined in terms of strategies for retrieval and for indexing new items in the store. Furthermore, we require that the model be programmable on the computer. This ensures that the processes and structures of the model are defined explicitly enough and in enough detail to run in a computer implementation. The algorithms presented in this book and the structures that hold the knowledge those algorithms use are implemented in the CYRUS system.

The integrated approach to memory, along with our attempt to define memory's processes and structures as explicitly as possible, leads to a third novel feature of this model. Because we want to define what drives retrieval and organizational strategies, and because we have had to implement the model in a computer program, we have had to very explicitly define the structures in memory that organize individual memories with respect to each other. This is what we call *memory organization.* While psychologists have been looking at memory organization in the form of schemata, the organization proposed here goes beyond current schemata theory in a number of ways. First, it provides ways of organizing schemata with respect to each other. Second, it examines change in schemata over time. Third, it studies the use of schemata in organizing individual items represented by a particular schema with respect to each other. All of this adds up to a level of detail unique in the study of memory.

The need to look at these features of schemata arises from a fourth novel feature of the approach. We are studying memory for everyday events over time. The memory items we are examining are personal events. How are everyday events remembered? How does memory for a particular event change as similar experiences are encountered? How does generic memory for particular kinds of events change as similar experiences are encountered? These are some of the questions we attempt to answer. Most approaches to long-term memory have not looked at the relationships between things as complex as individual events.

The fifth novel feature is a by-product of the others. In coming up with a memory organization that reflects human retrieval capabilities, we have defined a memory organization that integrates generic and episodic memory. Both are organized in the same structures and are thus accessed and updated via the same strategies. This is in line with recent studies that show a blurred distinction between the two stores (e.g., Anderson & Ross, 1980, McKoon & Ratcliff, 1979).

Finally, a last novel feature is in our way of looking at reconstruction. Psychologists use reconstructive memory to refer to the producing of plausible scenes or making plausible guesses at what a targeted event might have been. This model, on the other hand, uses reconstruction to refer to constructing a description of a target event, adding features to progressively differentiate it from its nearest neighbors, and finally ''finding'' its hiding place in a well-organized memory. There are two primary differences in emphasis. First are assumptions about the organization of memory—to psychologists, organization of items in memory doesn't come into play in reconstruction. In this model, memory's organization drives the process.

The second difference in emphasis concerns the process itself. We have, in effect, included a verification process in the reconstructive process itself. Thus, reconstruction is a two-step loop: (1) coming up with a description and (2) discovering if it is in memory, or searching for it, and going back to (1). In this way, the contents of memory drive the reconstructive process. Because verification is part of the procedure, however, mistakes are not always obvious. While errorful descriptions of a targeted event may be produced during elaboration in our model, the verification process or search through memory suppresses their output. The primary problem with this is that it does not directly explain how people can generate gross errors and yet have complete confidence that they are correct. On the other hand, the search (or verification) part of the process allows more and more detail to be generated about a targeted event and provides a means by which memory can guide the elaboration process.

10. SUMMARY

A reasonable goal in the design of intelligent fact retrieval systems is to give them memories with many of the same capabilities people have. To do so, we must discover how information can be organized in a large, constantly changing memory, and how it can be retrieved to answer natural language queries. We turn to people as a model of the intelligent processes we wish the computer to have. People use a reconstructive process to remember, reasoning about "what must have happened" rather than directly retrieving what did happen. We base our model on that. CYRUS, the computer program that implements our process model, was designed to store and retrieve information about important dignitaries. Its memory organization and strategies support processes we see in people.

2 Background and Motivation

1. MEMORY AND UNDERSTANDING

The original motivation behind this research was to jointly address the problems of how long-term memory is used in understanding and how long-term memory is built up through understanding. Numerous researchers in psychology and artificial intelligence have shown that understanding and memory cannot be considered separately (Anderson & Bower, 1973; Lebowitz, 1980; Norman & Rumelhart, 1975; Quillian, 1968; Rieger, 1975a; Schank, 1980; Schank & Abelson, 1977). While all these researchers agree that memory is an important part of understanding, they do not agree on its form and organization. Quillian, Anderson, and Bower emphasize a semantic memory organization based on inheritance, Rieger emphasizes organization of inferences around primitives, and the others emphasize more complex episodic organizations.

Within the field of natural language understanding, researchers have recognized the need for long-term memory in understanding but for the most part have not addressed the problem. Research within that field has emphasized algorithms for machine analysis of text, and inference (e.g., Collins, 1978; Rieger, 1975a, 1975b; Riesbeck, 1975; Schank, 1975). Knowledge structures have been developed for use in representing the knowledge necessary for understanding (e.g., scripts [Schank & Abelson, 1977], frames [Minsky, 1975]). Their use in the understanding process has been illustrated in a series of computer programs that understand simple texts (e.g., SAM [Cullingford, 1978], FRUMP [DeJong, 1979a], Ms. Malaprop [Charniak, 1977], see also Schank & Riesbeck [1981]).

A simplifying assumption in most understanding systems was that the necessary knowledge structures would be available when needed during understanding. This assumption allowed emphasis to be placed on the knowledge and knowledge structures needed for understanding and on the process of using those structures. As a result, however, little emphasis was placed on the organization of those structures with respect to each other in a long-term memory. The problem of organizing individual instances with respect to generalized structures was not addressed at all. Knowledge structures organized inferences into packets of various kinds, but the organization of those packets with respect to each other was largely ignored.

As we have gained a better understanding of "understanding," it has become clear that previous knowledge and its organization in long-term memory play a major role in understanding, generalization, and inference. Furthermore, this knowledge must be built up during the understanding process (Lebowitz, 1980; Schank, 1980). A memory that can build up its knowledge base (i.e., learn) in the course of processing will be more adaptable to new and unanticipated inputs than one whose knowledge is static. In addition, to make sure that our natural language systems are able to access all of the relevant knowledge in memory when necessary, and also to make sure that irrelevant information does not get in the way of that processing, we must consider how that knowledge is organized and retrieved. The study of memory organization and access, then, is the logical next step in the study of natural language understanding.

Although this book will not explicitly address the relationship between memory and understanding, it is important to recognize that our approach to memory comes from considering what a memory involved in understanding would have to be like. Thus, our approach differs markedly from that of psychologists who have looked at long-term memory without considering its function in everyday cognitive tasks.

Our approach builds on previous research in artificial intelligence and natural language processing by examining how knowledge structures are organized with respect to each other. Because of this perspective, it has been possible to formulate a theory of memory that built upon previous theoretical notions of language processing. CYRUS is an extension of memory-processing theories that originated with the study of natural language understanding, inference, and question answering. Some of the concepts adopted from those studies are presented below.

2. CONCEPTUAL MEMORY

The major concept underlying CYRUS is conceptual memory. In a conceptual memory, knowledge is organized around concepts. Knowledge about "traveling," for example, is organized around the concept "travel." Expressions such as "going somewhere," "taking a train," "going away," or "travel" express a similar concept. Because they express the same concept, they can all reference the same concept in memory (i.e., "travel"), making information about travel available for understanding and inference no matter which words are used to express it. The questions "Has Vance ever been to Egypt?" "Has Vance traveled to Egypt?" and "Has Vance ever taken a trip to Egypt?" can all be answered in a similar fashion because they all reference the same conceptual category.

A conceptual organization has quite a few advantages over conventional lexical systems. Contrast the capabilities of the organization just described with those of a lexical information retrieval system such as the New York Times Data Base, which keeps track of news stories from the New York Times. Instead of providing natural language communication, it must be queried with key words. Although anyone can ask for information using key words, it takes practice to use them effectively. Queried by a novice, a key-word system will return many extra irrelevant items the user wasn't expecting and will miss relevant articles. A system such as this, then, is hard for the man in the street to use. A technician trained in its use must be consulted to retrieve information from it. If, instead of being organized as a lexical system, newsworthy items were organized conceptually, then memory organization could be utilized to create a natural language query system that anyone could use. It is the similarities between the concepts reported in news stories and those expressed in people's questions that must be exploited to do that.

2.1. Conceptual Representation

Since it is the meaning of facts that must be retrieved from a fact retrieval system, it is the meaning of those facts that should be stored. The representations that should be stored in memory, then, should be representations of meaning, independent of the language used to express that meaning. By the same token, it is the meanings of questions that must be used to retrieve an answer from memory. Consider, for example, the following question:

(Q1): Has Vance talked to Begin recently?

To answer this question, a fact that expresses the *concept* "Vance had a meeting with Begin" must be retrieved from memory. It is irrelevant how that fact was worded when it was entered into the system. It may, for example, have been reported in either of the following two ways:

EV1: Cyrus Vance met with Begin yesterday in Geneva to discuss control of the Sinai.

EV2: During their conversation yesterday in Geneva, Vance and Begin discussed sovereignty over the Sinai.

Though expressed differently, the two sentences report the same event. Either would answer the question above, though neither is worded exactly like that question. Both reports of the event refer to "yesterday." The question says "recently." The question has the word "talked." Neither report uses that word—one uses "met," one uses "conversation," and both use "discuss."

If a memory is going to store representations of the meanings of facts, and not raw facts themselves, then there must be some means of analyzing the raw facts and producing a representation of their meaning. Although this research has not addressed that problem, it has been addressed by other researchers in the field of natural language processing. Schank's theory of *conceptual dependency* (Schank, 1975) (described below) provides a set of primitives for representing low-level actions, and a process of conceptual analysis to extract meaning from sentences. A descendent of that analyzer, CA (Birnbaum & Selfridge, 1981) is a computer program that analyzes sentences in detail, producing representations of their meaning. Two other computer systems analyze at a higher level to produce representations of connected events in individual stories. DeJong's (1979b) FRUMP skims news stories and produces summaries in certain domains that it "knows about." IPP (Lebowitz, 1980) reads stories about terrorism, produces representations of their events, and integrates those representations into its memory.

2.2. Conceptual Organization

Three criteria must be satisfied by the organization of memory in a system for fact retrieval. Memory should be organized so that any given fact can be extracted from the data base when appropriate. The organization must also allow inferences to be drawn from information in the data base in order to retrieve information only implicitly there. A third factor in memory's organization is that it must facilitate natural language communication.

A *conceptual organization* of facts based on meaning of data items addresses all of these issues. If two items express similar concepts, they will be organized in the same conceptual category. Instead of being based on similarities between key words, categories are based on similarities between meanings.

Meaning is important in drawing inferences and in communication with the data base. The same sorts of inferences should be able to be drawn about items in the same category. In a conceptually based memory, the following two facts, although expressed differently, would be stored in the same category.

EV3: Cyrus Vance met yesterday with Gromyko in Geneva to discuss SALT.

EV4: During their conversation Monday at Blair House, Vance and Begin discussed sovereignty over the Sinai.

Both involve communication between Vance and a foreign dignitary. If one were to define Vance's "diplomatic meetings" as "bilateral communication between Vance and a foreign dignitary about a matter of international concern," then both of these meetings could be stored in that "diplomatic meetings" category. In general, any fact with those properties would be recognized as a diplomatic meeting and stored in that category. Suppose the following two questions were asked of a system with facts EV3 and EV4:

(Q2): Why did Vance meet with Gromyko about SALT yesterday?

(Q3): Why did Vance and Begin discuss the Sinai?

Despite the fact that neither EV3 nor EV4 gives the reasons why it occurred, the following inference rule, if associated with the category "diplomatic meetings," could be used to answer these questions:

> Diplomatic meetings are often instrumental to negotiations involving the countries the meeting participants represent, and concerning a contract which includes the meeting topic.

Applying this inference to events EV3 and EV4, questions Q2 and Q3 could be answered "to negotiate the SALT treaty" and "to negotiate an aspect of the Camp David Accords" respectively.

In order for inference rules like that given above to be useful, categories in a conceptual memory must store only facts which are amenable to the same inferences, and each category should have associated with it generalized information that can be used for drawing inferences about items in the category.

To see that this is so, suppose that a retrieval system held the following fact in addition to the two above, that it was stored in a category with the two events above, and that the inference above was associated with that category:

EV5: During their conversation Monday at Blair House, Vance and his wife discussed sovereignty over the Sinai.

In that case the following dialog could take place:

(Q4): Why did Vance discuss the Sinai with his wife Monday?

A: To negotiate the Camp David Accords.

Obviously, applying the "diplomatic meetings" inference above to an event which is not a diplomatic meeting leads to an absurdity.

A fact retrieval system, then, should have the following property:

Conceptual categories in memory should hold items related through the inferences that can be drawn about them. These categories should have associated generalized information that will enable inferences to be drawn about their members.

In the following sections, the actual theories of conceptual representation and organization underlying CYRUS are presented.

3. CONCEPTUAL DEPENDENCY

Underlying conceptual memory is a theory of memory representation called "Conceptual Dependency" (CD) (Schank, 1972). The major point of CD theory is this: If memory processes are to operate on the concepts underlying sentences and not on sentences themselves, then our computer simulations must rely on conceptual representations of meaning. Conceptual dependency encodes the meanings of sentences by decomposing them into a small set of meaning primitives. When two sentences have identical meanings, the conceptual dependency representations are the same. For example, "John took the train to New York" and "John went to New York on the train" have the same CD representation.

There are many advantages to a representational system based on primitives.

1. *It provides canonical representation.* This means that any two sentences or utterances or stories with the same content will be encoded in the same way. Memory representations and processes will not have to deal with differing styles of expression or word choice in doing their reasoning.

2. *Conceptual primitives provide a natural way of organizing memory.* Inferences and conceptualizations referring to the same meaning primitive can be grouped together in memory.

3. *A representation based on conceptual primitives allows inferences to be stored economically in memory.* Instead of storing an inference along with each word or conceptualization it is associated with, an inference can be stored once along with the primitive it is associated with. When a new concept is added to memory, only the inferences associated with its primitives need be considered.

4. *A canonical representation of meaning allows easy recognition of the similarities between similar concepts.* If similar concepts are represented in the same way, then their similarities and differences become transparent.

As a result of such organization and representation, memory access is based on meaning rather than on words. Once the meaning of a sentence or story is encoded in CD, memory processes need deal only with that representation and not with the words used to express it. Thus, answering a question expressed differently from the sentence in a story that answers it becomes a problem of matching the meaning of the question to the meaning of the story encoded in memory rather than having to deal with the actual words. Since there are many fewer primitives than words or phrases, and because primitives organize knowledge efficiently, the matching process becomes less complex.

Conceptual dependency includes a set of meaning primitives called the primitive ACTs, described below. It should be noted that the important concept here is the use of primitives for encoding rather than the particular set of primitives used. The following set of primitives has proven useful in a number of domains that deal with real world actions and events:

ATRANS—The transfer of possession, ownership, or control. Requires an actor, object, donor, and recipient. This primitive is used to represent actions such as giving, taking, buying, selling, trading, and stealing. "John gave Mary a book," for example, is represented as an ATRANS with actor John, object the book, recipient Mary, and donor John. "Mary took the book from John" is represented identically, except that the actor is Mary instead of John.

PTRANS—Physical transfer of an object from one place to another. Requires an actor, object, source, and destination. Often, the actor and object are identical. "John ran home from the store" is a PTRANS with John as the actor and the object, home as the destination, and the store as the source. This act is used to represent actions such as going somewhere, taking a train, leaving the room, crawling, walking, running, putting something somewhere, and moving an object from one location to another.

Notice that primitive ACTs are not associated with particular English verbs. Both "John took the book to Boston" and "John took the train to Boston" are represented using PTRANS, while "John took the book from Mary" is an ATRANS (which happens to have an instrumental PTRANS). "Take" by itself does not designate one primitive over another. Rather, the entire action articulated in the sentence must be taken into account to figure out what "take" means.

PROPEL—Applying a physical force. Requires an actor, object, source, and destination. If movement takes place, then there is also an associated PTRANS. PROPEL is often *instrumental* to PTRANS, i.e., an object moves (PTRANS) because of a force that is applied (PROPEL). Throwing a ball, pushing something, falling, and shooting a gun are all examples of PROPELs.

INGEST—To take a foreign object internally into the body of an animal. Requires an actor, object, origin, and destination. Eating, drinking, smoking, and taking medicine are all examples of INGEST.

EXPEL—To push an object out of the body. Requires an actor, object, origin, and destination. Crying and spitting are examples of EXPEL.

MTRANS—Transfer of information from one mental location to another. Requires an actor, a mental object (i.e., the information being transferred), a source and a destination. Memory is divided into three locations: the Conscious Processor (CP) which holds information which we are consciously aware of, Immediate Memory (IM), which holds contextual information associated with what is in CP and which can be accessed easily when necessary, and Long Term Memory (LTM), which is the long-term store. An MTRANS can occur between people, as in John telling Mary something. It can also occur between different mental locations within the same person. Remembering, for example, is an MTRANS from long-term memory to conscious memory. Seeing is an MTRANS from the eye to CP.

MBUILD—A thought process that constructs new information from old concepts. An MBUILD happens in IM. It takes input (a set of known concepts) from CP and outputs a new concept to CP. Conclude, decide, and infer are all examples of MBUILD.

ATTEND—To focus a sensory organ on a stimulus. Requires an actor, object (sensory organ being focused), a recipient (the stimulus being focused on). This ACT is most often instrumental to an MTRANS. Seeing, for example, is an MTRANS with an instrumental ATTEND in which the actor is the animal doing the seeing, the object is his eyes, and the recipient is whatever is being looked at. Similarly, hearing, touching, smelling, and tasting are represented by ATTEND.

SPEAK—To make a noise. This ACT also is usually instrumental to MTRANS when people do it. The object of a SPEAK is the words being spoken. The destination is the person being spoken to and the source is the mouth of the person doing the vocalizing. SPEAK is used to represent talking, singing, screaming, and barking.

GRASP—To hold on to an object. Requires an actor, object being held, a recipient (the body part holding on, usually a hand). Holding and grabbing are represented by GRASP. Letting go of or throwing something are represented as completing a GRASP.

MOVE—To move a body part. Requires an actor, an object (the body part), a source and destination. MOVE is often instrumental to PTRANS. Kicking, throwing, shaking hands, and kissing all involve MOVEs.

4. RELATING EVENTS TO EVENTS

Understanding requires more than just being able to extract the explicit meaning from a set of sentences. It is also necessary to be able to connect those sentences together causally. For example, when told that John hit Mary and Mary cried, most people will infer that John's hitting Mary led to Mary's being hurt, which in turn initiated her crying. Meaning includes the connections between events. If we are to represent meaning, then we must be able to represent the relationships between actions in addition to representing the actions themselves. We do this through causal chains.

Causal chains connect actions and states together based on their causal relationships. Events can result in states or state changes, and states can enable and disable future events. There are six different types of causality that we consider in CD (Schank, 1975):

RESULT—An event can result in a state or state change. This causal link can connect any of the primitive ACTs to any states expect mental states. John hitting Mary resulting in Mary being hurt is an example of a RESULT link between an event and a state.

ENABLE—A state can enable an event to occur. Getting a high school diploma is one of the enablements for attending college. Having enough money is one enablement for going on a trip. Putting a switch in an on position results in a circuit being closed, which enables a light to go on.

REASON—A mental activity (MBUILD) can be the reason for doing some action.

INITIATE—A state or an event can initiate an MBUILD.

LEADTO—This relates two events in an unexpanded causal chain. It is used when there is a causal relationship known to exist between two events, but that relationship is unknown or not explicit.

CANCAUSE—This link flags potential causality. It is equivalent to a conditional expression. "If John brings me a present, then I will be happy" is represented using a CANCAUSE link to connect the two concepts (John ATRANS a present and I am happy). The events and states connected by a CANCAUSE link are hypothetical.

The list above provides a very general causal syntax. Events can result in states that can enable potential actions. A state or event can initiate a thought process (MBUILD), which is the reason for doing another action. This causal syntax can be used to tie together loose ends in extended texts or utterances. In this work, we concentrate mostly on RESULT and ENABLE relationships.

5. SITUATIONAL CONTEXT

One problem with the causal syntax above is that it does not give a way of tying together parts of a situation. Often, the causality in a situation is based on social or cultural protocol rather than causality. The relationships between standing in line, giving money to a woman, standing in line, giving tickets to a man, for example, are based on time relationships associated with the stereotypic situation "going to the movies," and not on strict causality.

Scripts (Schank & Abelson, 1977) are used to describe situational causality. A script is a knowledge structure that describes a stereotypic type of event. It provides world knowledge about often-experienced situations. Scripts are often associated with *situational nouns*, as in going to a restaurant, taking the subway, going to a football game, a birthday party, or a meeting. In addition, scripts exist for each type of mundane situation we can be involved in, such as getting up in the morning, going to weddings, shopping for groceries, and taking a train or bus.

Scripts, like the primitive ACTs, are conceptual primitives. They are higher level primitives than the ACTs, however, grouping together situation-related sequences of actions. As conceptual primitives, they have many of the same properties as the ACTs. They provide canonical representation, a natural way of organizing memory, and an economical way of storing information. The script provides the predetermined sequence of actions that defines a situation. Use of scriptal knowledge during understanding allows parts of a situation that are not told to be filled in. An interesting feature of scripts is that after being told a script-based story, the listener usually cannot later recall which aspects of the story were given and which he inferred.

Scripts provide a context for understanding a situation or for behaving in an appropriate manner. Thus, it is necessary to trigger the appropriate script during understanding in order to continue understanding correctly. Once the appropriate script is triggered or instantiated, it will provide expectations of what will or should come next.

6. E-MOPs AND MEMORY ORGANIZATION

Two interesting problems associated with scripts are (1) how they are learned and (2) how they can be grouped together to form more complex situational descriptions. In studying long-term memory, both of these problems are important. Since scripts describe generalized episodes, learning them must involve compilation of the similarities between individual experiences. An implication of this learning process is that scripts must organize the episodes they are compiled from. Thus, organizational structures in long-term memory must organize both general information and individual episodes.

Scripts can be connected through causality and situations to other scripts. A diplomatic trip, for example, involves flying, a welcoming ceremony, travel in a limousine, a series of meetings, press conferences, state dinners, and a return flight. Each of the scenes of a diplomatic trip is a script to a diplomat. Thus, in addition to scripts, memory needs higher level structures than scripts provide.

The structures that organize related scripts are called E-MOPs (Episodic Memory Organization Packets). A script is the simplest form of an E-MOP. Like scripts, E-MOPs provide conceptual categorization for events. The emphasis of E-MOPs is different, however. While script research emphasized the structure of generalized episodes and its use in understanding, the emphasis in studying E-MOPs is the organization of individual episodes with respect to each other and to appropriate generalized episodes. Scripts were thought of primarily as processing structures, while E-MOPs are looked at as both storage and processing structures.

E-MOPs organize similar events with respect to each other by indexing them according to their differences. The similarities between the events an E-MOP organizes make up the descriptions of the generalized episodes and provide the same processing information scripts provided. In fact, this organization gives memory the ability to learn generalized episodes from particular experiences. E-MOPs will be referred to generically as "MOPs."[6]

6.1. What Kinds of Situations Correspond to E-MOPs?

E-MOPs organize both individual events and general information. Because events must be organized in E-MOPs for easy retrievability, E-MOPs correspond to situations that are *similar* to each other, but which can be *distinguished by domain-relevant criteria*. The situations should be similar to each other so that generalized information can be maintained on the E-MOP. Differences between events in E-MOPs should be *domain-relevant* so that retrieval strategies can be used to retrieve them. As we shall see, retrieval strategies are most powerful in predicting domain-related information. Domain-relevant features of meetings,

[6]These structures are related to Schank's (1980) MOPs and to Lebowitz's (1980) S-MOPs, but the concerns in defining MOPs and S-MOPs were different than those in defining E-MOPs. In particular, Schank's (1980) concern was with showing the interrelatedness of structures in memory. Thus, in his example domain of professional office visits, he described how visits to doctors, dentists, lawyers, and other professionals are similar, and how the structures they are stored in are related. My concern, on the other hand, is with the processes for retrieval of individual episodes, and the organizational requirements those processes place on memory. If my domain were professional office visits, I would be describing how particular visits are stored in memory in relation to each other and the generalized information that would allow them to be retrieved.

Lebowitz (1980) used S-MOPs to store terrorism events derived from newspaper stories. E-MOPs are more experientially oriented and hold more detailed information than his S-MOPs.

for example, include their topics, participants, and purpose. For home buying, domain-relevant features are the condition and price of the house.

"Speeches," for example, would be a good E-MOP for organizing the speeches of a person who does not go to or give many speeches. Its events have a similar structure, but can be differentiated. They consist of the speech maker being introduced, giving his speech, and receiving questions from the audience. Furthermore, they normally take place in large lecture halls. Some aspects of speeches that can differentiate them from each other are the speaker, the topic of the speech, and the reaction of the audience.

When situations are too much alike or too different, they will not correspond to useful E-MOPs. If a person gave a number of speeches every day, for example, all about the same topic, then "speeches" would not be a good E-MOP for organizing that person's experiences. The speeches would not be easily distinguishable from each other. Although "speeches" would organize a great deal of generalized information about speeches, it could not provide discriminability for the events. We shall see that when an E-MOP is overwhelmed by similar episodes in that way, retrieval strategies can use the generalized information associated with the E-MOP to search for related situations that might enable reconstruction of the designated event.

"Meeting somebody" and "talking to somebody" also are not usually good E-MOPs. They happen frequently and in many different situations. Thus, there is not a great deal of generalized information that can be built up about them, and there are no domain-related criteria for distinguishing between individual episodes. They are best stored as part of the situation in which they occur. If one talked to somebody or met somebody during a conference, it would best be stored as part of the conference situation.

In general, situations that are too much alike are not good E-MOPs because their instances cannot be distinguished. Those that are too different are not good because no generalized information ties them together. We see in later chapters that generalized information is necessary to direct retrieval, constrain indexing, and guide understanding.

6.2. The Internal Organization of an E-MOP

Internally an E-MOP is a network in which each node is either an E-MOP or an event. Each E-MOP has two important aspects: (1) generalized information characterizing its episodes, and (2) tree-like structures that index those episodes by their differences. The generalized information associated with an E-MOP is called its *content frame,* following Schank's (1980) usage for MOPs. An E-MOP's content frame holds information describing its events, including their usual cast of characters, settings, props, and topics, and their usual relationships to other events and E-MOPs.

One of the E-MOPs CYRUS uses is "diplomatic meetings." Each of Vance's or Muskie's diplomatic meetings that is entered into CYRUS' memory is indexed in that E-MOP. CYRUS knows that the participants of diplomatic meetings are foreign diplomats, that their topics are international contracts, that they include discussion between the participants about the topic, that their goal is usually to resolve a disputed contract, and that they are normally instrumental to a larger negotiating episode. That is some of the information that makes up the content frame of "diplomatic meetings." In addition, CYRUS' E-MOP for Vance's diplomatic meetings holds the information that Vance is the actor in those meetings. That content frame is illustrated below.

content frame:

the actor is Cyrus Vance participants are foreign diplomats topics are international contracts participants talked to each other goal is to resolve disputed contract instrumental to negotiations

FIG. 2.1. 'Diplomatic meetings' content frame.

The second important feature of an E-MOP is its indices. Events are indexed by those of their features that differentiate them from other events in the E-MOP. An E-MOP's indices can index either individual episodes or specialized E-MOPs. When an E-MOP holds only one episode with a particular feature, the index corresponding to that feature will point to the individual episode. When two or more episodes in an E-MOP share the same feature, its corresponding index will point to a specialized sub-MOP (with the structure just described) that organizes the subset of events with that feature. In this way, MOP/sub-MOP hierarchies are formed.

Consider, for example, how the following two events are indexed in CYRUS' "diplomatic meetings" MOP.

EV1: "diplomatic meeting" with:
    actor (Vance)
    others (Begin)
    topic (the Camp David Accords)

EV2: "diplomatic meeting" with:
    actor (Vance)
    others (Gromyko)
    topic (SALT)

Both of these meetings are diplomatic meetings with foreign diplomats about international contracts. One is with Begin about the Camp David Accords (EV1), and one is with Gromyko about SALT (EV2). These two meetings are discriminated in CYRUS' "diplomatic meetings" MOP ($MEET) as follows:

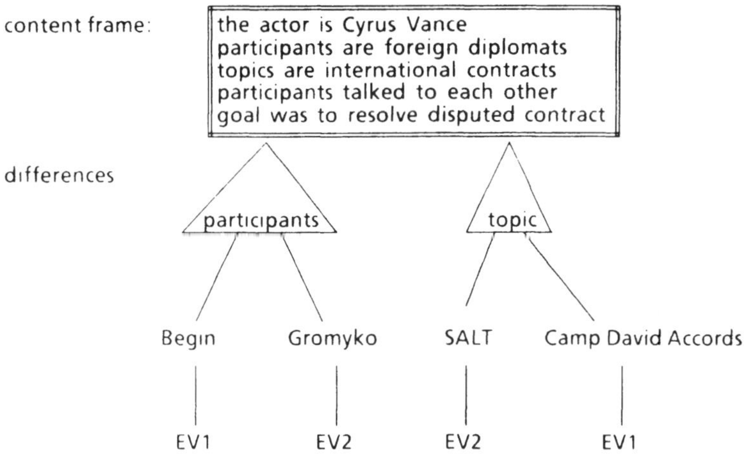

FIG. 2.2. 'Diplomatic meetings'—$MEET.

Notice that indexing in an E-MOP is two-tiered. The first tier points to the type of index (e.g., participants, topic), the second its value for a particular event or group of events (e.g., Begin, SALT).

As additional meetings are added to memory, generalized content frame information is refined, and additional indices for events are created. As that is happening, new E-MOPs are created where multiple episodes are indexed. Each of those new E-MOPs has a content frame based on the similarities between the episodes it indexes. Episodes are indexed in each new E-MOP according to their differentiating features. (There will be fewer of these features as E-MOPs get more specific.) These newly created specialized E-MOPs inherit content frame properties from the more general E-MOPs they are specialized from, and in addition have their own more specialized content frame information. Thus, E-MOPs and their specializations form a hierarchy discriminated by differences from content frame features.

After many meetings with Begin are added to the memory structure in Fig. 2.2 above, its organization looks like Fig. 2.3.

MOP1, "diplomatic meetings," is a refined version of the diplomatic meetings MOP in Fig. 2.2, while MOP2 and MOP3—"diplomatic meetings with Begin" and "diplomatic meetings about the Camp David Accords," respectively—are at the points in MOP1 where the meeting with Begin about the Camp David Accords is indexed. SALT and Gromyko remain indices to EV2, an

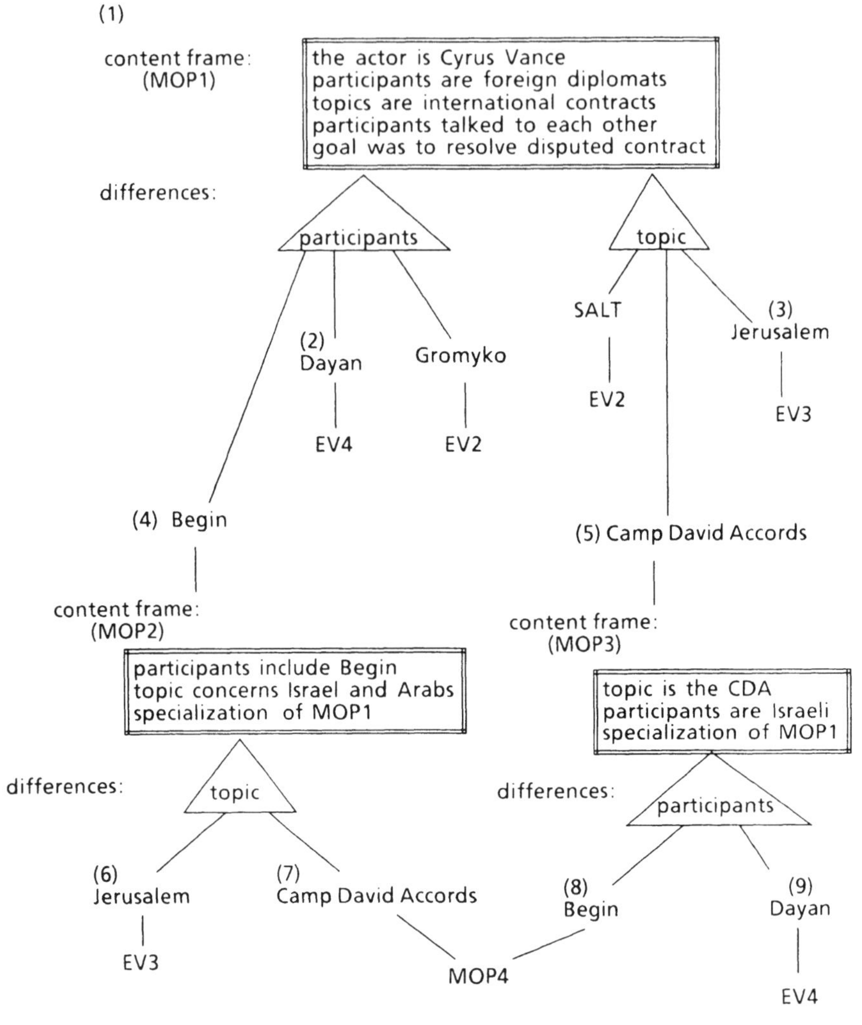

FIG. 2.3. 'Diplomatic meetings.'

individual event, since no additional similar meetings were added to the MOP. Thus there would be no MOPs created at those index points until additional meetings about SALT or with Gromyko were added. Index points (2) and (3) index meetings with Dayan and about Jerusalem, respectively, in "diplomatic meetings." Index points (6), (7), (8), and (9) are new indices in MOP2 and MOP3, and index differences from the content frames of those newly created MOPs. The meeting with Dayan and the meeting about Jerusalem are indexed in MOP1 and also in appropriate specialized E-MOPs.

An organization such as this provides rich cross-indexing of events in memory. Specification of any discriminating set of event features within an E-MOP should allow retrieval of the corresponding event. When a richly indexed organization such as this is used, enumeration of a memory category should never be necessary for retrieval. Rather, specification of indexed features allows search to be directed only to categories and subcategories whose events are relevant.

6.3. Classifying E-MOPs

E-MOPs can be classified according to the kinds of information they hold in their content frames. As we see later, this classification can constrain search strategy application, since only strategies appropriate to the kinds of information an E-MOP holds in its content frame need be applied.

Scripts (Schank & Abelson, 1977) are the simplest form of E-MOP. Scripts represent events that take place over a short period of time, usually in one location, and with very stereotyped sequences of events. Some of the scripts CYRUS uses are diplomatic meetings ($MEET), speech ($SPEECH), fly ($FLY), and welcoming ceremony ($WELCOME). Scripts are the smallest event unit that can be searched for. Individual actions (such as talking) must be found by searching for episodes (often scripts) they could have been embedded in.

Scriptal events are often embedded in the sequence of events of larger episodes. Some of the larger types of episodes CYRUS uses are diplomatic trip (sM-VIPVISIT) and summit conference (sM-SUMMIT-CONFERENCE). Diplomatic trips and summit conferences are examples of *simple MOPs* (Schank, 1980). Simple MOPs have less stereotyped sequences of events than scripts do and often include scriptal situations and other simple MOPs in their sequences of events. A diplomatic trip, for example, includes flying ($FLY), being welcomed ($WELCOME), doing a series of diplomatic activities, and flying home ($FLY). Instead of a standard sequence of events, some simple MOPs have a set of scripts, which are their standard ways of being done. Travel (sM-TRAVEL), for example, can be done by flying, driving, taking a train, taking a bus, or taking a boat.

The third kind of E-MOP that can be distinguished is an *Intentional MOP* or *I-MOP* (Schank, 1980). I-MOPs are episodes that normally take place over a long period of time and have a standard goal. Negotiating (I-NEGOTIATE), for example, takes place over a long period of time and always has the goal of solving the problem being negotiated. It is not usually embedded in any other episode, except perhaps a more encompassing negotiating episode. Vacation (I-TRIP) is also an I-MOP. Its goal is relaxation. CYRUS' E-MOPs are listed in Fig. 2.4.

$MEET -- diplomatic meetings with foreign dignitaries
$CONSULT -- consultations with American officials
$PUB-REL-MEET -- political meetings with non-diplomats
$STATE-DINNER -- state dinners
$FLY -- flights
$REPORT -- press conferences
$SPEECH -- speeches

sM-MEETING -- political meetings
sM-CONFERENCE -- political conferences
sM-SUMMIT-CONFERENCE -- specialized political conferences
sM-TRAVEL -- traveling
sM-TRIP -- generalized trip
sM-VIPVISIT -- diplomatic trip
sM-SIGHTSEE -- sightseeing
sM-SOCIAL-POL-ACTIVITY -- social political activities
sM-DIPLOMATIC-ACTIVITY -- diplomatic activities

I-NEGOTIATE -- negotiations
I-DIPLOMACY -- diplomacy
I-SOCIALIZE -- socializing

FIG. 2.4. CYRUS' E-MOPs.

6.4. Organizing E-MOPs with Respect to Each Other

Just as individual events can be related to each other causally, E-MOPs can be related to other E-MOPs through causality. When we say that an E-MOP is causally related to another E-MOP, we mean that most of the events in the first E-MOP are related by the same causal link to an event in the second E-MOP. When we say that the start of "negotiations" enables "diplomatic meetings," we mean that each diplomatic meeting in the "diplomatic meetings" MOP has a corresponding negotiating episode in the "negotiations" MOP that enabled discussion of the meeting topic.

Events (and therefore E-MOPs) can also be related to each other through containment and time. "Diplomatic meetings" often happen during "diplomatic trips," for example. This is a containment relation. "Press conferences" often happen after important "diplomatic meetings." This is a time relationship.

MOPs can be related to other MOPs in two other ways. They can be generalizations or specializations of other MOPs. The E-MOP "diplomatic meetings about the Camp David Accords," for example, is a specialization of "diplomatic meetings." The E-MOP "travel" is a generalization of the E-MOP "taking an airplane."

CYRUS' E-MOPs are related to each other through the causal, temporal, containment, and specialization relationships shown in Fig. 2.5.

Causal relationships
- --usual events and states that enable these events to happen
- --their normal preconditions
- --events and states that usually cause these events to happen
- --events and states these events usually cause
- --events and states these events usually enable

Containment relationships
- --E-MOPs these events are usually part of
- --the typical sequence of events for these episodes

Temporal relationships
- --what kinds of events usually come before these episodes
- --what kinds of events usually follow these episodes
- --what kinds of events usually go on at the same time

Specialization/generalization relationships
- --parent E-MOPs
- --standard methods of achievement

FIG. 2.5. Relationships between E-MOPs.

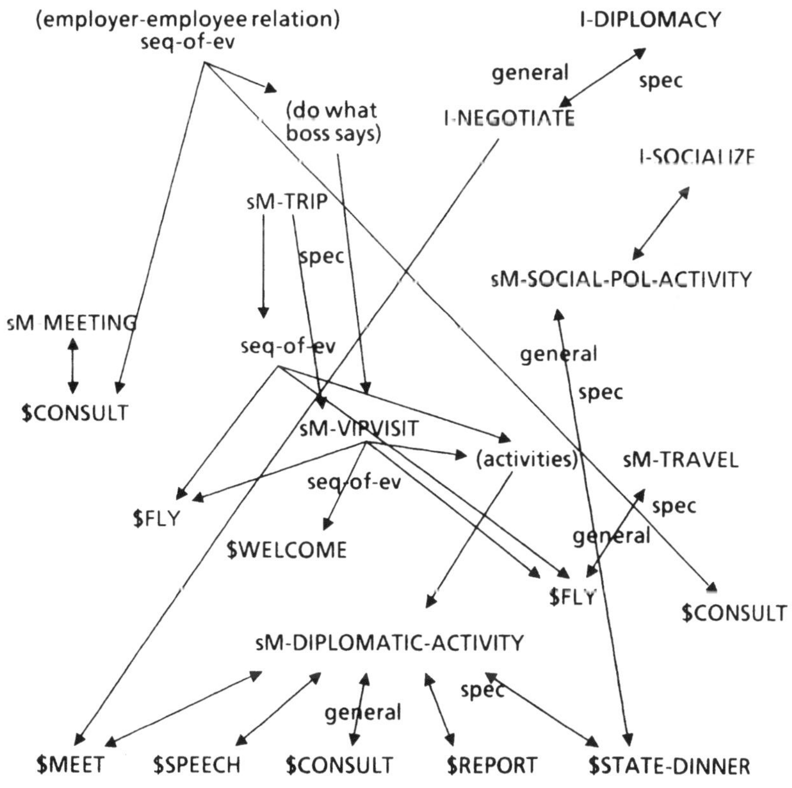

FIG. 2.6. Relationships.

Fig. 2.6 shows some of the interconnections between CYRUS' E-MOPs. The sequence of events for a trip (sM-TRIP) includes flying, doing trip activities, and flying home. Its specialized E-MOP "diplomatic trip" (sM-VIP-VISIT) includes, in addition to that, a welcoming ceremony. Instead of general trip activities, it specifies diplomatic activities. The reasons for Vance's and Muskie's diplomatic trips usually stem from some world problem (not shown) that initiates a consultation with Carter in which Carter advises travel. When the trip is finished, the secretary of state reports back. We can think of that as a generalized sequence of events describing an "employer-employee relationship" (at the top).

In addition to their relationships to other E-MOPs, E-MOPs must specify default values for their components. The following are the kinds of components CYRUS' E-MOPs can have:

1. animate participants -- people, countries, organizations, etc.
2. inanimate participants -- associated objects
3. topic of discussion
4. location
5. time
6. duration

FIG. 2.7. Role-fillers for E-MOPs.

Each of CYRUS' E-MOPs specifies both the other MOPs it is related to and the relationships between its components. "Diplomatic meetings" ($MEET), for example, are specialized "political meetings" (sM-MEETING), as are "consultations" and "public relations meetings." A "political meeting" has a sequence of events and typical setting common to all meetings. In addition to those attributes which it inherits from "political meeting," "diplomatic meeting" specifies that its participants be foreign diplomats, that it is usually part of "negotiations," that its instances happen during "conferences" and "diplomatic trips," that the topic of discussion is usually an international contract, and so on. Fig. 2.8 shows the generalized information CYRUS has about "diplomatic meetings" ($MEET).

Like "diplomatic meetings," "public relations meetings" ($PUB-REL-MEET) is also a specialization of "political meeting," but has different specialized features than does diplomatic meeting. Their participants are representatives of lobby groups and are non-politicians, while for "diplomatic meetings," the participants are foreign diplomats. In addition, public relations meetings happen during important negotiations, but do not usually have direct bearing on those negotiations.

Notice that the relationships between E-MOPs cannot be stored as simple links. Rather, they must also specify correspondences between their components. Thus, CYRUS' "diplomatic meetings" MOP specifies not only that it is

larger episodes:
"negotiations" (I-NEGOTIATE)
participants = diplomats of same nationality as meeting participants, and of other countries involved in meeting topic
topic = generalization of meeting topic
"diplomatic trips" (sM-VIPVISIT)
destination = country or area involved in meeting topic, or country of residence of meeting participant
"conferences" (sM-CONFERENCE)
participants = diplomats of same nationality as meeting participants, and of other countries involved in meeting topic
location = location of meeting
topic = generalization of meeting topic

enables:
"treaty signing" ($TREATY)
sides = sides of meeting topic

sequence of events:
participants MTRANSing to each other about meeting topic

preceding and following events:
"diplomatic meetings" ($MEET)
participants = subset of meeting participants
topic = aspect of meeting topic

more general E-MOPs and classifications:
"political meetings" (sM-MEETING)
all components correspond
"diplomatic activities"
all components correspond

role fillers:
participants: foreign dignitaries of countries involved in contract being discussed
location: conference room in capital city of country of residence of some important participant
topic: international contract
duration: one to two hours

FIG. 2.8. 'Diplomatic meetings' ($MEET)—generalized information.

related to "negotiations," but that the participants in the "negotiations" it is related to are the countries the participants of the meetings represent, and that the topic of the negotiations includes the topic of the meeting.

7. EPISODIC VERSUS SEMANTIC MEMORY

CYRUS' memory is an episodic memory. The episodic view of memory claims that memory is organized around personal experiences or episodes and not around abstract semantic categories. In such a memory, repeated or similar sequences of events are recognized as similar and used to build up generalized knowledge about episodes. This generalized knowledge can later be used for understanding. Thus, every person's episodic memory will be different from every other person's.

Other proposals for memory organization have stressed "semantic memory" organizations. A semantic memory is a memory for words or concepts that is organized hierarchically using class membership as the major link. For example, "elephant" is linked to "mammal," which is linked to "animal" in a hierarchy.

In an episodic memory, on the other hand, propositions are linked together based on their occurrence in the same event or time span. Objects in an episodic memory are defined by their place in an event sequence, or their "function" in a particular type of situation. Particular events are stored as the set of conceptualizations making up their sequence of events.

A person searching his episodic memory for an object will search for episodes that object was part of. Searching for a particular episode might require search for possible related episodes. Of course, often search is not episodic, as in attempting to remember something learned in school, or in remembering the last thing one heard about a certain person or object.

Our emphasis throughout this document is on episodic memory organization and episodic retrieval. Thus, we discuss organization of information about episodes. Although we recognize that knowledge about things other than episodes is organized in memory, and that search is not always episodic, we do not discuss such organization or search. Our preference for episodic memory has a dual basis: (1) We are interested in storing episodes; (2) in observing people, we've found that episodic retrieval is reported more often than semantic. One of the conclusions of this research is that episodic and semantic memory are not necessarily different, but are integrated in such a way that they cannot always be told apart.

Because some episodes are similar to each other, and because we can talk about general types of episodes, memory must have economy measures for dealing with similarities. This is what E-MOPs do for us. They store the similarities between events as a generalized standardized episode that can be used in understanding instead of accessing all of the episodes relevant to a particular new situation. This also means that it is not necessary for memory to store the full sequence of events for each new episode added to memory if it is similar to other episodes already there. Instead, the particular E-MOPs it fits into can be determined, and only its differences from those E-MOPs need be stored. The rest can be reconstructed from the standardized E-MOP if needed. This economy of storage of course has a side effect—forgetting. That side effect, however, may be necessary to give memory its power.

8. QUESTION ANSWERING

Thus far, we have discussed representations in memory and memory's organization. The other important aspect of long-term memory is its retrieval processes and capabilities. The theory of retrieval presented in this document has its roots in a previous theory of question answering (Lehnert, 1978). Question answering differs from data base retrieval in an important way: the emphasis in question answering is on appropriate answers rather than on correct answers. In querying a data base about the existence of some item, "no" would be a perfectly good answer if the item did not exist. A question-answering system, however, must give a better answer than that. Along with the "no," it must explain why the item did not exist or what existed instead of it. In other words, the question-answering system must respond to both the *content* and the *intent* of a question. Making a system "smart" in this way makes the user's job easier. He can phrase questions as he would if he were asking a person, expecting his intent to be understood and the added information he implicitly requested to be supplied.

Question answering requires understanding a statement or question, inferring its intent, retrieving the requested information from memory, and formulating an answer. To answer a question, the question must be analyzed and its question category and question concept must be extracted. The *question concept* (Lehnert, 1978) of a question is the part of the question that must be searched for initially. To answer "Why did John go to the store?" or "What did John do after he left

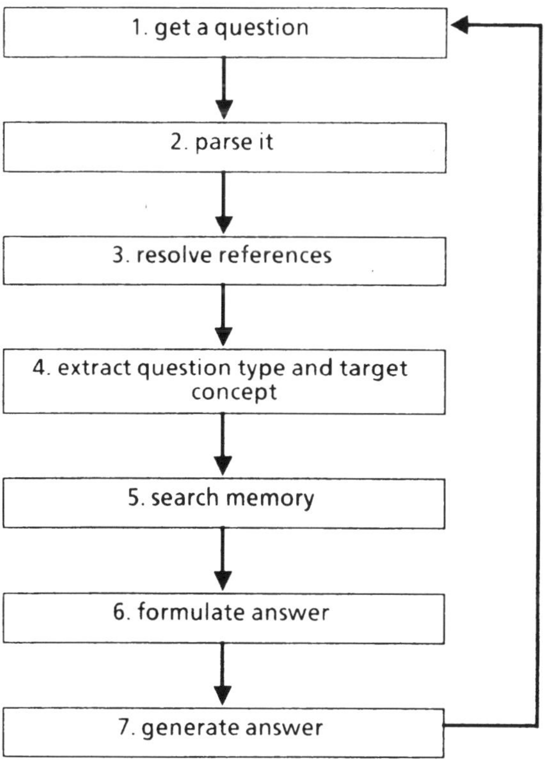

FIG. 2.9. Question-Answering Loop.

for the store?'' for example, memory must first be searched for ''John's trip to the store,'' the question concept of the two questions above. We refer to Lehnert's question concept as the *target concept,* the event that must be retrieved before further processing can be done.

When an event corresponding to a target event is found in memory, processes associated with the *question category* are applied to it to formulate an answer. The question's category specifies the process to be used to extract appropriate features of the retrieved item. If the question asks ''why,'' for example, the causes of the retrieved event are extracted and expressed. The entire question-answering process can be described by the algorithm in Fig. 2.9.

In formulating her theory of question answering, Lehnert's emphasis was on steps 4, 5, and 6. Answers to steps 4 and 6 describe what it means to interpret a question for intent and to give an appropriate answer. In step 5, Lehnert concentrated on searching the memory representation of a single story. Our emphasis is on step 5 of this process—memory search. It is different than Lehnert's description since we are dealing with an entire long-term memory including representations of many events rather than just a single detailed episode. The new problems we must address include choosing an appropriate starting point for search and directing search from that point. The retrieval processes and strategies introduced in chapter 1 are the strategies used to search a long-term memory for a target concept. When the term ''retrieval'' is used throughout this text, it refers to memory search, the primary step in the retrieval process.

9. SUMMARY

CYRUS' memory organization and retrieval processes have their roots in previous theories of natural language understanding, including conceptual dependency, causal chain construction, scripts, and question answering. CYRUS answers some of the questions associated with memory organization and retrieval brought out by those previous theories.

II RETRIEVAL STRATEGIES

Q: Have you been to Saudi Arabia recently?

A: Yes, most recently last month, to discuss the Camp David Accords with King Khalid and Prince Fahd.

Q: Where did you go afterwards?

A: To Syria. I was touring the Middle East talking to each of the Arab leaders about the Accords.

Q: How many times have you been to the Middle East in the past 6 months?

A: I was in Israel and Egypt this past summer on two separate trips, and after the Camp David Summit, I was in the Middle East to talk to Arab leaders about the Camp David Accords.

Taking part in a dialog or discussion often requires retrieval of past events from memory. The answers given in this hypothetical dialog are reasonable ones for Cyrus Vance to have given while he was secretary of state. What are the processes that allow such retrieval to happen? How can a list of events be retrieved from a memory which does not allow enumeration of its categories? In this section of this book, we examine the processes of memory retrieval and search.

To see which processes are involved in retrieval, consider retrieval's prerequisite: before searching memory, what is being sought must be described. Such a specification is called a *context for search.* A context for search has two components: a specification of a category to begin the search and a set of features describing the item to be extracted from that category. Retrieval processes derive from failures in specifying a search context. When no category specification is given in a question, one must be chosen by considering available question components. When poor contexts are given, better ones must be constructed—either by elaborating the given one with better features or by choosing a new related category. When search for an initial context fails, search for something related can help. Retrieval, then, includes at least the following:

1. choosing a conceptual category (E-MOP) for search (context construction)
2. filling in hypothetical features of a target concept (elaboration)
3. search for episodes related to the target concept (alternate-context search)

These tasks are done by *retrieval strategies.* There are two types of retrieval strategies—processes for constructing and further specifying contexts for search, and processes for directing search and application of constructive strategies. Those which direct search we call *executive strategies.* Those which construct and elaborate contexts are called *instantiation strategies.*

The functions served by strategies were illustrated in chapter 1. They are reviewed below:

1. Strategies can be used to better specify contexts for retrieval by filling in details and providing cues. In searching for museum experiences, descriptions of museum experiences can be better specified to include where the activity took place and what type of museum it was.

2. Strategies can be used to hypothesize contexts for search when none are explicitly available in a retrieval specification. In searching for famous people they had met, people searched for the kinds of situations where they could have met famous people (e.g., political rallies, scientific conventions).

3. Strategies can be used to choose contexts for search from already specified events. Museum experiences can be found by recalling trips.

4. *Strategies can be used to search within specified contexts to find a targeted event.* After recalling a trip to find a museum experience, the context of each trip must be searched for the museum experiences it included. The diagram (Fig. 1.3) is shown here again, indicating the focus of the following chapters of this book.

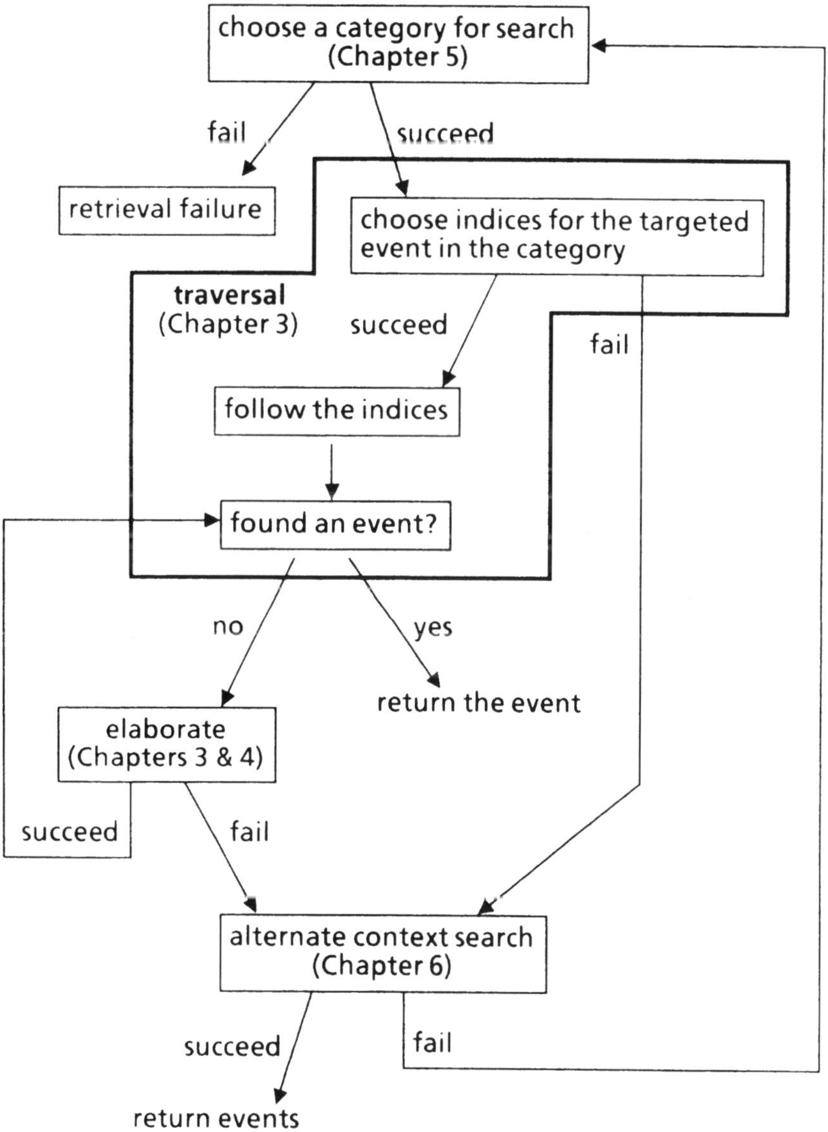

In the next four chapters, we explain the retrieval process in detail, focusing on strategy application. Among the issues which will be addressed are the following:

1. What is the retrieval process?
2. Where do retrieval strategies fit into that process?
3. What kinds of strategies are there?
4. When are they applied?
5. What information do they use, and where can that information be found?

Chapter 3 presents traversal, the core search process, and motivates the need for elaboration during retrieval. Chapter 4 presents strategies for elaboration. Chapter 5 presents strategies for choosing a context for search, and chapter 6 presents the process of using alternate contexts to aid retrieval.

3 Traversal and Elaboration

1. RETRIEVING AN EVENT FROM AN E-MOP

Strategies for searching memory derive from failures in the process of searching a particular E-MOP to find an event. In order to motivate retrieval strategies, we must therefore first explain that procedure in detail.

Because events are organized in E-MOPs by their differentiating features, an event can be found in an E-MOP by traversing indices corresponding to its features. Consider, again, the E-MOP presented in chapter 2 (see Fig. 3.1).

The retrieval process for an indexed structure such as this can be characterized as a *traversal* process. Traversal involves following appropriate indices down the tree until the sought item is found. An event to be retrieved from an E-MOP is called a *target event,* and the features that describe it make up its *context specification.* A target event, or event that must be retrieved, can be said to be *targeted for retrieval.*

Traversal of an E-MOP is guided by the particular event targeted for retrieval. Indices for traversal are chosen from among the features specified in that target event. To search for "a diplomatic meeting with Gromyko" in this MOP, the participant index corresponding to Gromyko would be followed, and the event indexed at that point (EV2) would be found. Similarly, to find a "diplomatic meeting about SALT," the topic index corresponding to SALT would be followed and a matching event (EV2) would be found.

Rich cross-indexing, such as that found in E-MOPs, enables *directed search* of memory. In a directed search, categories need not be sequentially enumerated. Rather, indices corresponding to specified features are traversed. To ensure directed search, traversal's first step must thus be to specify appropriate paths for traversal. We call this process *index selection.*

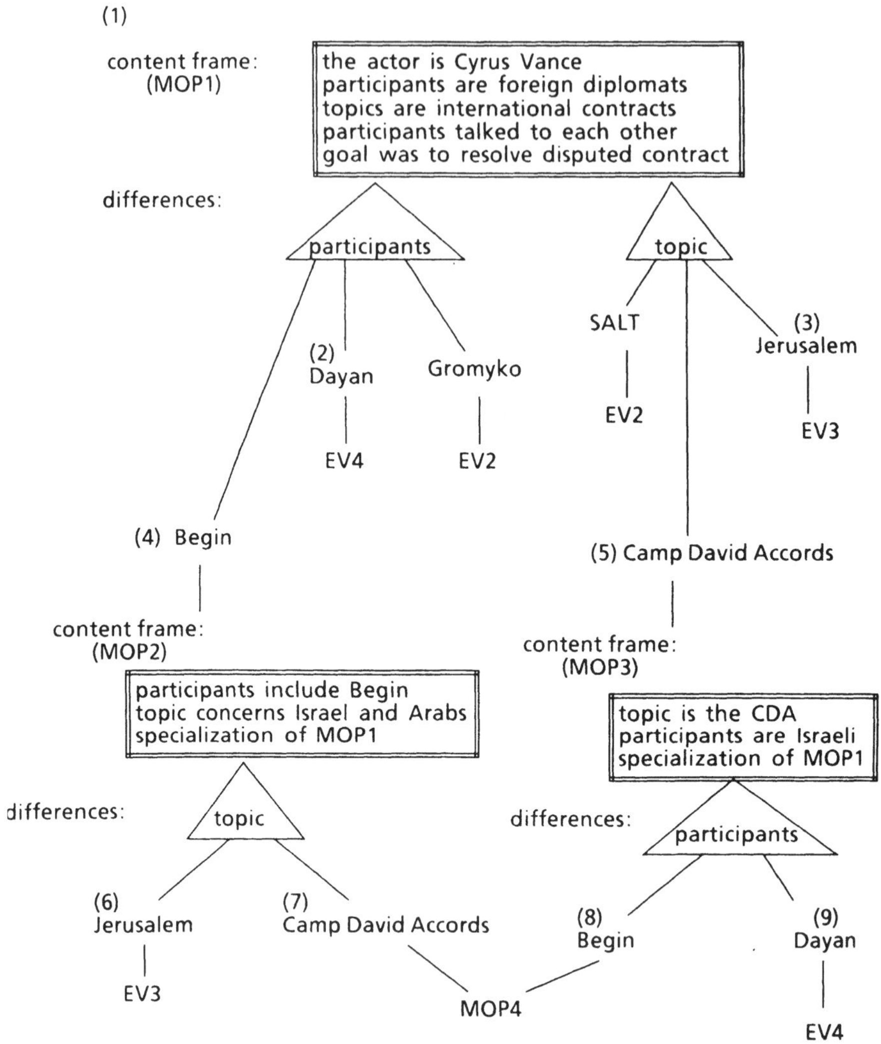

FIG. 3.1. Diplomatic meetings.

Index selection is based on features specified in the target event. Indices chosen for use in retrieving any target event should be features that would have been chosen as indices for that event if it had previously been indexed in the E-MOP. The same process of index selection is used both when an event is added to memory and when it must be retrieved. When an event is added to memory, the index selection procedure chooses features that should be indexed, and indices are built. During retrieval, the index selection procedure chooses features that would have been indexed if the target event had been added to memory, and those indices are traversed. The actual process of choosing indices is discussed in chapter 7.

Consider, for example, how we might answer the questions below using the MOP illustrated in Fig. 3.1.

(Q1): Have you ever discussed SALT with Gromyko at a diplomatic meeting?

(Q2): Have you ever attended a diplomatic meeting about the Camp David Accords with Dayan?

As a first step, answering a question requires extraction of its *target concept,* that is, the concept that must be searched for in memory. The target concept for (Q1) is a "diplomatic meeting about SALT with Gromyko." Answering (Q1) requires retrieval of an event with that description. A real event corresponding to this event description can be retrieved from the structure in Fig. 3.1 by traversing either the topic index corresponding to SALT or the participant index corresponding to Gromyko. Events that are retrieved are checked to see if their features correspond to the target concept. Since EV2, found at both index points, is a meeting with Gromyko about SALT, it has all the features of the target event and can be used to answer "yes" to the question.

When a target event specifies an event feature that is unique in an E-MOP, the event can be found by traversing the index associated with that feature. Question (Q1) had two unique features in the "diplomatic meetings" MOP—its participants and its topic. Either can be followed to retrieve the appropriate event. The target concept for (Q2) is a "diplomatic meeting with Dayan about the Camp David Accords." One can be retrieved from Fig. 3.1 by traversing the participant index corresponding to Dayan (index point 2 in Fig. 3.1), since there is only one event in the MOP with that feature. EV4 is found. It is checked to make sure its topic "the Camp David Accords" corresponds to that specified in the target event. Since EV4 is a meeting with Dayan about the Camp David Accords, it has all specified features and can be used to answer the question.

There is also a second way the "meeting with Dayan about the Camp David Accords" can be found in that tree. Since it has a topic specified, it can be found by traversing the topic index corresponding to the Camp David Accords. Following that index, MOP3, "diplomatic meetings about the Camp David Accords," is reached. When a specialized E-MOP is reached during the traversal process, it must be searched for the target event in the same way its parent E-MOP is searched. Thus, its indices are traversed after selecting appropriate indices for traversal to find the target event. In this case, the participant index in MOP3 corresponding to Dayan (index point 9 of Fig. 3.1) would be traversed and EV4 would be found, again a sufficient answer to the question.

Because there is no way of knowing before traversal whether or not a feature is unique to an E-MOP, indices associated with all features selected for retrieval must be traversed. If one is unique, an event will be found and traversal can end. Otherwise, traversal continues at the next E-MOP level. Thus, in answering (Q2), both indices "has Dayan as a participant" and "has topic the Camp David Accords" are traversed. Since one is unique, an event is found, and traversal can stop. If, however, the index "has Dayan as a participant" had not been unique (i.e., if there had been more than one meeting with Dayan indexed in the E-MOP), then traversal would have continued within the E-MOP at that point, as well as within the "meetings about the Camp David Accords" MOP.

Thus, traversal is a *recursive process* involving choice of indices and traversal of those indices. It stops when an event is found, or when there are no more specified indices to be traversed. If there are multiple paths to a target event, it will be retrieved from the shortest path that has all of its indices specified in the target event. We can think of traversal as a breadth-first search, which implements parallel traversal of all appropriate indices.

We can thus specify the following algorithm for traversal:

1. Select possible indices for the target event based on its specified features and their differences from the norm of the E-MOP being traversed.
2. IF there are no indices, THEN return "not found".
3. ELSE follow all of those indices in the E-MOP.
4. IF events are found, THEN check that they have all features of the target event. If any do, return them, and finish.
5. IF E-MOPs are found, traverse them in parallel using this algorithm.

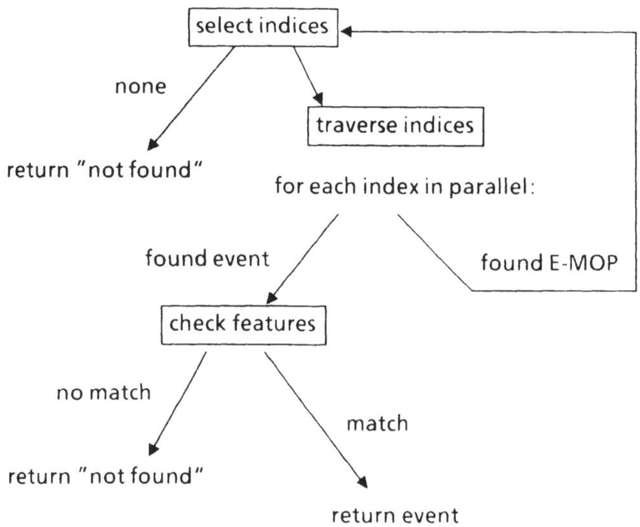

FIG. 3.2. E-MOP Traversal.

2. THE NEED FOR ELABORATION

In each of the examples above, traversal continued until a unique event was found. Each of those target concepts specified some event feature that was both indexed in the E-MOP and unique to one event in the E-MOP. Thus, we can conclude that retrieval of a target concept that specifies an event feature or combination of features that is both *indexed* and *unique* can be done easily through traversal.

We cannot expect that every question asked, however, will specify unique, indexed features. When a target concept specifies unindexed features or does not specify a unique combination of features, the traversal algorithm presented above will fail.

For example, suppose we wanted to answer the following question using the MOP in Fig. 3.1:

(Q3): How many times have you met with Begin about the Camp David Accords?

One way to answer this question is to find all meetings with Begin about the Camp David Accords. Because enumeration of events is not allowed, answering this question requires individual retrieval of each appropriate meeting. In order to traverse E-MOPs to find those meetings, the indices to be traversed must be specified.

Meetings with Begin about the Camp David Accords can be reached by first traversing the branch from MOP1—"diplomatic meetings"—indexing Begin as a participant, arriving at MOP2—"diplomatic meetings with Begin." That E-MOP's topic index with value "the Camp David Accords" can then be traversed, arriving at index point (7) in the tree, where all diplomatic meetings with Begin about the Camp David Accords are organized in MOP4. Alternatively, these meetings can be reached by first traversing a topic index in MOP1 with value equal to the Camp David Accords, arriving at MOP3—"diplomatic trips about the Camp David Accords." From that E-MOP, the index specifying Begin as a participant can be traversed, arriving at index point (8), also an index to MOP4—"diplomatic meetings about the Camp David Accords with Begin." Breadth-first traversal, in this case, will arrive at MOP4 in two different ways.

At this point, the traversal process, as specified above, must abort. There are no additional features specified in the target concept that correspond to indices in the "meetings about the Camp David Accords with Begin" MOP. Thus, no further traversal can be done. Although all meetings between Vance and Begin about the Camp David Accords can be found in MOP4, they are indexed in that E-MOP and can only be retrieved through specification of the differences that index them.

The problem is that an E-MOP has been retrieved instead of an event. Individual events from that E-MOP must be extracted from it, but there are no

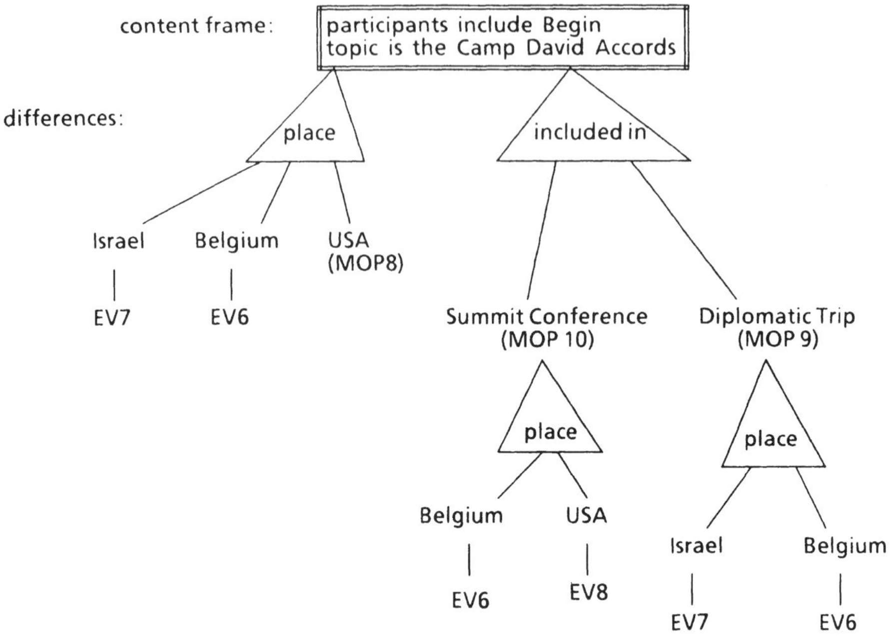

FIG. 3.3. Meetings with Begin about the Camp David Accords—MOP4.

specifications in the target event that can be used to traverse the E-MOP. This happens when a retrieval specification is *too general*. If a retrieval specification does not specify a unique event but specifies an entire class of events, then additional event features must be specified in order to traverse deeper into the corresponding E-MOP.

Consider how retrieval could continue if MOP4—"diplomatic meetings about the Camp David Accords with Begin"—had the structure shown in Fig. 3.3. This E-MOP has indices corresponding to meeting locations and episodes the meetings were part of. If possible places for these meetings could be inferred, or if the episodes they were part of could be imagined, then individual meetings could be retrieved from the MOP.

The process of specifying additional features of a target event is called *elaboration*. Elaboration provides additional event features, serving to "unlock" memory's networks. It allows downward traversal through memory. The processes CYRUS uses for elaborating a retrieval specification are called *instantiation strategies*. They use information specified in a target concept and information associated with the E-MOPs the target concept fits into to fill in or better specify target concept features.

Instantiation strategies are used to elaborate two classes of event features: event components and event contexts. Event components include such descriptive features as participants, location, and topic. An event's context includes other episodes related to it through time, causality, or containment.

Consider, for example, the following instantiation rule:

To infer the country an event might have taken place in, use the participants' country of residence, country they habitually travel to, or their nationality.

FIG. 3.4. Infer-Country.

Applying this rule to "meetings with Begin about the Camp David Accords"—the target event of (Q3)—"Israel" can be inferred as a plausible place for one of these meetings. The index for "location is Israel" can then be traversed in the E-MOP, and EV7 will be found. The set of strategies that infer event components and slot fillers are called *component instantiation strategies*.

Besides "location" indices, the "meetings with Begin about the Camp David Accords" MOP (specified in Fig. 3.3) has indices for types of E-MOPs its events were included in. Thus, elaborating the kinds of episodes a "meeting with Begin about the Camp David Accords" was part of can also help in retrieving individual events from that E-MOP. The set of instantiation strategies that construct event contexts related to a target event are called *context-to-context instantiation strategies*. These strategies use information from the E-MOPs the target event fits into to elaborate on contexts related to the target event.

One of these strategies, called "Instantiate Larger Episodes," uses information about the kinds of larger E-MOPs its episodes are normally part of to predict episodes the target event could have been embedded in. Because "diplomatic meetings" often occur during negotiations and summit conferences, and because "diplomatic meetings" are "diplomatic activities" (another E-MOP), which often happen during "diplomatic trips," that strategy can be used to elaborate the target event "meetings with Begin about the Camp David Accords" in the following three ways:

meetings with Begin about the Camp David Accords, which took place during a diplomatic trip to Israel

meetings with Begin about the Camp David Accords during a summit conference, which included Begin as a participant and whose topic was related to the Camp David Accords

meetings with Begin about the Camp David Accords, which were part of negotiations with Israel about the Camp David Accords

Retrieval of each of these can then be attempted. The first will retrieve EV7 by following the indices "included in a diplomatic trip" and then "place is Israel." Retrieval of the second will include traversal of the index "included in a summit conference," and further elaboration will be needed to retrieve an individual event. The third will not be successful in the E-MOP illustrated.

2.1. When is Elaboration Appropriate?

There are two circumstances when elaboration should be used:

1. When traversal has failed because there are no additional features to use as indices (i.e., the target event is too generally specified).
2. When traversal has failed because the only features available for use as indices do not correspond in type to E-MOP indices (i.e., when a target concept specifies features which are not indexed).

The first case, illustrated in the example above, results in *plausible-index generation*—generation of additional event features. The second case results in index fitting, a process of transforming given features to correspond to E-MOP features. Suppose, for example, that we wanted to answer the following question:

(Q4): Where did Vance go on diplomatic trips last April?

The target event of this question is "diplomatic trips by Vance last April." Suppose that the following "diplomatic trip" MOP were the one being traversed to answer this question:

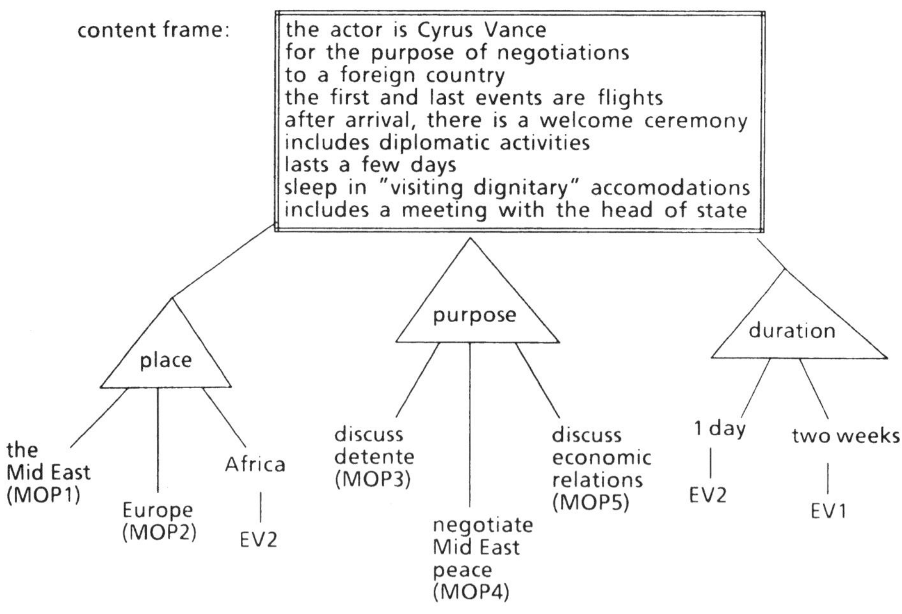

FIG. 3.5. Diplomatic trips.

The only feature the target event specifies is a time, but this E-MOP has no indices for time. The same elaboration rules that can be used to elaborate additional features when none are available can be used to *transform* inappropriate indices into appropriate ones. By recalling what kinds of important international problems were going on last April, for example, possible places and purposes for diplomatic trips can be inferred. Suppose, for example, that one of the international problems going on last April had to do with setting up the Zimbabwe government. It would be plausible in that case to hypothesize that Vance spent some time last April in Zimbabwe, and to attempt retrieval of a trip to Zimbabwe last April. Thus, the feature "place is Zimbabwe" could be inferred and traversal attempted. This, however, would still not be sufficient in the E-MOP above. Its place indices are parts of the world, not countries. Thus, elaboration would be used again to transform "place is Zimbabwe" into "place is Africa." That index could be followed, finding EV7, and its description could be checked to see if it had occurred last April.

We call the process of transforming an inappropriate index into one that can be used for traversal *index fitting*. There are three ways a feature can be "fit" to an E-MOP.

1. A given feature can be specialized.
2. A given feature can be generalized.
3. Given features can be used to derive other possible features.

Transforming the feature "place is Zimbabwe" to "place is Africa" as in the example above is an example of feature generalization (2). Using the time specification to infer a purpose or place in the example above is an example of using given features to derive other possible features (3). This type of index fitting is equivalent to the elaboration done when a target specification is too general.

Feature specialization (1) can be done when a specified feature is too general to be traversed in the E-MOP, but when some of its more specific instances might be indexed. Suppose, for example, that we wanted to answer the following question using the "diplomatic meetings" MOP in Fig. 3.1:

(Q5): How many times have you talked to Begin about Arab-Israeli concerns?

This question has target concept "meetings with Begin about Arab-Israeli issues." Using the "diplomatic meetings" MOP in Fig. 3.1, traversal can be directed to MOP2 "meetings with Begin." The problem at this point is that the remaining feature that has not yet been traversed—"topic concerns Arabs and Israel"—is too general to use in traversing the E-MOP. In fact, it is one of the norms of that E-MOP. More specialized topics involving the Arabs and Israel are used as indices in the E-MOP, however. It would thus be appropriate to specialize "topic concerns Arabs and Israel," and to infer particular Arab-Israeli issues that might be indexed.

2.2. Guiding Elaboration

Elaboration of a context involves specifying or elaborating some aspect of the context, often filling in a place, participant, or time specification. Instantiation strategies are the reasoning rules for filling in contextual details. After using these strategies to fill in details during retrieval, traversal can be attempted again on the better specified context. In this way we can imagine a dialog going on between elaboration processes and traversal processes.

Recall that in the second step of the traversal process, if there are no indices specified for traversal, traversal fails. If, instead, the traversal process sends a message stating that it needs more information, then elaboration can take over, and traversal can be continued using the new specifications. We can envision that process as follows:

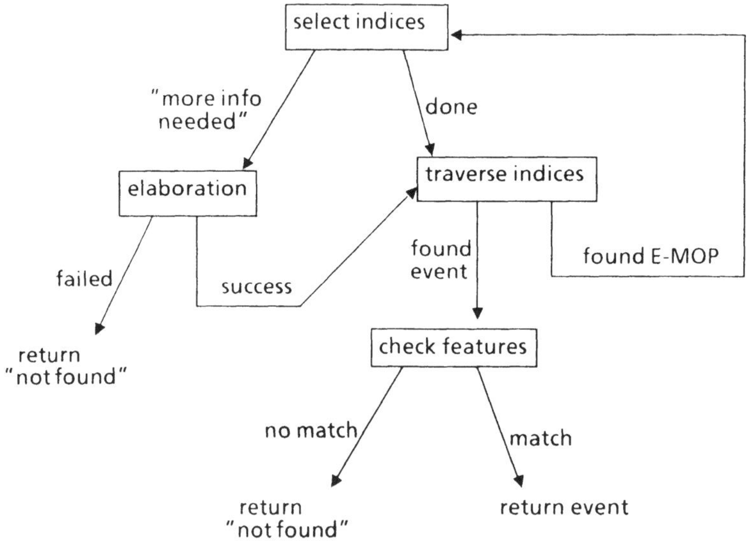

FIG. 3.6. Traversal/Elaboration

An E-MOP's two-tiered indexing structure can be utilized to guide elaboration. Recall that the first tier holds the *types of features* that are indexed in the E-MOP (e.g., place, purpose, duration in Fig. 3.6). The second tier is indexed off the first and has values for each type of feature (e.g., the Middle East, Africa, 2 weeks, in Fig. 3.6).

If the first tier is available to the traversal process, then when it aborts, it can specify the E-MOP it stopped at and the types of indices in that MOP. Only instantiation strategies associated with those types of indices need be applied. Note that this does not mean that values for every feature indexed in an E-MOP must be available, but only that *the nature of the indices* (i.e., the types of indices) be known or derivable. Instantiation rules associated with each appropriate type of feature will generate values for the indices. Values of features do not need to be enumerable since application of instantiation strategies provides reasonable values for particular target events. Thus, the second tier can be accessed directly (e.g., via a hashing scheme).

Using the E-MOP in Fig. 3.6 to answer (Q4), for example, traversal would return with the information that the MOP had "place," "purpose," and "duration" indices. Elaboration rules associated with each of those would be applied to compute actual indices. In this way *memory organization guides choice of features to be elaborated*, limiting choice of instantiation rules.

We can amend the traversal strategy presented in Fig. 3.2 as follows to include elaboration:

1. Select possible indices for the target event based on its specified features and their differences from the norm of the E-MOP being traversed.
2. IF there are no appropriate indices, THEN return (a) the E-MOP being traversed and (b) the nature of its indices. Call instantiation strategies to elaborate on the target concept and attempt traversal/elaboration of the newly-elaborated target
3. ELSE follow all of those indices in the E-MOP.
4. IF events are found, THEN check that they have all features of the target event. IF any do, return them, and finish.
5. IF E-MOPs are found, traverse them in parallel using this algorithm.

FIG. 3.7. Traversal/Elaboration

This algorithm describes the diagram in Fig. 3.6. The significant change in this algorithm over the initial traversal algorithm is that it specifies that instantiation strategies be applied to elaborate an underspecified target concept. Step (2) above is equivalent to a message from memory saying "I don't have enough information to traverse deeper in my E-MOP structures. If you give me the following *types* of information, I may be able to search deeper." When traversal returns that message, instantiation rules fill in necessary details, and traversal is attempted again. This dialog continues until appropriate events are found or until no more elaboration can be done. In this way, memory organization guides retrieval.

2.3. Types of Elaboration

Recall from section 2.1 that particular features can be specialized, generalized, or used to derive new features during elaboration. E-MOPs direct this process by specifying which types of features they need, and instantiation rules specific to each type of feature are applied. These rules are used during elaboration to perform three different functions on the target event:

(1) feature specification
(2) feature inference
(3) feature enumeration

In feature specification, a particular feature of the target event is better specified. In feature inference, a feature not specified in the target event is inferred. In feature enumeration, a set of possible values for some feature is computed. Instantiation strategies do these things by considering the given features of the target event to derive the new features.

Consider the following question again:

(Q6): Where did Vance go to on diplomatic trips last April?

We explained above that in order to answer this question, features indexed in the "diplomatic trips" MOP had to be inferred. We suggested using information about what was going on in the world last April to infer possible trouble spots where Vance might have been, and made the inference that Vance might have been in Zimbabwe. In this way, the following transformation of the target event was made:

target event:
"diplomatic trips last April"
| | infer-location
\ /
modified target:
"diplomatic trips to Zimbabwe last April"

A new feature (location) that had not been previously specified in the target event was inferred. One task elaboration can do, then, is to *infer event components not previously specified.*

In attempting retrieval of the new modified target event "diplomatic trips to Zimbabwe last April," retrieval failed because the place index in the "diplomatic trips" MOP specified parts of the world and not countries. To traverse the E-MOP, elaboration had to be applied to generalize "Africa" from "Zimbabwe." The following target event transformation was done:

target event:
"diplomatic trips to Zimbabwe last April"
| | infer-part-of-world
\ /
modified target:
"diplomatic trips to Africa last April"

In this case, a feature that was already specified in the target event (location) was better specified to correspond to E-MOP indices through generalization of its value. Both generalization and specialization of particular features can be used to *better specify* an already-specified event feature for traversal.

Often, specification of features involves *enumeration of possibilities*. Both partially specified or previously unspecified features can be enumerated. Consider, for example, the following question:

(Q7): How many of the states in the United States has Vance been to?

If a map of the United States could be reconstructed and each state named as that reconstruction was going on, then the 50 states could be named and retrieval of events in each state attempted. Enumeration of this type has been referred to as "map search" by Schank (1980). Map or chart application, or well-ordered enumeration, can be helpful in specifying possible features of a target event. *Well-ordered enumeration* is a useful type of elaboration.

3. ELABORATION IN HUMAN PROTOCOLS

Let us return to some of the questions we asked people and explain their answers in terms of instantiation strategies and elaboration. The following two protocols illustrate traversal and application of component instantiation strategies for elaboration in answering "Name all the museums you've been to."

Protocol 1

What kinds of museums have I been to? Art museums, there have been a lot of them. I'll come back to them. Science museums—there's a good one in Philadelphia, the Franklin Institute, there's one in Boston that I've been to, and there's an air and space museum in Washington that I've been to. Wax museums—there's one in London—Mme. Taussaud's.

Protocol 2

I know I've been to a lot of museums in Europe. I've been to England, and I went to a number of museums there—some in London—the British Museum, the National Gallery, and a few smaller galleries. . . . I was at a museum in Brighton—the Royal Pavilion. I've been to museums in Paris—the Louvre and some smaller ones. In Rome, I've been to. . . . In Naples, to. . . . In Florence, to. . . .

In the first protocol, the respondent seems to be elaborating types of museums first, then elaborating places where those museums might be. Thus, we can imagine that component instantiation was initially used to supply a museum type. Elaboration continued for each type of museum by enumerating places.

We can explain this protocol using the traversal/elaboration process described above. In recalling museum experiences, the traversal process returned a message saying "I need more information. The type of museum would be useful." At that point, component instantiation rules were applied to enumerate museum types and traversal continued. As traversal was attempted for each type of museum, the traversal process could have returned the message "I need more information, place would be useful." Component instantiation strategies could then be used to enumerate places and retrieval of each newly specified target could be attempted.

The second protocol was from a person familiar with Europe. He remembered museums he had been to in Europe by enumerating places in Europe. We can imagine him mentally walking through a map of Europe stopping at each familiar or important point and attempting to use it to further specify the target event.

4. IMPLICATIONS OF TRAVERSAL/ELABORATION

In the traversal algorithm described, indices must be specified in order for an E-MOP to be traversed. There are two disadvantages that stem from this requirement. First, an event cannot be retrieved unless a suitable discriminating index for it can be inferred. Because the process does not allow enumeration and search of all E-MOP indices, but requires determination of plausible indices, all events matching a particular specification will not always be found. Events can be forgotten.

A second disadvantage of this method of retrieval is that memory is too sensitive to incorrectly specified questions. Partial matching is not allowed. A question may get details of an event wrong. For example, a question could ask about an event that happened in the spring, when in fact the event happened in the summer, or it could ask for a meeting in Jerusalem that actually took place in Tel Aviv. As people, we are often able to recognize and point out another person's mistaken presuppositions and retrieve what he was "really" asking for. In the scheme described, a mistaken presupposition will keep memory from returning a correct answer.

It should be possible to incorporate a solution to this problem into the retrieval algorithm, even though it is not there now. In the retrieval scheme described, memory finds partial matches during its search but discards those that are inconsistent with the question concept. An evaluation procedure added to the search process might be able to save those matches that are close. In general, however, the problem of partial matching and finding the best partial match has not been solved.

Advantages of this retrieval scheme far outweigh the disadvantages. The major advantage of this algorithm is that it directs search only to relevant places in an E-MOP. Thus, if a MOP has hundreds of indices organizing thousands of events, they do not all have to be searched. Only the ones directly related to the targeted context specification are traversed.

The second advantage of this algorithm is that it allows generalized information to be retrieved in exactly the same way events are retrieved. Thus, retrieval for a question such as "When you go to Europe, where do you usually stay?" will proceed exactly as for "Last time you were in Europe, where did you stay?" To answer the second question, the particular trip to Europe would be retrieved by the traversal process (as described above), and its context would then be searched for where the actor stayed. In traversing memory to answer the first question, an E-MOP corresponding to "trips to Europe" would be returned by the traversal process in exactly the same way a particular event is retrieved. Generalized information associated with that MOP would then be used to answer the question.

4.1. Recognizing Whether or not an Event is in Memory

When an event cannot be found, either it is not in memory or it is in memory but not retrievable because the proper indices cannot be specified. There are two ways of evaluating whether or not an event is in memory. In the first step of the traversal algorithm, possible indices for the target event are selected. The same process that chooses features of an event to be indexed when it is added to memory is used during retrieval to choose features that *would have been* indexed if the target event were in memory. A procedure for deciding that an event is not in memory will take a target's possible indices into account.

If some possible index of the target event is unique in an E-MOP, and the event that it indexes does not match the target event, then we can assume that the target event is probably not in memory. Using the E-MOP in Fig. 3.1, suppose we wanted to answer the following questions:

(Q8): Have you met with Gromyko about the Afghanistan invasion?

(Q9): Have you met with Dayan about the status of Jerusalem?

One of the indices that should be traversed to answer the first question is the participant index corresponding to Gromyko. This E-MOP indexes one meeting with Gromyko (EV2), and that meeting is about SALT. Thus, the index "has Gromyko as a participant" indexes a unique event. Since that event does not correspond to the target event "a meeting with Gromyko about the Afghanistan invasion," we can safely assume that there is no meeting corresponding to that target event. If there were, it would be indexed at that point.

A negative answer to the second question can be derived similarly. Its target concept is "diplomatic meetings with Dayan about Jerusalem." The indices "participants include Dayan" and "topic concerns Jerusalem" can be followed, retrieving EV3 and EV4. If neither matches the target specification, we can assume there is nothing in memory corresponding to it.

There is a second heuristic for deciding whether or not an event is in memory. Just because an E-MOP does not index a particular given feature of an event does not mean that the event is not in memory. However, if an E-MOP has indices of the same type as an index selected from the target, but it has no particular index corresponding to the value of that feature in the target, then we can conclude that the event is not in memory. This heuristic corresponds to what Collins, Warnock, Aiello, and Miller (1975) and Collins (1978) call a "lack of knowledge" inference.

Consider, for example, how the following question could be answered using the E-MOP in Fig. 3.1.

(Q10): Has Weizmann been to any of your diplomatic meetings about the Camp David Accords?

The target event in the first question is "diplomatic meetings with Weizmann about the Camp David Accords." One of its features, appropriate for indexing in that E-MOP, is "participants include Weizmann." Since there are indices for participants in that E-MOP and they index individual people, and Weizmann is not one of those people, the MOP does not include an event corresponding to the target event.

Similarly, suppose that an E-MOP "diplomatic meetings about Arab Israeli peace" had the structure in Fig. 3.8, and that we wanted to answer the following question:

(Q11): Was King Hussein ever at a diplomatic meeting you attended about Arab-Israeli peace?

According to that E-MOP, only Israelis and Egyptians have attended "diplomatic meetings about Arab-Israeli peace." Since (a) Hussein is a Jordanian, (b) there are indices for participants' nationalities in the E-MOP, and (c) Jordan is not one of them, we can assume there has never been a meeting with Hussein about Arab-Israeli peace. If there had been, there would be an index for it.

It is not always possible to determine with certainty whether or not an event that cannot be found is actually in memory. If all known possibilities for features have been enumerated and retrieval has been attempted on all of them, then there is a good chance that the event is not in memory. If, however, appropriate indices in an E-MOP cannot be completely enumerated, there is no way of

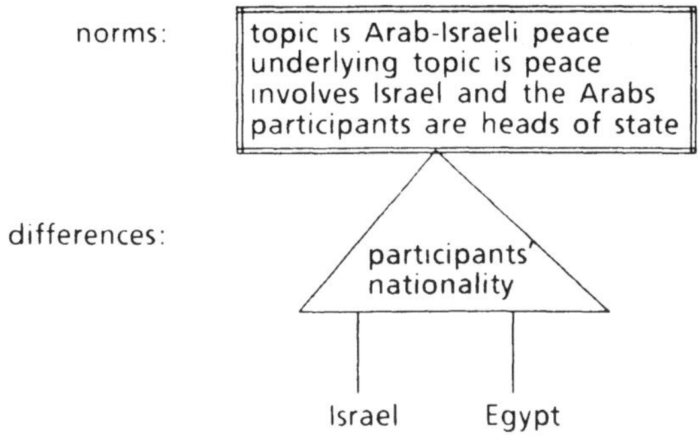

FIG. 3.8. Diplomatic meetings about Arab-Israeli peace

knowing if a target event is in memory or not. The assumption can be made that it is probably in memory but can't be found. Instantiation strategies can be used to infer information that cannot be found directly.

This uncertainty seems to correspond to what Collins (1978) and Norman (1973) have called a "feeling of knowing." When people experience a feeling of knowing, they think, but cannot verify, that a fact is true. They have a "feeling of knowing" that it did happen, but cannot find the appropriate information to verify its occurrence. That feeling of knowing can happen when (1) the traversal/elaboration process arrives at an E-MOP that may contain the target event, and (2) elaboration processes are inadequate for specifying indices for the target event in that MOP. When that happens, an answer of "probably" or "possibly" can be given rather than answering "no" or "I don't know."

4.2. Representations of Events in E-MOPs

Another important implication of the ability to make the inferences made by instantiation strategies is that *all details of events need not explicitly be stored.* Instantiation processes are used during retrieval to infer aspects of a target event's context. They are also used to elaborate on specifications stored in memory. They use generalized knowledge to reconstruct plausible scenarios. Thus, if generalized knowledge is available, it can be used to infer normative details when needed, and those normative details need not be stored.

If reconstructive processes can be used to reconstruct unspecified details of events, then the question arises as to how much detail is necessary within memory to refer to events stored there. Up to now, the assumption has been that E-MOPs organize pointers to actual events, and that events in memory point to the other events they were related to. CYRUS' memory has this organization. In terms of a computer model, this organization has the advantage that large chunks of episodes can always be retrieved in detail without mistakes. The inference we can make by looking at the elaboration process, however, is that all of that direct reference is not necessary.

References to actual events can be costly in terms of storage. Since E-MOPs store the similarities between the events they organize, and since the apparatus for reconstruction from partial descriptions is available in memory, references to complete events are overly redundant. They repeat normative information found at the E-MOP level. All we really need to store are those aspects of an event that are different than, or add to, an E-MOP's specifications. Merging those differences and the E-MOP's norms during retrieval produces a specification of an entire event. References to events in E-MOPs need only enough information to enable that reconstructive process to happen.

Consider, for example, how the following event could be stored in a "diplomatic meetings" MOP.

> EV1: Vance went on a diplomatic trip to China to discuss Chinese-American relations with Chinese leaders.

If that E-MOP held the information that diplomatic trips are to foreign countries, usually for negotiations, and include diplomatic activities, then this particular trip could be stored in that E-MOP as in Fig. 3.9.

Its differences and additions to the norms include the features that (1) it was to China, (2) its purpose was diplomacy (as opposed to negotiations), and (3) it included at least one meeting about Chinese-American relations in its sequence of events. Thus, those three features are features that the episode is indexed on. The descriptions of the event at each of those index points, however, need hold only the features that differ from the E-MOP's norms and that are not part of their index. They do not need to hold an entire event description. Thus, the event is described by the features "included a meeting about Chinese-American relations" and "purpose was diplomacy" when indexed under "destination is China." Using those features plus the norms for "diplomatic trips," there is enough information to reconstruct the trip as follows:

> Vance went on a diplomatic trip to China for diplomatic reasons. The trip included a meeting about Chinese-American relations. Its first event was a flight to China; there was a welcome at the airport there; there were a number of diplomatic activities, one of which was a meeting about Chinese-American relations; and there was a flight back to the United States.

Events in memory refer to other episodes they are related to. How much detail must those references include? If events stored in E-MOPs must include only enough information to enable their reconstruction, then it follows that references to episodes a particular event is related to should need to specify only those

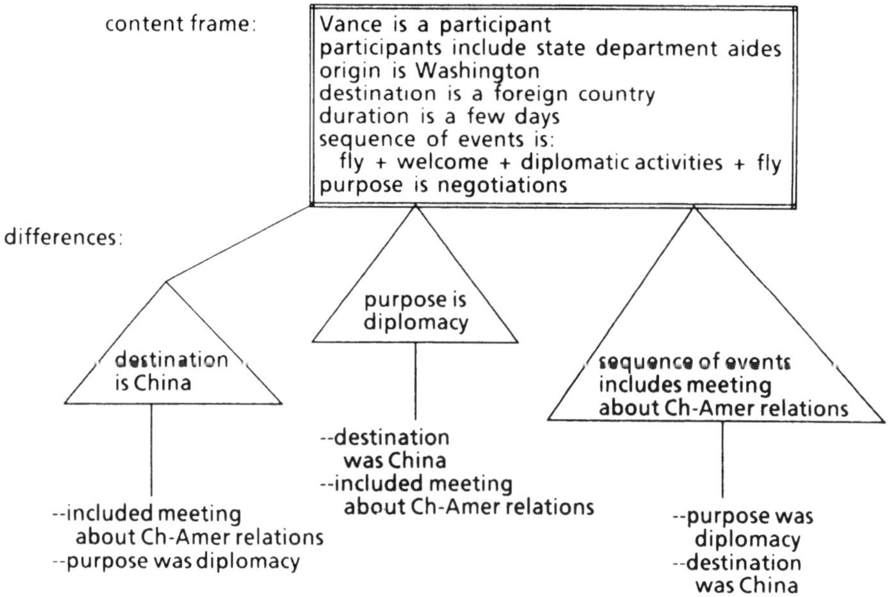

FIG. 3.9. Diplomatic trips.

features that are necessary for its reconstruction. A reference to a meeting that happened during EV1, for example, should need to specify no more than the fact that it was a meeting, its topic was Chinese-American relations, and its participants were Chinese leaders. Using that information, plus generalized information about "diplomatic meetings" and information relating "diplomatic trips" to "diplomatic meetings," a more complete description of the meeting, including its place and location, can be inferred.

A meeting that happened during EV1, however, is itself stored in a "diplomatic meetings" MOP. All of its meeting-relevant features are recorded in that E-MOP. That information, then, does not need to be part of the trip specification. Instead, all that is needed is enough detail to recognize the meeting in the "diplomatic meetings" MOP. With that amount of detail, the meeting could be retrieved and reconstructed from the "diplomatic meetings" MOP if necessary. If, for example, that meeting were the only one about Chinese-American relations, then it would be sufficient for the trip to specify that it had as an embedded event a "diplomatic meeting about Chinese-American relations." The meeting could be recognized with that specification and no additional details of the meeting would need to be specified among the features of the trip to China.

References to events related to an episode, then, need contain only enough features to enable their retrieval. A more complete description can be obtained by retrieving and reconstructing other details of that description. This organization provides economy of storage by storing only differences from and additions to generalized E-MOP information at any index point. Similarities are stored only once at the E-MOP level.

5. SUMMARY

Searching an E-MOP to find a particular event involves choosing features of the event that correspond to E-MOP indices and then *traversing* paths in the E-MOP corresponding to those indices. Because features specified in a question do not always correspond to features used as indices in memory, an *elaboration* scheme is necessary.

Elaboration performs two functions: *plausible index generation,* or inference of additional features of an event, and *index fitting,* a process of transforming already specified features into features used as indices in the current E-MOP. Instantiation strategies, to be discussed in the next chapter, are the strategies used for elaboration.

4 Instantiation Strategies

1. INTRODUCTION

> I know I've been to a lot of museums in Europe. I've been to England, and I went to a number of museums there—some in London—the British Museum, the National Gallery, and a few smaller galleries. . . . I was at a museum in Brighton—the Royal Pavilion. I've been to museums in Paris—the Louvre and some smaller ones. In Rome, I've been to. . . . In Naples to. . . . In Florence, to. . . .

Instantiation strategies are the constructive retrieval strategies that elaborate poorly specified contexts. Two types of instantiation strategies used for elaboration are *component instantiation* and *context-to-context instantiation*. Component instantiation strategies elaborate components of events such as their participants, location, and time. *Context-to-context instantiation strategies* infer episodes plausibly related to a given event. This chapter presents component instantiation strategies and context-to-context instantiation strategies in detail.

Both component and context-to-context instantiation strategies use E-MOP information to elaborate on a given event. Using information about meetings to elaborate on a meeting between Vance and Begin, for example, instantiation strategies can infer that there was a negotiations episode going on, that the topic of the meeting was probably something related to Arab-Israeli peace, and that the meeting took place either in Tel Aviv or Washington. Context instantiation strategies would infer the negotiations episode, while component instantiation strategies would infer the place and topic of the meeting. Furthermore, if it were known that the meeting took place in Israel, then context instantiation strategies could infer that the meeting took place during a diplomatic trip by Vance to Israel. Conversely, if the meeting were in Washington, those strategies could be used to infer a diplomatic trip by Begin to the United States. In general, instantiation strategies and their related E-MOP information are used to infer "what must have happened," regardless of whether it is actually recorded in memory.

In addition to being useful for elaboration, instantiation strategies serve three other functions. First, they are used during alternate-context search. Recall from chapter 1 that alternate-context search is a process of searching memory for episodes related to a target event in the hope that they will refer to the target. Instantiation strategies are used during that process to construct the alternate contexts for search. Their use in that process is guided by executive strategies, which are explained in detail in chapter 6.

Another purpose for instantiation strategies is in reconstructing probable details of events when they are not specified, but are wanted. If asked, "Why did Vance and Begin meet last week?" content frame information and instantiation strategies can be used to answer "probably to negotiate Egyptian-Israeli peace," even if no actual reasons are known. In answering this question, the meeting between Vance and Begin (mentioned in the question) is first retrieved using the retrieval process described previously. Instantiation strategies are then applied to the retrieved event to infer its reason.

In a related way, these strategies can be used to predict the kinds of things to look for in memory to reasonably answer a question. In answering "why," for example (as above), plausible reasons for the event can be constructed using instantiation strategies, and memory can be searched specifically for those. Used in this way, these strategies can be thought of as the generation rules for constrained "generate and test" (Newell, 1973).

In answering the question, "How did Vance become secretary of state" for example, the strategy "Instantiate-Enablements" can be used to instantiate the normal enablement conditions for becoming secretary of state if no specific enablement conditions are known. Using that strategy, the question can be answered by "He was appointed by Carter" even if the appointment was not specifically recorded in memory.

2. ELABORATING COMPONENTS OF EVENTS

Component instantiation strategies are used to infer event components and role fillers of a target event. They get their guidance and information from three different sources:

1. the target event
2. content-frame information describing default values for components of items in some E-MOP the target event fits into

3. the general relationships (less dependent on content) between components and other components.

Component instantiation strategies take as input an event description and a MOP that event might fit into. They produce a set of possible values for the component in question. As a first step, each component instantiation strategy gets as much detail as possible about the event component from the event itself and the E-MOP content frame. It then uses general information about the relationships between event components to fill in more detail. There is a strategy associated with each type of event component or role filler.

Consider, for example, the "negotiations" MOP to see how these strategies use content-frame information:

content frame:

participants = representatives of countries involved in topic
topic = contract of international importance
duration = months to years

FIG. 4.1. Negotiations.

This E-MOP specifies that its participants are generally representatives of the countries involved in the contract under negotiation. Thus, if the target event were "negotiations about SALT," the participants in the event could be found by consulting the "negotiations" MOP to find the relationships between the different "negotiations" roles. After explicitly specifying fillers for these roles, the target event could be elaborated as "negotiations about SALT with Gromyko" or "negotiations about SALT with Brezhnev." Both E-MOP specifications and specific information from the target event are used to do this.

In addition to MOP-specific information, component instantiation also uses very general information about the usual relationships between different kinds of event components. Included in the information we have about people, for example, are their places of residence, interests, roles, and occupations. The general information that people often do things in their place of residence can be used by component instantiation strategies to infer the location for a particular event if the appropriate E-MOP cannot help in designating a place.

Sometimes both MOP-specific and general information are needed for elaboration. This happens when an E-MOP holds only a partial specification of a component to be fleshed out. In this case, MOP-specific information is used to constrain more general relationships between components. Consider, for example, a hypothetical "ski trip" MOP:

content frame:

location = mountains, ski resorts in the mountains
participants = ...

FIG. 4.2. Ski trips.

Although the E-MOP does not specify particular values for its components, it puts constraints on other instantiation strategies by providing partial knowledge. Suppose we wanted to retrieve particular "ski trips" from this E-MOP. Its default setting is "in mountains" or "resort areas in the mountains." That specification does not give particular settings, but does give enough information to apply other strategies to further specify the setting. Starting from that partial specification, mountainous areas or resorts in the mountains could be enumerated using other strategies (perhaps by mentally walking around a map).

When E-MOPs do not specify particular values for slot fillers, instantiation strategies use general information about the usual relationships between other components of the target event. Places of episodes, for example, often correspond to the residence or place of occupation of the participant, or a place where he can often be found. Thus, to answer a question such as "Where did you see Joe yesterday?" the places associated with Joe can be enumerated and checked without doing other memory search. Component instantiation strategies access those correlations.

There is a hierarchy of constraint associated with the sources of information component instantiation strategies use. The target event's features provide the first constraint, followed by full or partial specifications provided by an E-MOP's content frame. Only after those possibilities are considered are general relationships between components appropriate for consideration. In this way, target event and E-MOP constraints guide application of other component instantiation rules. Domain-related (i.e., MOP-specific) specifications are applied during component instantiation before weaker domain-independent correlations.

In memory, component instantiation strategies are associated with the types of components they elaborate. Strategies for participants are stored in a node in memory describing "participants." The strategy for inferring the country an event may have occurred in is associated with a memory node for "country," which is accessed through a more general strategy associated with "location." That strategy calls "Infer-Country" when the location to be inferred is already constrained to be a country.

Strategies for inferring locations, times, and participants are discussed below. It is always assumed that MOP-specific correlations are taken into consideration before using the general correlations presented below.

2.1. Instantiating Locations

Following are some of the rules for inferring place. Implicit in all of them is that the place inferred must not conflict with any partial specification of place (e.g., from an E-MOP's partial specification), that it must not conflict with other specifications in the target concept, and that all retrieval is for the time specified in the target concept.

1. Location can be inferred from important people participating in the target concept. Infer place from person specifications as follows:

   (a) If the location to be retrieved is related to occupation, and if the target concept refers to a person's occupation, retrieve his place of occupation.

   (b) Otherwise, use his place of residence, places he habituates, or nationality to the level of detail specified in the partial specification.

If, for example, this rule is applied when it is already known that the location should be a country, countries of residence of major participants are retrieved. If the location should be a city, his city of residence would be appropriate, and if a building, his house or some other appropriate type of building. As in the rule above, implicit in all of the following rules is that the specification should be to the level of detail implied in the partial specification in the target event.

2. Location can be inferred from organizations appearing in the target concept as follows:
   (a) Retrieve the organization's place of residence (i.e., its location).
   (b) Retrieve the place of the organization's affiliation (e.g., UNICEF is affiliated with the UN and can be expected to have its meetings there sometimes).
   (c) If an important representative of the organization is a participant, then retrieve his place of residence in the organization or places he habituates in the organization (e.g., his office or conference room).
   (d) If the partial location description specifies that the place is not the place of residence of the organization, retrieve places habituated by the organization in the locale of the target concept or places habituated by the important representative of the organization in the locale of the target concept.
3. Infer location from groups participating in the target concept as follows:
   (a) If the group is an ad hoc group, infer place by inferring place for important members of the group (rule 1).
   (b) If the group is affiliated with an organization, infer place by using rules for inferring place from rules for organizations (rule 2).
   (c) If the group is affiliated with a polity or locale, retrieve the polity or locale it is affiliated with.
   (d) Retrieve the place of residence of the group, its habitual meeting place, or its nationality.
4. Infer locations from locations by retrieving subparts and surrounding areas appropriate to the event class (e.g., for sightseeing, retrieve famous subparts; for trips, retrieve surrounding country or locale).

5. To infer location from contracts, use places associated with participants in the contract or appropriate known neutral locations.

CYRUS uses location information associated with people, places, contracts, groups, and organizations in order to infer possible locations for events. In answering the question, "Who have you discussed SALT with?" for example, CYRUS first infers a context of a political meeting (sM-MEETING). Because the locations of political events are often foreign countries, and because political meetings are political events, CYRUS makes use of the participants in the SALT contract to infer that a meeting about SALT may have taken place in the Soviet Union or the United States. It thus elaborates the meeting context it is looking for and searches for political meetings in both the Soviet Union and the United States. The following example is of CYRUS answering that question. Intermediate printout is included to show CYRUS' reasoning.

```
Enter next question:

>Who have you discussed SALT with?

The question is:
((ACTOR *VANCE* < = > (*MTRANS*) MOBJECT
        (*CONCEPTS* CONCERNING *SALT* TO (*?*)))
The question type is "concept completion"
The question concept is:
((ACTOR *VANCE* < = > (*MTRANS*) MOBJECT
        (*CONCEPTS* CONCERNING *SALT* TO (*?*)))
   applying INFER-FROM-TOPIC to *SALT*
      inferring political meeting context
The inferred question concept is:
((< = > (sM-MEETING ACTOR *VANCE* OTHERS (*?*) TOPIC *SALT*)))
searching memory for question concept
   additional information needed
applying strategies to elaborate question concept
  checking locative information on question concept
    sM-MEETING could have occured in USSR or USA
      searching for sM-MEETING in the USSR
      ...
      searching for sM-MEETING in the USA
      ...

Gromyko and Brezhnev at diplomatic meetings in the USSR, and Carter and
Brzezinski in consultations in Washington.
```

2.2. Inferring Participants

Participants in an event include people, organizations, groups, and countries that take part in the event. When an E-MOP does not specify the particular participants in an event, they can be inferred from locations, topics, and other participants. If we know, for example, that Vance attended a diplomatic meeting in Israel, then we can predict that one of the participants was probably Begin, and that other high-ranking representatives of the Israeli government, such as the foreign minister or defense minister might also have been present. We can make that prediction because we are aware of a correlation between topics and participants in political events. The following are rules for specifying participants.

1. Infer participating people by retrieving representatives of specified organizations, members of known groups, representatives of known countries, or persons associated with known organizations, groups, or countries fitting the initial description.

In answering a question such as "Have you met with NATO recently?" important representatives of NATO can be enumerated as meeting participants and meetings with each can be searched for.

2. Infer participating organizations by retrieving organizations known people or groups are affiliated with, and organizations affiliated with known countries.
3. Infer participating groups by retrieving groups known people belong to, and groups affiliated with known organizations and countries.
4. Infer participating countries by retrieving nationalities, affiliations, and places of residence of known people, groups, and organizations, or by retrieving sides of a known contract or issue.

CYRUS' "political meetings" E-MOP (sM-MEETING) specifies that its participants are people or organizations representing the sides of a contract being discussed or negotiated. Thus, in answering a question such as "Who have you discussed the Camp David Accords with?" CYRUS consults its knowledge about the Camp David Accords to find out who it involves. After discovering that it involves Israel, Egypt, and the United States, CYRUS uses component instantiation strategies to infer that participants in these meetings would be representatives of those countries. CYRUS further specifies possible participants by recalling important diplomats of those three countries and checking whether Vance had met with any of them about the Camp David Accords. The following example is of CYRUS answering that question.

```
Enter next question:

>Who have you discussed the Camp David Accords with?

The question is:
((ACTOR *VANCE* < = > (*MTRANS*) MOBJECTS
    (*CONCEPTS* CONCERNING *CDA*) TO (*?*)))
The question type is "concept completion"
The question concept is:
((ACTOR *VANCE* < = > (*MTRANS*) MOBJECTS
    (*CONCEPTS* CONCERNING *CDA*) TO (*?*)))
```

```
   applying INFER-FROM-TOPIC to *CDA*
      inferring political meeting context
 The inferred question concept is:
 ((< = > (sM-MEETING ACTOR *VANCE* OTHERS (*?*) TOPIC *CDA*)))
 searching for question concept
    searching directly for sM-MEETING
       additional information needed

 applying strategies to elaborate question concept
    ...
 elaborating OTHERS
    OTHERS are RT-DIPLOMAT of Israel, Egypt or the USA
  searching for sM-MEETING with OTHERS RT-DIPLOMAT of Israel
    additional information needed
    elaborating OTHERS
       OTHERS could be Begin, Dayan, or Weizmann
     searching for sM-MEETING with OTHERS Begin
       ...
     searching for sM-MEETING with OTHERS Dayan
       ...
     searching for sM-MEETING with OTHERS Weizmann
       ...
   searching for sM-MEETING with OTHERS RT-DIPLOMAT of Egypt
    additional information needed
    elaborating OTHERS
       OTHERS could be Sadat
     searching for sM-MEETING with OTHERS Sadat
       ...
   ...
```

Israeli and Egyptian diplomats including Begin, Dayan, Weizmann, Sadat, and Khalil, and American diplomats including Carter and Brown.

2.3. Inferring Time

Time cues can often be provided by generalized E-MOP information. Many activities are specific to a particular time of the year (e.g., sledding in the winter, final exams in the early winter or spring), while others are specific to a particular time of one's life. Exams, for example, are particular to times when one is a student. For Cyrus Vance, meetings with heads of state are probably particular to times when he has had a diplomatic role. Each E-MOP includes temporal information on its content frame.

In addition, some objects, people, and places have temporal information associated with them. Boots and heavy coats are winter clothing and an event involving either of them is not likely to have occurred in the summer. Similarly, experiences with a person one knows only through summer camp can be inferred to have happened during the summer and at a time of life that included going to summer camp. Experiences with a person one associated with only in college would have happened during college years.

Time information inferred from objects, people, and places can be found directly associated with the object or person, or can be inferred from characteristic activities associated with the object or person. If a person who has gone to the Caribbean during the winter is asked about an experience that would have happened in the Caribbean, he will be able to attach time information to the experience by retrieving the default time from a characteristic Caribbean activity, namely, vacationing there.

Time representations can refer to particular times or can be specified in terms of events, characteristic events, role themes (Schank & Abelson, 1977), or eras. An *era* (Kolodner, 1978) is a time span in a person's life characterized by some long-term role he is playing. Eras are usually associated with occupational, family, and social roles. Thus, for Vance, the time period when he worked as a lawyer was an occupational era characterized by his being a lawyer. Associated with an era are the characteristic roles and activities a person is involved in during that time span, as well as other eras going on at the same time and other eras related to it in time. An educational era comprising going to professional school must come after an era of going to college. Thus, eras can be helpful in better specifying the time for an event.

The specification, "while I was a lawyer," has an occupational era associated with it, which can be consulted to infer better time specifications. "When I was a teenager" can be expanded upon to include eras going on at that time (such as high school) and events characteristic of that time, which might serve as time specifications on events in memory.

Time cues, then, can be provided by E-MOPs, people, objects, places, and partially specified times. Similarly to the way locational specifications are inferred, time specifications should first be retrieved from content frames of the relevant E-MOPs. The constraints posed by those specifications can be used to retrieve time information from other event components. Also, as the example above shows, time specifications themselves can be used to expand on time cues. Following are some rules for inferring time.

1. Infer time cues by retrieving times associated with already-specified components, such as people, organizations, and countries.
2. Infer time cues by retrieving times associated with characteristic events associated with already-specified components.

3. ENUMERATION STRATEGIES AND MAPS

Q: Which of your colleagues at work have you had lunch with?

A: There's the regular lunch crew, I've had lunch with all of them. Then, there's Smith at the end of the hall, I've never had lunch with him.

> Next to his office is Jones. We had lunch the other day. In the office across from there is . . .

Often component instantiation requires enumeration of possibilities. How is that possible if memory is not organized in lists? One way we've observed people doing enumeration is by using some well-known map or organizational chart. In the example above, we imagine the person reconstructing and going through the floor plan of his office building to enumerate all the employees he might have lunched with. Recall that in answering "What museums have you been to?" some people seemed to recall museums by mentally walking through a map of a familiar area, stopping at each important place and recalling whether they had been to a museum in that place. Thus, their answers were something like "Let me see, have I been to a museum in Rome, in Naples, in Florence?" The set of component instantiation strategies that allow enumeration of this sort are called *enumeration strategies.*

Enumeration strategies allow cues to be enumerated in an orderly fashion. They work by sorting through well-known or easily constructed maps and charts to compute sets of possibilities for particular components of the target event. To enumerate trips to Europe, for example, it would be appropriate to walk through a map of Europe checking at each important point to see whether there had been a trip to that place. Similarly, to enumerate the players on a particular football team, we might expect a football fan to picture the playing field and go through each position on the field picking out the people on the team who play that position. Enumeration strategies, then, can be used for extensive search of both generalized and episodic memory, or for keeping track of a number of choices.

Any well-known map or chart can be used for enumeration. Imagining a map of the United States is the only way some people can name all 50 states. Similarly, well-known charts of organizations or objects are convenient for enumeration. A floor plan of offices might be convenient to use in enumerating the people who work in a building. A chart of organizational set-up can be used to name all the directors of a large organization. To remember all the doctors a person has been to, a chart of the human body could be used, and doctors specializing in each particular body part could be enumerated.

Williams (1978) suggests that people use an enumeration strategy to choose aspects of events to be elaborated. Although we do not consider this process in detail, it does provide a useful strategy for elaboration. Such a strategy involves choosing and examining a well-known event and using its features to choose instantiation rules to elaborate a target event. Such a strategy would be useful when a MOP holds too many types of indices to efficiently direct choice of instantiation strategies. To use such a strategy, we must define how to choose an appropriate well-known event.

One place where CYRUS does use enumeration is in elaborating place specifications. Often, CYRUS is asked questions about the Middle East, Europe, or

Asia. In retrieving episodes that happened in those places, it is usually helpful to specify each of the countries that could have been involved. Thus, in recalling whether Vance was in the Middle East last November, one of the things CYRUS does is to attempt elaboration of the trip description. In elaborating the destination of the diplomatic trip (sM-VIPVISIT), CYRUS enumerates the countries it knows to be in the Middle East. It thus attempts to recall trips to Israel, Egypt, Jordan, and Syria, and responds as follows:

```
Enter next question:

>Were you in the Mid East last November?

The question is:
((ACTOR *VANCE* IS (*LOC* VAL *MIDEAST*)) MODE (*?*) TIME G0832)
The question type is "verification"
The question concept is:
((ACTOR *VANCE* IS (*LOC* VAL *MIDEAST*)) TIME G0832)
   applying INFER-FROM-LOCATION to *MIDEAST*
      inferring a diplomatic trip context
The inferred question concept is:
((< = > (sM-VIPVISIT ACTOR *VANCE* DESTINATION *MIDEAST*)) TIME G0832)
searching memory for question concept
   searching directly for sM-VIPVISIT
      additional information needed

applying strategies to elaborate question concept
   checking locative information on question concept
      applying map of *MIDEAST* to specify place
        sM-VIPVISIT could have been to Egypt, Israel, Syria
          Jordan, or Saudi Arabia
      searching for diplomatic trips to Egypt
        ...
      searching for diplomatic trips to Israel
        ...
...

No.
```

Although maps and charts are used by people for enumeration, CYRUS does not have an extensive variety of maps. The ones it has are implemented as short lists. The reason for this lack in CYRUS is that the problem of organizing a map or chart in memory has not been addressed. Many of the maps and charts people seem to use are visual and easy to reconstruct through visual cues. Without a good handle on what a visual cue is, however, their implementation would be incomplete and probably list-like, at best.

4. INSTANTIATING EVENTS FROM EVENTS

Context-to-context instantiation strategies are used to elaborate the event context surrounding a target event. They use content frame information from E-MOPs the target event fits into to produce descriptions of events plausibly related to the target event. Context-to-context instantiation strategies produce a set of event descriptions as output. There is one such strategy corresponding to each possible relationship between events. Input to these strategies consists of an event (real or plausible) whose related episodes are to be inferred, an E-MOP that event fits into, and an optional partial description of the episode to be instantiated. The event descriptions output by the strategy describe events plausibly related in the specified way to the input event.

Recall from an earlier example that the context-to-context instantiation strategy "Instantiate-Larger-Episodes" produces descriptions of episodes an event might have been part of.

EVENT = target event

MOP = most specific E-MOP the target event fits into

EPISODE = framework for episode to be instantiated

EPISODES = output episodes, newly instantiated event descriptions

(1) If EPISODE is unspecified, then get the default larger episodes for MOP, else use EPISODE.

(2) For each of those specifications, transfer components as specified, producing EPISODES and make the following inferences when more specific information is not available on the E-MOP:

 (a) Time specifications on each EPISODE include the time specified in EVENT.

 (b) Place specifications on each EPISODE include the place specified in EVENT.

 (c) Participants of EVENT are included in the participants of each EPISODE, groups and organizations they belong to might also be involved.

 (d) Topic of each EPISODE includes that of EVENT.

(3) Use relevant Component-Instantiation strategies to further specify components of each EPISODE, using the already-instantiated partial descriptions of each component as constraints.

FIG. 4.3. Instantiate-Larger-Episodes.

Applying this strategy to a "meeting with Begin about the Camp David Accords," for example, and using content frame knowledge from the "diplomatic meetings" E-MOP, the following descriptions are generated of episodes the meeting could have been part of:

A "diplomatic trip" to Israel.

A "summit conference" with Begin as a participant and whose topic was related to the Camp David Accords.

"Negotiations" with Israel about the Camp David Accords.

larger episodes:
"negotiations" (I-NEGOTIATE)
participants = diplomats of same nationality as meeting participants, and of other countries involved in meeting topic
topic = generalization of meeting topic
"diplomatic trips" (sM-VIPVISIT)
destination = country or area involved in meeting topic, or country of residence of meeting participant
"conferences" (sM-CONFERENCE)
participants = diplomats of same nationality as meeting participants, and of other countries involved in meeting topic
location = location of meeting
topic = generalization of meeting topic

enables:
"treaty signing" ($TREATY)
sides = sides of meeting topic

sequence of events:
participants MTRANSing to each other about meeting topic

preceding and following events:
"diplomatic meetings" ($MEET)
participants = subset of meeting participants
topic = aspect of meeting topic

more general E-MOPs and classifications:
"political meetings" (sM-MEETING)
all components correspond
"diplomatic activities"
all components correspond

role fillers:
participants: foreign dignitaries of countries involved in contract being discussed
location: conference room in capital city of country of residence of some important participant
topic: international contract
duration: one to two hours

FIG. 4.4. 'Diplomatic meetings' ($MEET)—generalized information

Production of these episode descriptions allows the following elaborations of that target meeting:

> meetings with Begin about the Camp David Accords which took place during a diplomatic trip to Israel

> meetings with Begin about the Camp David Accords during a summit conference which included Begin as a participant and whose topic was related to the Camp David Accords

> meetings with Begin about the Camp David Accords which were part of negotiations with Israel about the Camp David Accords

In order for surrounding context to be inferred from a target event, E-MOPs must specify both the types of episodes (E-MOPs) they are often related to, and how those episodes are related, (how their roles correspond to those of the E-MOP). "Diplomatic meetings," for example, specifies that meetings are instrumental to "negotiations." It also specifies the types of negotiations they are instrumental to. That specification includes the information that the topic of related negotiations episodes is usually a contract involving the sides of the meeting and related to the meeting topic, that the participants in negotiations correspond to both the countries of nationality of the meeting participants and the participants in a contract being negotiated, and that the arbitrator might be a person from a country neutral to the conflict being negotiated and could be one of the meeting participants. Figure 4.4 (repeated from chapter 2) shows the relationships of "diplomatic meetings" to the other E-MOPs it is related to. Using these specifications, the "negotiations" episode any particular diplomatic meeting was part of can be inferred. A "diplomatic meeting with Gromyko about SALT," for example, must have been instrumental to "SALT negotiations including Gromyko and other Russian and American diplomats."

As with component instantiation strategies, context instantiation rules use both MOP-specific information and general information about containment, causality, and time relationships between events. The information in the MOP above is an example of MOP-specific information. An example of the general information these strategies use is that "events contained in other events have time and place which are contained in the time and place of the larger event."

Context instantiation strategies have three steps:

EVENT = target event

E-MOP = most specific E-MOP the target event fits into

EPISODE = framework for episode to be instantiated

EPISODES = output episodes, newly instantiated event descriptions

(1) If EPISODE is unspecified, then retrieve the requested content frame property from MOP resulting in a framework for a newly-instantiated event, else use EPISODE.

(2) transfer specifications on EVENT to the new events being instantiated producing EPISODES, making use of specifically-defined relationships and default content frame relationships.

(3) apply Component-Instantiation strategies to further specify underspecified role fillers of newly-instantiated EPISODES.

FIG. 4.5. Context-to-Context Instantiation Strategy Steps

The most specific E-MOPs a target concept can fit into are those that have no indices that can be traversed using target event specifications. Specific E-MOPs for a meeting between Vance and Begin about Egyptian-Israeli peace might be "meetings with Begin," "meetings with Israelis about Egyptian-Israeli peace," "meetings about Egyptian-Israeli peace," "meetings about Middle East peace," and so on.

Once a specific E-MOP has been found, the requested content frame property is retrieved from it. An E-MOP's specification of a related E-MOP will specify usual relationships between its role fillers and those of the context being constructed. "Negotiations," for example, specifies that the topic of a "diplomatic meeting" is a subtopic of the negotiations topic, and that participants are representatives of the countries involved in the negotiations.

In the second step, relevant specifications are transferred from the target event to the context being instantiated. Thus, if a particular negotiations episode is about SALT and with the Russians, the meeting constructed from it will be about some aspect of SALT and be with a Russian representative.

At this point, general information about the specified event relationship is used. When there are no specifications for instantiating some component of the new context, default information about the type of relationship between the target event and the event being constructed is used. In particular, time, place, and whole/subpart inferences can be made based on the relationship between the events. The time of an event contained in the target episode, for example, is during the time specified for the target event. The time for an enabling event is before the time specified by the target event. Participants of events in an episode contained in the target event include some of the latter's participants. The location of an episode contained within the target event is some location within or near the target event.

The last step in instantiating a new context is to apply component instantiation rules to better specify components. Already-specified constraints help to narrow the work of the component instantiation strategies.

These strategies infer as much as possible from MOP-specific and target event-specific information to fill in details of the events it is instantiating. They then use general knowledge about the specific event-to-event relationship they correspond to, to better specify the event being constructed. After applying domain-specific and event-relationship-specific information, component instantiation strategies are called to further specify particular components of the newly constructed events. In this way, the most domain-specific knowledge is used first, while the most general information is not used until the domain-specific constraints are set up.

Recall from chapter 2 that events and MOPs can be related to each other in 12 different ways. Events can be contained in episodes, contain other events themselves, or be before, after, or during other episodes. Events can also be causally related through enablement or direct causality. Events that cause or enable other

Instantiate-Enablements
Instantiate-Preconditions
Instantiate-Results
Instantiate-Reasons
Instantiate-Enabled-Events
Instantiate-Larger-Episodes
Instantiate-Seq-of-Events
Instantiate-Preceding-Events
Instantiate-Following-Events
Instantiate-Standardizations

FIG. 4.6. Context Instantiation Strategies

events come before them in time. Events caused or enabled by other events come after them. Each of these relationships has a context-to-context instantiation strategy associated with it. Those strategies are listed in Fig. 4.6.

The last step of each strategy is the same. The first and second depend on the relationship between the target event and the context being instantiated. Strategies are explained individually below.

4.1. Containment and Contained-in Relationships

''Instantiate-Seq-of-Events'' is used to construct specifications of events that might be included in a given episode. It takes as input an episode description (the target event), and optionally a sketchy description of the event to be instantiated. The default sequence of events is retrieved from the E-MOP the target event fits into, and each appropriate event in the sequence is instantiated. Because events of a sequence of events are part of a larger specified episode, time specifications of events within the episode will be within the time specifications of the episode, place specifications will be within the place specified on the given episode, and participants will include a subset of the people involved in the entire episode.

Applying this strategy to a diplomatic trip to Israel for the purpose of negotiating Arab-Israeli relations, and requesting instantiation of the trip's entire plausible sequence of events, would produce a list of events including flying to Israel, being welcomed at Ben Gurion Airport by a high Israeli official, meeting with Begin and Israeli officials at some unspecified place within Israel (probably in Jerusalem or Tel-Aviv), attending a state dinner hosted by Begin, and staying over at a diplomatic residence in Tel Aviv or Jerusalem. Applying this strategy to the same diplomatic trip and specifying that it should instantiate a diplomatic meeting would produce a diplomatic meeting with Israeli officials in Israel. The rules for ''Instantiate-Seq-of-Events'' are in Fig. 4.7.

The strategy ''Instantiate-Larger-Episodes'' constructs contexts for larger episodes an event could be part of. It uses specifications on E-MOPs the target episode fits into to choose contexts for larger episodes the target could be part of

EVENT = target event

MOP = most specific E-MOP the target event fits into

EPISODE = framework for episode to be instantiated

EPISODES = output episodes, newly instantiated event descriptions

(1) If EPISODE is unspecified then get the default sequence of events for MOP, else use EPISODE.

(2) Go through the event sequence one by one producing EPISODES by transferring components as specified and making the following inferences when more specific information is not available on MOP.

(a) Time specifications on each EPISODE are within the time specified in EVENT.

(b) Place specifications on each EPISODE are within the place specified in EVENT.

(c) Participants in any newly-instantiated EPISODE include a subset of the known participants of EVENT plus a number of as yet unspecified participants.

(3) Use relevant Component-Instantiation strategies to further specify components of each EPISODE, using the already-instantiated partial descriptions of each component as constraints.

FIG. 4.7. Instantiate-Seq-of-Events

(Fig. 4.8). The major difference between this strategy and "Instantiate-Seq-of-Events" is in step 2. In the latter strategy, knowledge about how larger episodes relate to the episodes they include is used. In the strategy below, general knowledge about how smaller episodes fit into larger ones is used to adjust the time, place, and participants of the episode. The time of a larger episode includes the time of the smaller one. Its place includes the place of the smaller one. Its topic includes that of the smaller.

Imagine, for example, attempting to retrieve sightseeing experiences in the Middle East. In order to do that, it might be appropriate to recall trips to the Middle East and sightseeing during those trips. Trips are *larger episodes* the sightseeing could be part of. In order to retrieve those trips, contexts for their retrieval must first be constructed. In constructing those contexts, contextual components must be transferred from the target concept (in this case, sightseeing) to the new retrieval concept (in this case, a trip). In this example, the place of the target sightseeing episode must be transferred to the trip instantiation. The actor of the sightseeing should be the same as the actor of the trip. Some of the other participants in the target sightseeing episode might be participants in the trip episode. And if the time of the sightseeing episode is known, the time of the

EVENT = target event

MOP = most specific E-MOP the target event fits into

EPISODE = framework for episode to be instantiated

EPISODES = output episodes, newly instantiated event descriptions

(1) If EPISODE is unspecified, then get the default larger episodes for MOP, else use EPISODE.

(2) For each of those specifications, transfer components as specified, producing EPISODES and make the following inferences when more specific information is not available on the E-MOP:

(a) Time specifications on each EPISODE include the time specified in EVENT.

(b) Place specifications on each EPISODE include the place specified in EVENT.

(c) Participants of EVENT are included in the participants of each EPISODE, groups and organizations they belong to might also be involved.

(d) Topic of each EPISODE includes that of EVENT.

(3) Use relevant Component-Instantiation strategies to further specify components of each EPISODE, using the already-instantiated partial descriptions of each component as constraints.

FIG. 4.8. Instantiate-Larger-Episodes

trip can be inferred from it. After construction of the trip context, its retrieval can be attempted.

4.2. Preceding Events

Enabling events, preconditions, and preceding events all happen before the target event they are being constructed from. Since those event relationships do not include containment, the relationships between other aspects of the input event and event to be constructed cannot be specified in general. The strategies Instantiate-Enablements, Instantiate-Preconditions, and Instantiate-Preceding-Events all have the same relationship in time to their target event—they come before it. Step 2 of each of those strategies is listed below.

(2) For each of those specifications, transfer components as specified producing EPISODES, and make the following inferences when more specific information is not available on MOP.

(a) The time of each new EPISODE is before that of the input EVENT.

FIG. 4.9. Instantiating-Preceding-Events

Consider, for example, a person who has lost his glasses trying to recall where he could have left them. He might try to reconstruct his previous sequence of actions until he recalls where his glasses might be. If he is at home while trying to recall where his glasses are, it would be appropriate to apply the strategy Instantiate-Enablements to construct the context for enabling his getting home. If he usually gets home by driving, he will construct a context for driving home and attempt to recall today's particular driving-home episode and whether he had been wearing his glasses or had put them down somewhere during the drive. If that doesn't help him, he may apply the strategy Instantiate-Preceding-Events to construct a context for what he might have been doing before driving home. In applying each of these strategies, he must know that the event being constructed happened before the event he is constructing it from. That time specification can be used to help him infer times for the events being reconstructed.

4.3. Following Events

In constructing resulting events, events a target event might enable, and events following a target, the time relationship of those events to the target is a "later than" relationship. Step 2 for Instantiate-Results, Instantiate-Enabled-Events (which infers events the target could enable), and Instantiate-Following-Events specifies that the default time of instantiated episodes is after the time of the target event.

(2) For each of those specifications, transfer components as specified producing EPISODES, and make the following inferences when more specific information is not available on MOP.

(a) The time of each new EPISODE is after that of the input EVENT.

FIG. 4.10. Instantiating-Following-Events

Suppose that instantiation strategies were used to recall ends of negotiations. The kinds of events that could result from ends of negotiations, and events that negotiations endings could enable, would have to be constructed and searched for. Those include treaty signings and perhaps the beginnings of cold wars, results of aborted negotiations. To construct the contexts for those episodes, the strategies Instantiate-Results and Instantiate-Enabled-Events would be applied. Knowledge on relevant negotiations E-MOPs would help in instantiating possible treaty signings and cold wars. General information about the relationship of resulting events would allow inference of sketchy time specifications for those events—sometime after the target negotiations episode.

4.4. Standard Methods of Doing an Activity

Standardizations are standard methods of achieving an E-MOP's state. Standard types of meetings for Vance include diplomatic meetings, consultations, and public relations meetings. Standard types of diplomatic ceremonies include welcomes, parades, and treaty signings. Travel can be by plane, train, bus, and so forth. The time of a standardization is that of the specification event it is being constructed from. A standard event is merely a specialization of a more general E-MOP. Thus, its participants, place, and duration are also the same. In instantiating a standard way of doing an activity, those features are transferred directly from the target event. Instantiate-Standardizations is the instantiation strategy that guides construction of standard ways of doing an activity. Step 2 of that strategy is illustrated below:

(2) For each of those specifications, transfer components as specified and make the following inferences when more specific information is not available on MOP.

(a) Time specifications are the same as those of the input EVENT.

(b) Place specifications are the same as those of the input EVENT.

(c) Participants are the same as those of the input EVENT, though there might be others in addition.

FIG. 4.11. Instantiate-Standardizations

In constructing a treaty-signing ceremony from the specification that there was a ceremony at the White House including Begin, Sadat, and Carter, the instantiated treaty-signing ceremony will have participants Begin, Sadat, and Carter, and location the White House.

5. SUMMARY

Component instantiation strategies use information about the relationships between objects and people in order to predict event features that are not specified. Thus, if a "speech" MOP held the information that their topics normally correspond to the interests of the participants, the topic of a speech could be inferred if the participants were known.

Context-to-context instantiation strategies use information about an event's probable surrounding context to predict episodes that may have been related to it. Thus, if a "negotiations" MOP specifies that a particular kind of "diplomatic meeting" is generally instrumental to it, details of a hypothetical meeting related to a known negotiations episode can be inferred.

5 Choosing a Context for Search

1. INTRODUCTION

(Q1): Mr. Vance, has your wife ever met Mrs. Begin?

The question above gives the answerer no idea about where in its memory to look or what kinds of situations to search for to answer the question. In terms of our model, it specifies no context for search. People are faced with questions like this every day, and they manage to figure out what they should search for. They know enough about the contents of their memories and the kinds of activities they've taken part in to direct memory search. How can a question such as this be answered from a memory which (1) keeps track of Vance's but not his wife's activities, and (2) has no category for ''meeting people''? This chapter explains in detail the strategies that allow retrieval from such incomplete specifications to happen.

2. CONTEXT CONSTRUCTION

To search a memory organized around categories, one or more categories for search must first be specified. Consider, for example, the following questions:

(Q2): Who have you talked to about SALT?

(Q3): Have you ever discussed the Camp David Accords with Dayan?

(Q4): Who is the most famous person you have ever met?

The first two questions are appropriate to ask the CYRUS data base about Vance. The last is a question we have asked a number of people. Suppose we wanted the CYRUS data base to answer the first two questions. CYRUS knows about many different situations in which Vance might talk to other people (in fact, almost any situation could apply), but it does not have an E-MOP for "talking to people." Although Vance could talk to somebody during any of his activities, it would not be appropriate for CYRUS to search every one of its E-MOPs to find discussions about SALT or the Camp David Accords.

In general, in order to search memory, a *context for search* must first be set up. A context for search specifies a memory category to be searched. Because CYRUS' memory is organized around event categories, or E-MOPs, a context for search in CYRUS must include a specification of an E-MOP for traversal. One way people's memories are organized is around events. Thus, in choosing a context for search, a person might also choose event categories. People's memories are also organized in other ways, and a person might choose any of those types of categories in this step. The point is, if a question does not already mention an available context for search, then one must be derived.

CYRUS chooses appropriate E-MOPs for traversal by looking at the kinds of situations associated with each of the given question components. In answering (Q2), for example, CYRUS uses information about SALT to choose an E-MOP. Because SALT is an international contract, CYRUS assumes that Vance would have discussed it at a political meeting of some sort—either with a foreign dignitary or with a United States official. Using that information, CYRUS knows to search its "diplomatic meetings" and "consultations" E-MOPs to find an answer. In answering (Q3) CYRUS uses knowledge about both "the Camp David Accords" and "Dayan" to decide that the correct E-MOP to search is "diplomatic meetings."

The strategies in CYRUS that construct contexts for search when none is specified in a target concept are called *component-to-context instantiation strategies*. These strategies make use of event information associated with each given question component to infer plausible E-MOPs for search. They are applied as a first step of memory search if a retrieval request (e.g., question) does not already refer to a category that can be traversed. The retrieval process, then, includes at least the following steps:

1. IF the target event does not specify an E-MOP for traversal, THEN apply component-to-context instantiation strategies to infer a context for search.

2. Traverse memory searching for that search context (using the traversal / elaboration process specified above).

3. IF an appropriate answer has not been found, go back to step 1, attempting to construct a new context.

FIG. 5.1. The retrieval process.

Component-to-context instantiation strategies are chosen by examining available question components and choosing strategies relevant to those components. In answering (Q3), two context instantiation strategies are used. The strategy "Infer-from-Topic" is applied to the "Camp David Accords" to infer a "political meeting" context, and the strategy "Infer-from-Participants" is applied to "Dayan" to infer a "diplomatic meeting" context, a refinement of "political meeting." "Infer-from-Topic" makes use of topic information to infer an E-MOP, while "Infer-from-Participants" makes use of participant information.

Since context-instantiation strategies infer event contexts from event components, memory must have information associating each of its people, places, contracts, and other role fillers with E-MOPs. In particular, in order to answer the questions above, the topic classification "international contract" must have the context "political meeting" associated with it, and the person classification "foreign diplomat" must have the event context "diplomatic meeting" associated with it. In the remainder of this chapter, the strategies and the knowledge they use are presented.

3. COMPONENT-TO-CONTEXT INSTANTIATION STRATEGIES

Component-to-context instantiation strategies use contextual information associated with given question components to infer contexts for search. They do this by retrieving standard contexts associated with the objects and people referred to in the query. Any type of contextual component can be used to retrieve a standard context, e.g., time periods, participants, and locations. Thus, there are context instantiation rules associated with each type of event component. CYRUS has context instantiation rules associated with participants, locations, topics, and time contexts.

3.1. Context Construction from Participant Specifications

Contexts can be inferred from particular participants or participant descriptions. Suppose, for example, that the only situation in which John had contact with Mr. Smith, his butcher, was in Mr. Smith's butcher shop. In that case, a context associated directly with Mr. Smith (buying meat in his store) could be inferred if John were asked the question "When was the last time you talked to Mr. Smith?" If, on the other hand, John did not have an event context associated with Mr. Smith. but did know Mr. Smith was a butcher, he could use information associated with "butchers" to infer a context for that question. The following two context instantiation rules account for context construction in both of those situations.

1. If particular participants, such as people, groups, or organizations, are specified, and if any has a particular event context associated, predict those characteristic events associated with each that could also include other already-specified components.

2. If classes of people, groups, or organizations (e.g., "butchers") are specified, predict characteristic events associated with each of them that could also include other already-specified components.

FIG. 5.2. Infer-from-Participants.

Notice that according to both of these rules, the event contexts suggested must be such that they could include other specified event components. This is a requirement of all context instantiation rules. Thus, if Dr. Jones is John's doctor and also belongs to the same swim club John belongs to, then in using this strategy to infer a context for "Did you see Dr. Jones at the pool yesterday?" the context of going to the swim club should be instantiated, and not a context of an "office visit," although that is associated with doctors. After choosing a possible context using these strategies, the context must be double-checked for correlation with other specified components. Because the place specification in the question above contradicts the "visit to the doctor" context for seeing Dr. Jones, it cannot be used.

CYRUS uses this strategy to answer questions such as "When was the last time you talked to a reporter?" "What heads of state have you met?" and "When was the last time you talked to Begin?" i.e., questions that do not specify an event context but that do specify event participants. When asked the question, "What heads of state have you met?" for example, it infers that it should look for "diplomatic meetings." It does that because it knows that "diplomatic meetings" are characteristic events associated with "heads of state" (and other diplomats). The following is a protocol of CYRUS answering that question:

Enter next question:

>What heads of state have you met?

```
The question is:
((ACTOR *VANCE* IS (*PROX* VAL G0749)) TIME G0751)
The question type is "concept completion"
The question concept is:
((ACTOR *VANCE* IS (*PROX* VAL G0749)) TIME G0751)
    applying INFER-FROM-PARTICIPANTS to RT-STATE-HEAD
        inferring a diplomatic meeting context
The inferred question concept is:
((< = > ($MEET ACTOR *VANCE* OTHERS G0749)) TIME G0751)

searching memory for question concept
    searching directly for $MEET
    ...
```

Anwar Sadat, President Assad, King Hussein, Hassan, and Menachim Begin.

If CYRUS is asked "what heads of state have you talked to?" it would apply the same rule to infer the same "diplomatic meeting" context inferred above. Talking to someone does not imply an event context. Thus, in this question, like the one above, the specification "heads of state" is used to infer an event context. If, on the other hand, CYRUS is asked "What heads of state have you gone out to dinner with?" it will not apply these rules, since the question already implies the event context "dining."

3.2. Context Construction and Personal Relationships

One particular aspect of participants that can be used to infer an event context is the relationship between the respondent and others involved in a situation to be retrieved. This is the case when we ask CYRUS the question, "Has your wife ever met Mrs. Begin?" There are many types of activities Vance's wife normally takes part in. Thus, applying the strategy Infer-from-Participants would not help in choosing categories for search when his wife is the only other known participant. Moreover, the CYRUS data base doesn't include Mrs. Vance's activities unless Vance was involved also. Thus, the inference is made that Vance must also have been a participant in the episode when Mrs. Vance and Mrs. Begin met. Using the relationship of Vance to his wife, the types of situations in which his family group and others would be involved can be inferred. Those situations are social situations. Applying "Infer-from-Participants" to the family group composed of Cyrus Vance and his wife, CYRUS can infer that the occasion must have been a social occasion. The inference that this was a social occasion that included both the Vances and Mrs. Begin allows the inference that Mr. Begin was also a participant in the event. "Infer-from-Participants" can be applied again to the occupational group set up by Vance and Begin's relationship to infer that the occasion was probably political. The following output from CYRUS shows how it applies these rules to answer this question.

```
Enter next question.

>Has your wife ever met Mrs. Begin?

The question is:
((ACTOR *MRS-VANCE* is (*PROX* VAL G1571)) TIME G1572 MODE (*?*))
The question type is "verification"
The question concept is
((ACTOR *MRS-VANCE* IS (*PROX* VAL G1571)) TIME G1572)
   applying INFER-FROM-PARTICIPANTS
      to family group (*VANCE* *MRS-VANCE*)
     inferring social occasion
   applying INFER-FROM-PARTICIPANTS
      to occupation group (*VANCE* *BEGIN*)
     inferring political occasion
   inferring political social occasion
The inferred question concept is:
((< = > (sM-SOCIAL-OBL ACTOR *VANCE* OTHERS (*MRS-VANCE* *BEGIN*
G1571)))
```

```
    TIME G1572)
searching memory for question concept
 searching directly for sM-SOCIAL-OBL
    searching for $PARTY
    searching for $DINE
    searching for $STATE-DINNER
    ...
```

yes, most recently at a state dinner in Israel

Using the relationships between the people, CYRUS answers this question by inferring that if it knew that Mrs. Vance and Mrs. Begin had met, then Vance would also have been present. It applies Infer-from-Participants twice to infer that it would have been a political social occasion. The political social occasions CYRUS knows about (sM-SOCIAL-OBL) include entertaining officials privately at parties and dinner, and state dinners. It searches for instances of each that involve both couples and finds a state dinner in Israel.

3.3. Context Construction From Topic Specifications

Topics of conversation can also be used to infer event contexts. In answering "When did you first hear about the Boston Tea Party?" some people infer a context of a high-school history class. The Boston Tea Party is a historical event, and the event contexts they have associated with historical events as topics are classroom situations. The following rule can be applied to infer event contexts from specified topics of communication:

> If topics of discussion or classes of topics of discussion are specified, and if any of them have communicatory event contexts associated with them, predict appropriate communicatory events associated with the topic or class of topic.

FIG. 5.3. Infer-from-Topic.

CYRUS uses this rule to answer questions such as "Who have you discussed the Camp David Accords with?" and "Have you ever talked to anyone about Zimbabwe independence?" Both the Camp David Accords and Zimbabwe independence are international concerns, and event contexts associated with international concerns as event topics are political meetings. Thus, in retrieving people Vance has discussed the Camp David Accords with, CYRUS infers that the discussions would have been at political meetings (as opposed to parties, speeches, etc.) and searches for those types of meetings.

```
Enter next question:
```

>Who have you discussed the Camp David Accords with?

```
The question is:
((ACTOR *VANCE* <=> (*MTRANS*) MOBJECT
   (*CONCEPTS* CONCERNING *CDA*) TO (*?*)) TIME G1380)
```

```
The question type is "concept completion"
The question concept is:
((ACTOR *VANCE* <=> (*MTRANS*) MOBJECT
    (*CONCEPTS* CONCERNING *CDA*) TO (*?*)) TIME G1380)
    applying INFER-FROM-TOPIC to *CDA*
        inferring undifferentiated political meeting
The inferred question concept is:
((<=> (sM-MEETING ACTOR *VANCE* OTHERS (*?*) TOPIC *CDA*))
    TIME G1380)

searching memory for question concept
 searching directly for sM-MEETING
    searching for $MEET
    searching for $CONSULT
    searching for $PUB-REL-MEET
    ...
```

Begin, Sadat, Dayan, Hussein, and Assad at diplomatic meetings, Carter during consultations, and a group of Jewish leaders at a public relations meeting.

The only specification in the question that suggests an event context is the Camp David Accords (*CDA*), an international contract. Characteristic events in which international contracts occur as topics are political meetings (sM-MEETING to CYRUS). Thus, CYRUS applies the strategy "Find-from-Topic" to infer that Vance would have discussed the Camp David Accords during political meetings. It then searches for political meetings. Because there are a number of different types of political meetings it knows about, CYRUS traverses memory individually for each of those. The context instantiation and search strategies that guide that search are discussed in chapter 6.

Consider the following question:

(Q5): Have you talked to Begin recently about Arab-Israeli peace?

Because Arab-Israeli peace is an international issue. it has the context "political meetings" associated with it. Because Begin is a foreign diplomat, he has the context "diplomatic meetings" associated with him. "Diplomatic meetings" is a specialization of "political meetings." The more specific context is searched for in a case like this.

3.4. Using Locations for Context Construction

Location specifications can also be used by context instantiation rules to infer event contexts. In answering "Did you see Mr. Smith at the pool yesterday?" a context associated with "pools" as locations would be appropriate for searching memory. "Swimming at the gym" or "going to the swim club" could be inferred and searched for. Similarly, in answering "When was the last time you were at a ski resort?" the location specification "ski resort," which has "ski trips" associated with it, can be used to direct search to a "ski trip" context.

The context instantiation strategy that allows for processing of this sort is "Infer-from-Location."

If locations or classes of locations specified have associated event contexts, predict the characteristic events associated with each of them that could also include other already-specified components.

FIG. 5.4. Infer-from-Location.

In CYRUS, this strategy is used in answering questions such as "Were you in Europe last week?" and "Have you been to Asia recently?" CYRUS knows that events associated with foreign places are "diplomatic trips." Thus, in answering these questions, CYRUS predicts that it should look for diplomatic trips.

```
Enter next question:

>When was the last time you were in Egypt?

The question is:
((ACTOR *VANCE* IS (*LOC* VAL *EGYPT*)) TIME TIME0)
The question type is "time"
The question concept is:
((ACTOR *VANCE* IS (*LOC* VAL *EGYPT*)))
   applying INFER-FROM-LOCATION to *EGYPT*
      inferring diplomatic trip context
The inferred question concept is:
((< = > (sM-VIPVISIT ACTOR *VANCE* DESTINATION *EGYPT*)) TIME TIME0)
searching memory for question concept
   searching directly for SM-VIPVISIT
   ...

on DEC 10, 1978.
```

CYRUS uses the facts that Egypt is a foreign country and that Vance would have been there as part of his job to infer that he would have gone there on a diplomatic trip. It thus uses "Infer-from-Location" to infer a diplomatic trip to Egypt as the search context.

3.5. Context Construction and Time

Time specifications can also be used to infer event contexts. Consider, for example, the following two questions:

(Q6): While you were a lawyer, what did you usually discuss with your partners?

(Q7): What kind of exercise did you get last winter?

The first question can be answered by referring to event contexts characteristic of lawyers, which would include partners in the law firm. The second can be answered by inferring winter sports contexts. The following context instantiation rule guides construction of event contexts from time specifications.

If the time specification refers to a time period with characteristic events (an era) or a long term role with characteristic activities associated with it, predict those characteristic events of the time specification that could include other already-specified components.

FIG. 5.5. Infer-from-Time-Specification.

The time period necessary to answer (Q6) above is an *era* (Kolodner, 1978, Schank & Kolodner, 1979). An era is a time span characterized by some long-term role (Schank & Abelson, 1977) or long-term state. Thus, eras can coincide with job situations, family roles, home ownership and school, to name a few. The most important piece of information an era holds is the role or state that characterizes it. If that role or state has event contexts associated with it, then they can be instantiated when an era is specified. Sports contexts associated with high school, for example, include pep rallies and football games. The question "While you were in high school, did you ever meet a football player?" might be answered by recalling "pep rallies," a kind of situation that happened during high school that involved football players.

4. MEMORY ORGANIZATION FOR CONTEXT CONSTRUCTION

In order for component-to-context instantiation strategies to work, role fillers must specify contexts they are associated with. In CYRUS, that means that non-event concepts must point to E-MOPs they are related to.

Recall, for example, the following two questions, discussed previously:

(Q8): Who have you talked to about SALT?

(Q9): Has your wife ever met Mrs. Begin?

In the first question, the international contract "SALT" is available to aid context construction. In the second question, the two people mentioned, their relationship, and Vance's relationship to them can be used for context construction. Thus, we expect "SALT," "Mrs. Begin," "Mrs. Vance," "family relationship," and "business relationship" each to refer to possible E-MOPs for search.

In practice, this does not have to be a direct pointer. To answer (Q8), for example, the description of SALT must be used to infer a search context, or E-MOP for traversal. "SALT," as a concept in CYRUS' memory, has no contexts associated with it. It is defined in memory, however, as an "international contract," which does have contexts associated with it. An "international contract" can be talked about in a "political meeting" (sM-MEETING). Using that information, a "political meeting" context with topic "SALT" can be constructed and searched for.

There are two important points about the organization of concepts in memory that are shown in this example. First, context construction requires association of an E-MOP specification with non-event concepts in memory. In order to infer a context for "talking about SALT," "international contract," which has an E-MOP associated with it, was used. If it had no references to E-MOPs, context construction could not have happened.

Second, a *hierarchy of concepts* will allow contexts to be associated with more general concepts than those specified in a question, and through *inheritance* of properties, an E-MOP can be inferred from those more general concepts. Although SALT had no contexts associated with it, the contexts associated with "international contract" could be used.

An important conclusion to draw from these two observations is that context construction can proceed in exactly the same way whether a particular entity or a class it falls into is specified in a question. Compare, for example, the following two questions:

(Q10): Who have you talked to about the Camp David Accords?

(Q11): Who have you talked to about international contracts?

The "Camp David Accords," like "SALT," is an "international contract." Thus, using the information that "international contracts" are talked about at "political meetings," the target concept "political meetings about the Camp David Accords" can be inferred. In answering (Q11), information from the concept "international contract" is also used, and the target concept "political meetings about international contracts" can be inferred. The only difference here is that after inferring a context in (Q10), the specific contract mentioned in the question is filled in.

Thus, in exactly the same way "political meeting about SALT" can be inferred from the original target "talking about SALT" in (Q9), a context can be constructed for answering (Q10) and (Q11). The hierarchical organization of contracts in memory shown in Fig. 5.6 allows that construction.

"International contracts" have countries as their sides and are the topics of political meetings. "SALT" is an "international contract" with sides Russia and the United States, and underlying issue "arms limitations." "The Camp David Accords" is another "international contract" with underlying issue peace and involving Israel and Egypt. Other international contracts in memory can be represented similarly.

In addition to this organization of particular contracts as international contracts, each of the particular contracts above might belong to other classifications of contracts. "The Camp David Accords," for example, is a "peace contract" (a contract with underlying issue peace), and if there were any contexts associated with "peace contract," those also could be used during context construction. It is also a specialization of "Arab-Israeli peace," also an "international

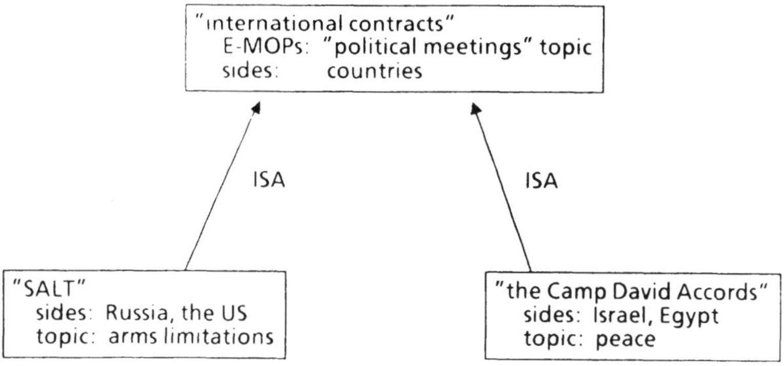

FIG. 5.6. International contracts.

contract,'' and if there were contexts associated with that classification of contracts, those too would be used during context construction.

The actual hierarchies of concepts there are in memory depend on how the concepts are used. Thus, unless ''peace contract'' has some necessary generalized information for processing associated with it, it does not need to be an explicit classification in the contract organization, although there may be many examples of peace contracts among the particular contracts organized there.

Similarly, the types of concepts that have E-MOPs associated with them should be those concepts (and classes of those concepts) that are associated with events. In CYRUS' memory, that includes animate participants, such as people and organizations, and inanimate participants, such as objects, locations, and times. In addition, the classifications each particular person, country, or object fits into should have E-MOPs associated with them.

In a political context, people can be described by the political roles they play, their nationalities, their affiliations to political groups, and their occupations. Thus, generalized information about people and classifications of people should be based around those specifications. Menachim Begin, for example is ''Israeli,'' a ''prime minister,'' and acts as a ''delegate'' or ''negotiator.'' A ''prime minister'' is a ''head of state.'' ''Heads of state,'' and most other high political officials, are ''diplomats.'' ''Negotiators,'' too, are ''diplomats.'' Anwar Sadat is a ''president,'' which is also a ''head of state,'' and fits into many of the same classifications Begin fits into. Information in memory about Begin and Sadat, and the person categories they fit into, are organized as in Fig. 5.7.

As a head of state, the ''summit conference'' MOP is associated with Begin. As a ''diplomat,'' ''negotiations'' and ''diplomatic meetings'' are associated with him. Begin, himself, is closely associated with ''Camp David negotiations,'' a specialization of the ''negotiations'' MOP. Consider how the following question can be answered using this information:

(Q12): Under what circumstances have you talked to Begin?

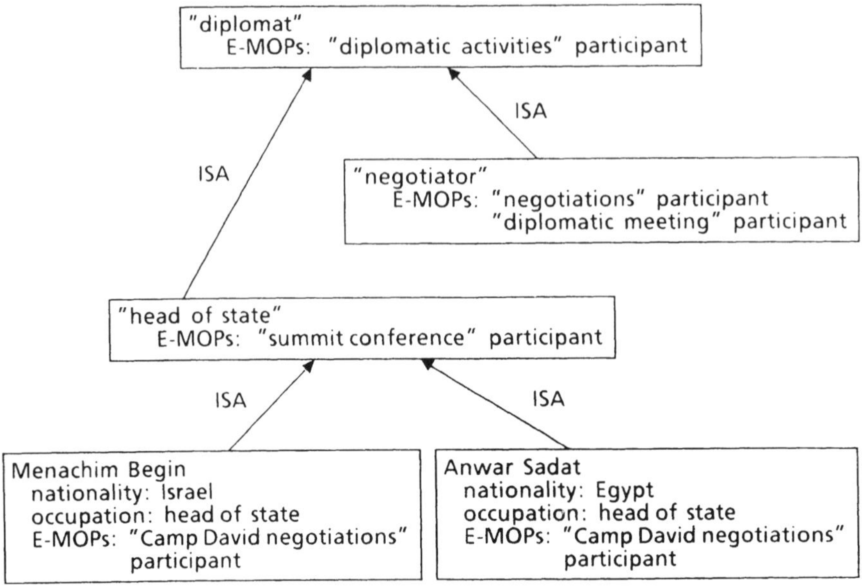

FIG. 5.7. Heads of state.

Using the information about Begin above, along with component instantiation strategies, any of the following contexts can be constructed for search in answering this question:

> ''negotiations about the Camp David Accords with Begin''
>
> ''summit conferences about the Camp David Accords including Begin''
>
> ''diplomatic meetings about the Camp David Accords including Begin''

The first can be constructed from E-MOP information directly associated with Begin, the second from ''head of state'' information, and the third from ''diplomat'' information. Since there is a particular type of ''negotiations'' context associated with Begin, himself, the general ''negotiations'' context associated with ''diplomats'' is not constructed.

Location and object information can be organized similarly. What is important for them, as for contracts and people, is that they be organized in *functional* hierarchies and that classifications in the hierarchies specify associated E-MOPs. Thus, with information that ''airplanes'' have ''flying'' associated with them, the question ''Have you been in a plane recently?'' could be answered by constructing and searching for a recent ''flying'' episode. With E-MOP information associated as above with ''resort area,'' ''trips'' can be inferred.

5. HUMAN PROTOCOLS AND CONTEXT CONSTRUCTION

When we asked people to recall the most famous person they had ever met, we found that people used a retrieval process similar to that just described. The following two protocols are typical of the answers we got to "Who is the most famous person you have ever met?"

Protocol 1

Since I've been at Yale, I've met famous people at the Chubb Fellow seminar series. I met President Carter at one of those seminars, before he was president.

Protocol 2

First I thought how somebody could be famous, and politics was the first thing I thought of. Then I thought about circumstances where I could have met a famous politician. I searched political experiences I have had—mostly political rallies I participated in and experiences campaigning for candidates. I remembered that I had met McGovern. But since you said "most famous," I went on to think of other famous people I might have met. Next I thought of entertainers, and how I could have met them. . . . Then I thought of famous scientists, and places I could have met scientists.

What people seem to be doing in these examples is constructing situations during which they would have met famous people. The person in Protocol 1 could have used the strategy "Infer-from-Participants" to infer a context he had associated with "famous people." The second protocol can be explained as the result of a failed initial attempt to apply that strategy. We can assume that person had no event contexts associated with "famous person," or he would have attempted retrieval of those contexts. Because the only specification given in the question was participants, that was the only choice for elaboration. By specializing "famous person," concepts with associated event contexts (e.g., politician, entertainer) could be inferred, and "Infer-from-Participants" could be applied to each of those. Our explanation of why that person enumerated types of famous people, then, is so that he could then search individually for contexts associated with each.

In recalling famous people they had met, people applied context instantiation to construct and then search for political rallies, participation in political campaigns, and visits backstage after the theater, to name just a few. Each of these is a kind of situation in which a particular kind of famous person could have been met. Each is an instance of inferring an E-MOP for traversal from participant information available in a target concept. In order for this to happen, "politician," as a memory concept, must have the fact that they normally take part in political rallies and campaigns associated with them. Similarly, ''entertainer'' must have associated with it the fact that they can be found in plays.

Using these strategies, we can predict a plausible reasoning process for answering the following question about Cyrus Vance:

(Q13): What heads of state have you met?

Vance meets people in many different types of situations every day—at meetings, parties, conferences, on the street, in his office, and so forth. Furthermore, meeting heads of state is probably not very different from meeting any other person (for Vance). Thus, it doesn't seem like ''meeting people'' or ''meeting heads of state'' would be good E-MOPs for Vance. This question can be answered, however, by applying ''Infer-from-Participants'' to infer E-MOP-related situations in which he would have met heads of state.

In order for that to happen, we assume that ''heads of state'' or ''diplomats'' has associated with it knowledge about the kinds of activities they are most often involved in with him. Heads of state are involved in ''summit conferences.'' They are also diplomats, and diplomats are normally involved in ''diplomatic meetings'' and ''negotiations.'' Thus, by applying ''Infer-from-Participants'' first to ''head of state'' and then to ''diplomat,'' ''summit conference,'' ''diplomatic meeting,'' and ''negotiations'' situations involving heads of state can be inferred and their E-MOPs traversed. Thus, the following reasoning sequence is one way of answering this question.

1. Heads of state are often involved in summit conferences. Have I been to any recently?
2. Heads of state are diplomats. What kinds of episodes am I involved in with foreign diplomats? Negotiations and diplomatic meetings. What countries have had problems that I've negotiated? Who did I meet with during those negotiations? Have I been to any meetings recently? Who was at those meetings?

6. IMPLICATIONS OF CONTEXT CONSTRUCTION

In using these strategies, there is always the chance that something relevant will not be retrieved because its context was not inferred. Vance's discussions about the Camp David Accords outside of political meetings are not recalled by CYRUS in answering ''Who have you talked to about the Camp David Accords?'' He may have given a speech about the situation or have talked to somebody about the accords at some social political situation (such as a state dinner). Similarly, if Vance's wife had met Mrs. Begin in some situation other than a social activity when the Vances and Begins were present, then retrieval would have failed.

Choice of contexts for retrieval is dependent on the information or cues available at the time of retrieval. A context can be chosen for search only if some aspect of the given retrieval specification refers to that context. In answering "Who is the most famous person you've ever met?" a person might fail to remember meeting a famous person in a museum because there is no available cue to initiate retrieval of museum experiences. On the other hand, if the person were prompted with "how about in a museum?" there is a better chance of his retrieving that experience.

In judging the advantages and disadvantages of traversal/elaboration, a similar problem was mentioned. As in that case, the advantages of directed context construction seem to outweigh its disadvantages, since search is directed only to areas of memory with potential relevance.

7. SUMMARY

An important component of the retrieval process is choosing a context or category for search. This is done by considering the contexts associated with given question components. "International contracts," for example, are known to be associated with "diplomatic meetings" and "negotiations" in the domain of international diplomats. This knowledge directs search to either of those two categories to answer a question such as "Who has Muskie talked to recently about the Camp David Accords?"

Because context construction requires information from concepts other than E-MOPs to infer E-MOPs for traversal, concepts in memory must refer to event contexts they are normally associated with. In fact, automatic context construction in any data base requires that data base concepts refer to the types of valid retrieval contexts they can be associated with.

6 Alternate-Context Search

1. INTRODUCTION

Name all the amusement parks you've been to.

Protocol 1

There's an amusement park near my parents' house that we used to go to when we were kids—Willow Grove. When I've gone to amusement parks since then, it's been either as part of an outing when a friend was in town or as part of a trip. Once, we went to an amusement park before going to a concert at the summer music school. That was with Howard and Lauri. Another time we went to an amusement park when John and Wendy were visiting, one around here someplace. I've been to Disney World twice, and to Disneyland last summer while we were in California. And I've been to Great Adventure once when I was in Philadelphia visiting my parents. I've also been to a bunch of amusement parks on the beach—in Atlantic City, Coney Island, Santa Cruz, probably some others I can't remember.

In searching memory extensively to remember an event, it is often helpful to search for episodes related to the target event. In trying to remember experiences at amusement parks, for example, the person above recalled friends visiting, trips around the United States, and amusement parks at the beach, in order to recall her experiences. Alternate contexts people choose for search are not chosen randomly. The person above thought about the kinds of episodes that could have been related to amusement parks. She did not think about football games, conferences, or reading mystery books to remember amusement park experiences. Searching for a different type of event than the one targeted for retrieval is called *alternate context search*. Once a related event is retrieved, it can provide cues to use in reconstructing the originally targeted event.

2. ALTERNATE-CONTEXT SEARCH

The traversal/elaboration process must halt when no further elaboration can be done. Often, when appropriate elaborations have been exhausted, however, there are still additional events to be found. Consider the following example:

(Q1): Enumerate all of Vance's meetings with Gromyko.

Suppose that memory held a large number of "diplomatic meetings" with Gromyko, some in the United States, some in Russia, and all to discuss various aspects of SALT. Because they are so similar, it is not likely that elaboration by itself would be enough to specify unique event descriptions for retrieval of all of them. If traversal/elaboration were the only retrieval process, then many of these meetings might not be retrievable.

Because events happen in the context of other events, and because they refer to those related events, an event can be found by finding an episode it was related to. When a related event is found, its context can be searched for the target, or its features can be used to reconstruct features of the targeted event. To search for a meeting with Brezhnev, for example, it might be appropriate to recall a summit conference that would have included Brezhnev and to recall a meeting with Brezhnev from the summit conference's sequence of events. Since summit conferences are less common than diplomatic meetings, they might be easier to retrieve.

Search for alternate episodes can aid retrieval in answering (Q1). For example, some of those meetings were parts of diplomatic trips, some were parts of summit conferences, some were called for crisis reasons, and some enabled a breakthrough in negotiations. If diplomatic trips, summit conferences, crisis situations, and negotiations breakthroughs related to those meetings could be found, the meetings themselves could be remembered.

Searching for alternate contexts can aid retrieval, since an alternate context might be less common than a target event and thus need less specification in order to be retrieved. Summit conferences, for example, happen less frequently than diplomatic meetings do. Although a specification "diplomatic meetings about SALT" might describe many meetings, the specification "summit conferences about SALT," which can be derived from that, describes only a small number of events.

Alternate-context search can also aid retrieval of a target event if the alternate context can be better specified with respect to the E-MOPs it is indexed in than the target event can. "Diplomatic meetings with Begin" might be an ambiguous

1. IF the target event does not specify an E-MOP for traversal, THEN apply context instantiation strategies to infer a context for search (explained in chapter 5).

2. Traverse memory searching for that target event (using the traversal / elaboration process specified in chapter 3).

3. IF an appropriate answer has not been found, THEN apply executive search strategies to search for alternate contexts related to the target.

4. IF an appropriate answer has not been found, THEN go back to step 1, attempting to construct a new context.

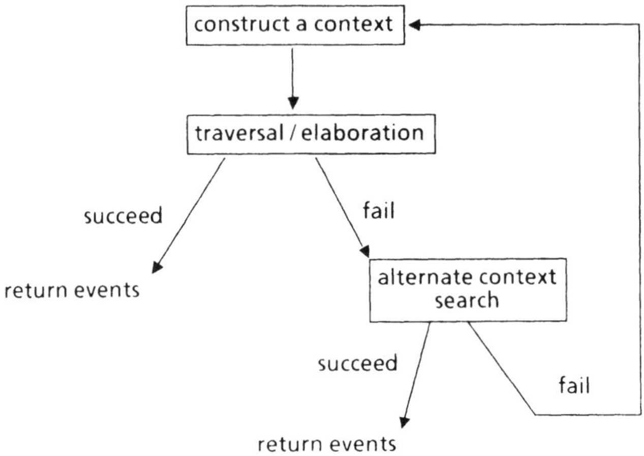

FIG. 6.1. The retrieval process.

target event. Although "diplomatic meetings" might often happen as a result of "crisis situations," if there had only been one crisis situation that involved Israel, then it would be better specified in its E-MOPs than "meetings with Begin" are in "diplomatic meetings." Thus, it would be more retrievable and aid retrieval of at least one meeting with Begin.

Alternate-context search is the last step of CYRUS' retrieval process. It happens when traversal/elaboration fails. We hypothesize that it is also a step of last resort in human processing, since it requires so much more effort than simple elaboration. The following picture describes the entire reconstructive retrieval process and shows where alternate-context search fits into that process.

Executive strategies direct search for alternate contexts. They first call context-to-context instantiation strategies (explained in chapter 4) to construct descriptions of episodes plausibly related to the target event. They then pass control to the traversal/elaboration process, directing that process to attempt retrieval of each of those hypothetical events. If any such event is found, its episodic context is searched for the original target event. If no event is found that way, any plausibly related events are used to elaborate the original target event, and it is searched for using traversal/elaboration. Executive strategies, then, have four steps:

1. Call the appropriate context-to-context instantiation strategy to construct a (hypothetical) episode related to the target event.
2. Use traversal/elaboration to retrieve that episode from memory.
3. Search for the target event in the episodic context of the events retrieved in step 2.
4. If step 3 fails, use events retrieved in step 2 to elaborate the target event. Search for the elaborated target using traversal/elaboration.

To search for a particular "diplomatic meeting," for example, executive search strategies trigger appropriate context instantiation strategies to construct contexts related to diplomatic meetings (e.g., negotiations, summit conferences, crisis situations, diplomatic trips), traverse memory to retrieve those hypothetical related contexts, and if one is found, direct search within the episodic context of that episode to find the original target event—a diplomatic meeting. Steps 1 and 2 of executive strategies have been described previously. Search of surrounding context (step 3) and elaboration of the target event in step 4 will be described in more detail.

Recall from the discussion of instantiation strategies that an event's context includes events it was related to through containment, time, or causality. Search of the episodic or surrounding context of one event to find a target event means reconstructing the appropriate part of the first event to see if it corresponds to the target event. In our model, there are two mechanisms for doing this. First, an event itself might point to or describe another event related to it. If a particular museum experience was the highlight of some trip, for example, then the trip's description in memory may point directly to the museum experience or describe it in enough detail to retrieve it from its own MOP. In this case, to find a target event in the surrounding context of another event, the possible relationship between the two events is determined, and appropriate parts of the context of the second event are checked to see if events it points to or describes correspond to the target. If an event does not explicitly point to episodes related to it, a second procedure is available. The content frame of the E-MOP that event resides in might specify the types of events related to it. "Diplomatic meetings," for example, are often parts of "conferences." In that case, the content frame description of a hypothetically related event is used by context-to-context instantiation strategies to reconstruct that aspect of the event's context. Again, correspondence to the target event is checked.

IF the Target Concept could have been embedded in a larger episode (sMOP)

THEN

(1) Use "Instantiate-Larger-Episodes" to hypothesize larger episodes (sMOP instances) the target concept could have been part of. Use component instantiation strategies to fill in each description.

(2) Search memory for each instance.

(3) For each one found, search its known sequence of events for a match to the target concept.

(4) If no match is found, use "Instantiate-Seq-of-Events", plus the additional information found in the sMOP instance, to better specify the target concept. Search for the new target concept in memory.

FIG. 6.2. Find-from-Larger-Episodes.

''Find-from-Larger-Episodes'' (see Fig. 6.2), for example, constructs, finds, and searches the episodic context of events a target event could have been part of. To aid in finding a particular ''diplomatic meeting with Gromyko,'' it would (1) call the context instantiation strategy ''Infer-Larger-Episodes'' to construct contexts for ''summit conferences about a Russian-American concern,'' ''diplomatic trips to Russia,'' and ''negotiations concerning a Russian-American contract''; (2) traverse memory searching for each of those; and (3) search (using the methods described in the previous paragraph) the sequence of events of each episode found for an appropriate diplomatic meeting.

If an event plausibly related to the target event is found, but it does not point to an event corresponding to the target event, it can nevertheless aid in retrieval of the target. This second way of using alternative events to find a target is a process of using features of the alternative event to flesh out the target. Its use in ''Find-from-Larger-Episodes'' is listed in step 4 of that strategy. As an example of its use, consider the following: The target event is ''museum experiences.'' In searching for museum experiences, some trips are recalled, say a trip to England. While the sequence of events of the trip itself may not refer to any museum visits (step 3), transference of its features to a ''museum visit'' context might aid in describing a museum visit that did in fact happen. Its time, place, the weather, and so forth, applied to a museum visit might provide enough details to remember a particular visit to a museum. In this step, the context-to-context instantiation strategy describing the relationship of the hypothetically related event to the target event is used.

In guiding search for event contexts related to a target event, executive strategies direct search for ''what must have happened'' or ''what may have happened'' if the target event had taken place. If an event that must have happened along with a targeted event can be found, its specification in memory might refer to the target.

As for context-to-context instantiation strategies, there is one search strategy for each relationship between events. The full list is below:

Find-from-Enablements
Find-from-Preconditions
Find-from-Results
Find-from-Reasons
Find-from-Enabled-Events
Find-from-Larger-Episodes
Find-from-Seq-of-Events
Find-from-Preceding-Events
Find-from-Following-Events
Find-from-Standardizations

FIG. 6.3. Executive Search Strategies.

2.1. Sequence of Events

One event relationship useful in search is "sequence of events." Sometimes retrieval of an event that could have been part of the target episode can aid search for the target. In order to enumerate his trips to Europe, for example, one person we observed recalled significant sightseeing and museum experiences in Europe to remember particular trips he had made there. When CYRUS answers the question "What summit conferences have you been to recently?" it searches memory for diplomatic meetings and state dinners that could have been part of a summit conference. If it finds any, it retrieves the larger episodes they were embedded in to see if they were in fact summit conferences.

The strategy used in these examples is "Find-from-Seq-of-Events":

IF a possible sequence of events for the target concept can be inferred

THEN

(1) Instantiate each element of the sequence of events using "Instantiate-Seq-of-Events". Fill in their slots as well as possible by applying component instantiation strategies.

(2) Search for each inferred concept in memory.

(3) For each one found, see if one of the episodes it is embedded in corresponds to the target concept.

(4) If no dominating episodes are referred to directly, apply "Instantiate-Larger-Episodes" to instantiate a larger episode that it could have been part of corresponding to the target concept,and search for that episode in memory.

FIG. 6.4. Find-from-Seq-of-Events.

This strategy directs application of Instantiate-Seq-of-Events to infer a hypothetical event-component of the target concept and then attempts to retrieve that new event from memory. If retrieval is successful, the strategy directs search for the target event in the episodic context of the event found. In this strategy, the target event is checked against larger episodes the event was part of. If there are no specified dominating episodes, Instantiate-Larger-Episodes is called to reconstruct the dominating episodes that "must have been going on" along with the event found in memory. Those are checked against the target concept.

When we ask CYRUS to search memory for all of the summit conferences Vance has attended, one of the strategies it applies is Find-from-Seq-of-Events. Using this strategy, CYRUS calls instantiation strategies to construct contexts for diplomatic meetings with heads of state, addresses by heads of state, and state dinners (the kinds of meetings, speeches, and state dinners that could have happened during summit conferences) and searches for each of those. In the following example, we see CYRUS doing that.

```
Enter next question:

>How many Summit Conferences have you been to?

The question is:
((< = > (sM-SUMMIT-CONFERENCE ACTOR *VANCE*)) QUANTITY (*?*)
   TIME G0659)
The question type is "concept completion"
The question concept is:
((< = > (sM-SUMMIT-CONFERENCE ACTOR *VANCE*)) TIME G0659)
searching memory for question concept
   searching directly for sM-SUMMIT-CONFERENCE
    found (GN420)
applying strategies to search memory
   ...
   applying Find-from-Seq-of-Events to search for
     possible components of sM-SUMMIT-CONFERENCE
       searching for $WELCOME
       searching for $MEET
       searching for $SPEECH
       searching for $WORKING-MEAL
       searching for $STATE-DINNER
         found (GN475 GN526 GN577 GN514)

One about SALT and one about the Camp David Accords.
```

CYRUS first attempts to search for summit conferences that Vance has attended. Because he has attended many summit conferences, they are organized in an E-MOP that requires specification of indices for retrieval of individual events. By signaling the retrieval process that traversal has arrived at an E-MOP and not an event, memory in effect is telling retrieval that there are numerous summit conferences in memory and that search should continue. Operating without component instantiation strategies (one of CYRUS' modes of operation), CYRUS returns the most recent event in the summit conference MOP (most recent events are stored specially in CYRUS) and continues search by applying executive strategies to search for other contexts that might help it to find summit conferences.

One strategy CYRUS applies is "Find-from-Seq-of-Events." That strategy directs search for the kinds of activities that normally happen during summit conferences. Thus, CYRUS searches for welcomes by heads of state to conferences, meetings with heads of state about important topics, speeches by heads of state about important issues, and working meals and state dinners attended by heads of state. After finding events that match each specification given, it looks at the larger episodes each was a part of to see if they had happened during a summit. If so, it has retrieved the summit conferences it is looking for. CYRUS recalls two summit conferences in this way—one about SALT and one about the Camp David Accords.

Similarly, if we ask CYRUS to recall all of Vance's trips to Egypt, it applies the strategy "Find-from-Seq-of-Events" while searching its memory, and searches for meetings he would have had there, speeches he might have given, flights, and so forth.

```
Enter next question:

>How many times have you gone to Egypt recently?

The question is:
((ACTOR *VANCE* < = > (*PTRANS*) OBJECT *VANCE* TO *EGYPT*) TIME G0742
    QUANTITY (*?*))
The question type is "concept completion"
The question concept is:
((ACTOR *VANCE* < = > (*PTRANS*) OBJECT *VANCE* TO *EGYPT*) TIME G0742)
    applying INFER-FROM-LOCATION to *EGYPT*
     inferring diplomatic trip context
The inferred question concept is:
((< = > (sM-VIPVISIT ACTOR *VANCE* DESTINATION *EGYPT*)) TIME G0742)
searching memory for question concept
    searching directly for sM-VIPVISIT
     found (GN528)
applying strategies to search memory
...
  applying Find-From-Seq-of-Events to search for
   possible components of sM-VIPVISIT
    searching for $FLY
    searching for $WELCOME
    searching for sM-VIP-TRIP-DO
    searching for sM-CONFERENCE
    searching for $MEET
    searching for $SPEECH
    searching for $REPORT
    searching for $FLY
     found (GN539 GN531)

Four times in the past 6 months.
```

CYRUS first uses an instantiation strategy to infer that the context for being in Egypt must be a diplomatic trip. It then goes on to search directly for trips to

Egypt. Because there are many of them, it continues by applying search strategies to aid its retrieval. The flights ($FLY) CYRUS looks for while searching for trips to Egypt are flights to and from Egypt, the welcomes are welcomes by Egyptian diplomats at the Cairo airport. The conferences it looks for are about Egyptian concerns, involve Egyptian diplomats, and take place in Egypt, as do the diplomatic meetings ($MEET), speeches ($SPEECH), and press conferences ($REPORT) it searches for.

2.2. Using Standard Methods for Retrieval

Some E-MOPs don't have a standard sequence of events, but instead have more than one way of happening. For example, traveling can be done by air, by train, by car, and so on. In order to find traveling episodes, then, it is reasonable to think of different types of travel, and to retrieve instances of each. A person answering the question "How many times have you been to the Caribbean?" might try to think of times he had flown there and times he had gone there on a cruise. The strategy that directs retrieval of standard ways of doing an activity is called "Find-from-Standardizations" (see Fig. 6.5).

This strategy hypothesizes appropriate standard ways of doing the target activity and searches for each of them in turn. Retrieval of one of the standardizations constitutes a match to the target concept. That means episodic context need not be searched once a standardized method is found. To retrieve trips to England, for example, a businessman might first try to remember business trips to England and then try to remember vacations he took there. To remember diplomatic conferences, CYRUS searches for summit conferences.

We have observed that search strategies such as these are used extensively by people. Imagine how a person might attempt to remember trips he has taken. He might apply the strategy Find-from-Seq-of-Events to search for travel experiences. In order to search for travel, he may apply the strategy Find-from-Standardizations and search individually for standard types of travel. Let's suppose he searched for air trips and train trips, but did not search for cruises. Applying this strategy, he would fail to retrieve travel on ships and thus might fail to

IF the target concept has a number of standard ways of being done

THEN

(1) Use "Instantiate-Standardizations" to instantiate each standard way of doing the target concept's activity that is appropriate to the rest of the target specification. Use component instantiation strategies to fill slots in the hypothesized standardizations as well as possible.

(2) Search memory for instances of each of those standard ways.

(3) If one is found, it is a match.

FIG. 6.5. Find-from-Standardizations.

retrieve some of the trips he had been on. Failure to apply a strategy completely can result in retrieval failure.

One of CYRUS' E-MOPs with standard methods is "political meetings" (sM-MEETING). Standard political meetings include "diplomatic meetings" ($MEET, meetings with foreign government officials), "consultations" with other U.S. government officials ($CONSULT), and "public relations meetings" ($PUB-REL-MEET). Thus, when CYRUS is searching for undifferentiated political meetings, it applies the strategy Find-from-Standardizations to search for instances of each type of meeting individually.

```
Enter next question:
```

>Who have you talked to about SALT?

```
The question is:
((ACTOR *VANCE* < = > (*MTRANS*) MOBJECT
   (*CONCEPTS* CONCERNING *SALT*) TO (*?*)) TIME G1062)
The question type is "concept completion"
The question concept is:
((ACTOR *VANCE* < = > (*MTRANS*) MOBJECT
   (*CONCEPTS* CONCERNING *SALT*) TO (*?*)) TIME G1062)
 applying INFER-FROM-TOPIC to *SALT*
     inferring undifferentiated political meeting
The inferred question concept is:
((< = > (sM-MEETING ACTOR *VANCE* OTHERS (*?*) TOPIC *SALT*))
   TIME G1062)
searching memory for question concept
   searching directly for sM-MEETING
    found (GN545 GN525 GN517  GN486  GN453)
    applying FIND-FROM-STANDARDIZATIONS to search for
         standard types of sM-MEETINGs
      searching for $MEET
      searching for $CONSULT
      searching for $PUB-REL-MEET
       found (GN590  GN556  GN561)
```

Carter, Brezhnev, Gromyko, and other American and Russian diplomats.

In searching for situations where Vance talked about SALT, CYRUS first infers that those discussions would have been at political meetings. It then searches memory for instances of the kinds of political meetings it knows about—"diplomatic meetings" about SALT ($MEET), consultations about SALT with American government officials ($CONSULT), and public relations meetings about SALT ($PUB-REL-MEET). It finds meetings of each type with a number of people—consultations with Carter and other American diplomats, and diplomatic meetings with Gromyko, Brezhnev, and other Russian diplomats.

Another E-MOP with standard methods of implementation that CYRUS knows about is "ceremonies" (sM-CEREMONY). In trying to recall ceremonies, then, one strategy CYRUS applies is Find-from-Standardizations. Using this strategy, CYRUS searches for welcomes ($WELCOME), parades ($PARADE), and state dinners ($STATE-DINNER) individually as follows.

Enter next question:

>What ceremonies have you taken part in?

```
The question is:
((< = > (sM-CEREMONY ACTOR *VANCE* SPEC (*?*))) TIME G1057)
The question type is "concept completion"
The question concept is:
((< = > (sM-CEREMONY ACTOR *VANCE* SPEC (*?*))) TIME G1057)
searching memory for question concept
 searching directly for sM-CEREMONY
   found (GN300)
 applying FIND-FROM-STANDARDIZATIONS to search for
      standard types of sM-CEREMONYs
   searching for $WELCOME
   searching for $PARADE
   searching for $STATE-DINNER
    found (GN363 GN300 GN600 GN452 GN586 GN345)
```

A state dinner in Israel, a parade and state dinner in England, and a number of welcoming ceremonies.

Notice that by using this strategy, CYRUS can only retrieve standard types of ceremonies. In fact, one of the ceremonies Vance has taken part in, which was not retrieved using this strategy, was a ceremony commemorating the opening of commercial air traffic between Israel and Egypt. The ceremony consisted of taking off from Beersheba in Israel, flying over Cairo and Tel Aviv airports, and landing back in Beersheba. Because this was not a standard type of ceremony, CYRUS could not retrieve it using this strategy. In order to retrieve that ceremony, CYRUS would have to use other strategies to infer reasons why ceremonies might have taken place recently and what the form of those ceremonies might be.

As shown by CYRUS' failure above, one of the consequences of using event-oriented search strategies is that they can direct search only for standard types of related contexts. Because these strategies make use of content frame information, which is generalized or standard information about different types of episodes, unusual events cannot be retrieved using these strategies. They are useful, however, for finding more common types of episodes. More unusual events can be found in other ways—by using enumeration strategies, for example, to imagine possibilities, or by searching for interruptions or other standard ways that events can fail.

2.3. Using Larger Episodes

Most E-MOPs hold information about the types of larger episodes they are normally part of. For example, meetings generally occur in the context of negotiations, and sightseeing usually happens during trips. A person answering a question about sightseeing in a particular place is quite likely to try to remember a trip to that place. To remember meetings, CYRUS attempts retrieval of relevant negotiations episodes the meetings could have been part of.

There are two strategies that can guide this processing—Find-from-IMOP and Find-from-Larger-Episodes. Find-from-IMOP is used to search for IMOP-related episodes an event could have been part of. An IMOP (Schank, 1980) is a goal or intention-based type of episode that takes place over a long period of time. A vacation, for example, is an IMOP. It is done for relaxation. Negotiating is also an IMOP. It is done for the purpose of solving an important problem. Because an IMOP episode takes place over a long period of time, its sequence of events is not as important as the few particular events in its sequence of events that stand out as contributing to obtaining its goal. Thus, a "negotiations" episode does not refer to all of the meetings in its sequence of events, but only to those that were most instrumental in the attempt to reach the I-MOP's goal.

Find-from-Larger-Episodes is used to search for larger episodes in whose sequence of events a target event might have been. An sMOP (Schank, 1980) or simple MOP is a situation whose sequence of events is fairly stereotyped, and which can include other simple MOPs and scripts (Schank & Abelson, 1977) in its sequence of events. In both of these strategies, appropriate larger episodes the target concept could have been part of are inferred (using Instantiate-Larger-Episodes), and their contexts are searched to see if they could have included the target concept.

In searching memory for meetings with Begin, for example, CYRUS attempts retrieval of negotiations episodes involving Israel. After retrieving one of those episodes, CYRUS searches its instrumental events to see if they included a particular meeting with Begin. If such a meeting is not specified, CYRUS uses information in the negotiations episode to hypothesize a meeting with Begin that would have occurred in its context. In this way, it may be able to better specify the target concept. Memory is then traversed searching for the newly expanded target event. The meeting hypothesized from the negotiations episode would match the target concept but contain more information, since it was constructed from a particular negotiations context. Any meeting found in memory that

IF the target concept could have been dominated by an Intentional sequence (IMOP)

THEN

(1) Use "Instantiate-Larger-Episodes" to hypothesize IMOP episodes the target concept could have been part of. Use component instantiation strategies to fill in each description.

(2) Search memory for those instances.

(3) For each one found, search its goal progressions for instrumental events which could match the target concept.

(4) If no match is found, use "Instantiate-Seq-of Events", plus the additional information found in the IMOP instance, to better specify the target concept. Search for the new target concept in memory.

FIG. 6.6. Find-from-IMOPs.

IF the Target Concept could have been embedded in a larger episode (sMOP)

THEN

(1) Use "Instantiate-Larger-Episodes" to hypothesize larger episodes (sMOP instances) the target concept could have been part of. Use component instantiation strategies to fill in each description.

(2) Search memory for each instance.

(3) For each one found, search its known sequence of events for a match to the target concept.

(4) If no match is found, use "Instantiate-Seq-of-Events", plus the additional information found in the sMOP instance, to better specify the target concept. Search for the new target concept in memory.

FIG. 6.7. Find-from-Larger-Episodes.

matched it would also match the target concept. These two strategies are shown in Figs. 6.6 and 6.7.

Notice that there are two search strategies guiding search for larger episodes an event could be part of whereas there is only one instantiation strategy (Instantiate-Larger-Episodes) necessary to actually construct these larger episodes. Larger episodes, whether simple MOP episodes or IMOP episodes, have the same containment relationship to smaller episodes they contain. Thus, only one instantiation strategy is necessary.

On the other hand, the relationship of an event to simple MOPs is merely a containment relation through the sequence of events, while the relationship of an event to IMOPs it is part of is as an instrumental event. The smaller episode is instrumental in obtaining the goals of the larger intention-related episode. Meetings are instrumental to obtaining the goals of negotiations. They are merely part of the sequence of events of a diplomatic trip. Because IMOPs are closely related to goals, application of Find-From-IMOP is a way of implicitly using possible goals of an episode to search memory.

In terms of processing, Find-from-Larger-Episodes and Find-from-IMOPs are different in step 3. Those are the steps that guide search of the episodic context of an event. In Find-from-Larger-Events, the sequence of events of the simple MOP instance found can be checked or reconstructed to determine if it contained an event matching the target concept. Because IMOPs take place over long periods of time, and because their sequences of events are not as important as the changes in their goals, their sequences of events will not be well filled-out. Events instrumental to obtaining their goals will have to be found by remembering or reconstructing their goal progressions and remembering the events that prompted those changes.

CYRUS applies the strategy Find-from-Larger-Episodes whenever the type of episode it is looking for specifies which kinds of simple MOP episodes it is usually part of. "Diplomatic meetings" are often included in "conferences." "Sightseeing" is usually part of a trip. Thus, in searching extensively for sightseeing experiences, CYRUS searches for trips to the appropriate places, as illustrated in the example that follows:

```
Enter next question:

>Have you ever been sightseeing in Egypt?

The question is:
((< = > (sM-SIGHTSEE ACTOR *VANCE*)) TIME G0874 MODE (*?*)
   PLACE *EGYPT*)
The question type is "verification"
The question concept is:
((< = > (sM-SIGHTSEE ACTOR *VANCE*)) TIME G0874 PLACE *EGYPT*)
searching memory for question concept
   searching directly for sM-SIGHTSEE
    didn't find any
applying strategies to search memory
 ...
 applying FIND-FROM-LARGER-EPISODES to search for
  episodes sM-SIGHTSEE could have occurred in
   searching for sM-VIPVISIT
        found (GN528 GN536 GN551 GN407)
      searching sM-VIPVISIT instance for input
      searching sM-VIPVISIT instance for input
      searching sM-VIPVISIT instance for input
      searching sM-VIPVISIT instance for input
        didn't find any sM-SIGHTSEE
      ...

No.
```

After failing to recall sightseeing experiences in Egypt, we see CYRUS applying executive strategies to attempt to retrieve sightseeing experiences in some other way. Searching for trips might help CYRUS find sightseeing experiences for the following reason: In searching for "sightseeing in Egypt," CYRUS could not find an episode, perhaps because they were not indexed by country and that was all the information it had. If a well-specified trip to Egypt or the Middle East could be found, however, it might refer to sightseeing done during the trip. CYRUS attempts to retrieve trips to Egypt by traversing the "diplomatic trip" E-MOP. As it retrieves each trip to Egypt, CYRUS examines its sequence of events for a sightseeing episode. It doesn't find any.

In searching extensively for diplomatic meetings, CYRUS applies Find from Larger-Episodes to search for appropriate conferences the meeting could have been part of. Output from CYRUS follows:

```
Enter next question:

>What have you talked about with Gromyko?

The question is:
((ACTOR *VANCE* < = > (*MTRANS*) MOBJECT
   (*CONCEPTS* CONCERNING (*?*)) TO *GROMYKO*) TIME G1548)
```

```
The question type is "concept completion"
The question concept is:
((ACTOR *VANCE* < = > (*MTRANS*) MOBJECT
   (*CONCEPTS* CONCERNING (*?*)) TO *GROMYKO*) TIME G1548)
  applying INFER-FROM-PARTICIPANTS to *GROMYKO*
   inferring a diplomatic meeting
The inferred question concept is:
((< = > ($MEET ACTOR *VANCE* OTHERS *GROMYKO* TOPIC (*?*)))
   TIME G1548)
searching memory for question concept
  searching directly for $MEET
   found (GN453)
applying strategies to search memory
   ...
   applying FIND-FROM-LARGER-EPISODES to search for
   episodes $MEET could have occurred in
      searching for sM-SUMMIT-CONFERENCE
      searching for sM-CONFERENCE
      searching for sM-VIPVISIT
        found (GN540 GN481)
       searching sM-VIPVISIT instance for input
       searching sM-VIPVISIT instance for input
        found (GN561 GN564 GN567 GN485 GN488 GN489)
   ...
```

SALT and other arms limitations topics.

After first inferring that Vance would have talked to Gromyko at diplomatic meetings, CYRUS searches directly for those meetings. When memory returns the message that there are numerous meetings but more specification is needed to retrieve them, CYRUS attempts to retrieve them by applying search strategies. Thus, it applies Find-from-Larger-Episodes to search for conferences (sM-CONFERENCE, sM-SUMMIT-CONFERENCE) and diplomatic trips (sM-VIPVISIT) meetings with Gromyko could be part of. It calls Instantiate-Larger-Episodes to instantiate "summit conferences about Russian concerns with Gromyko" and "diplomatic trips to Russia," and searches memory for each of those. After finding those contexts, it retrieves the meetings with Gromyko that they included.

The strategy Find-from-IMOPs is similar. In applying Find-from-IMOPs, CYRUS applies Instantiate-Larger-Episode to construct an appropriate IMOP episode, traverses memory searching for that episode, and then searches the context of those episodes for the target. Because memory does not hold many IMOP episodes (because they are longer range), and because IMOP episodes do not have as well filled-out sequences of events as simple MOPs, CYRUS generally finds more of the existing relevant IMOP episodes than it would simple MOP episodes, but does not always find instances of the target concept within those episodes.

One of the IMOPs CYRUS knows about is "negotiations" (I-NEGOTIATE). Diplomatic trips are usually in the service of negotiations. Thus, one strategy CYRUS applies to search for diplomatic trips to Israel is Find-from-IMOPs.

```
Enter next question:

>How many times have you been to Israel?

The question is:
((ACTOR *VANCE* IS (*LOC* VAL *ISRAEL*)) TIME G0658 QUANTITY (*?*))
The question type is "concept completion"
The question concept is:
((ACTOR *VANCE* IS (*LOC* VAL *ISRAEL*)) TIME G0658)
    applying INFER-FROM-LOCATION to *ISRAEL*
        inferring diplomatic trip context
The inferred question concept is:
((< = > (sM-VIPVISIT ACTOR *VANCE* DESTINATION *ISRAEL*)) TIME G0658)
searching memory for question concept
    searching directly for sM-VIPVISIT
        found (CON131)
applying strategies to search memory
    applying FIND-FROM-IMOPS to search for episodes
            $MEET could have occurred in
        searching for I-NEGOTIATE
          found (GN524 GN522)
        searching I-NEGOTIATE instance for input
          found (GN533 GN546)
    ...

Twice to negotiate the Camp David Accords, and a few other times to negotiate
Middle East peace.
```

After first inferring that Vance would have been to Israel on a diplomatic trip, CYRUS searches memory for those trips. Because there are many, it recalls only the most recent and then applies executive strategies to find others. Because diplomatic trips are normally in the service of negotiations, it applies Find-from-IMOPs to search for negotiations episodes they could have been part of. CYRUS retrieves negotiations about the Camp David Accords and other negotiations about Middle East peace and recalls from their contexts a number of diplomatic trips.

2.4. Using Preceding Events

Enablements, preconditions, causations, and temporally preceding events of a target event all precede the target event. Enablements are the episodes and states that allow a state to be in existence or an event to happen. Enablements for Vance's being secretary of state include his being appointed by the president and approved by the Senate. Enablements for being a lawyer include going to law school and passing the bar exam.

Preconditions are states that must be true in order for an event to occur. The preconditions for a meeting are that all participants are present (unless it is a conference call). Preconditions for a successful telephone call are that participants be in different places, that they not be on the phone with someone else, that the person being called is in close proximity to the telephone being called, and that the phone lines be working.

Causations of an event are events that caused the target event to happen or states that require that an episode be done. When Vance is told to go to Russia to negotiate SALT with Gromyko, the fact that he is told to go by Carter is one of the reasons he goes on the trip, thus one of the trip's causations.

Events can be searched for in memory by attempting to recall preconditions, enablements, causations, or preceding events. To answer "Have you ever been to a summit conference in Belgium?" Cyrus Vance might attempt to recall reasons why such a summit conference would have been called. Reasons for summit conferences include the existence of international world problems that have to be solved. Recalling those problems might aid recovery of summit conferences.

The strategy "Find-from-Reasons" attempts to retrieve a target concept by hypothesizing the reasons for doing that event and searching for instances of those reasons. If they can be found, their resulting events might match the target concept. Alternatively, reasons can be used to further fill out the target concept, and the new fuller concept can be searched for. If Vance were trying to retrieve summit conferences he had attended in Belgium, he might try to retrieve reasons the summit conferences would have been called. Major world problems are reasons for summit conferences, so he might try to remember major world problems and see if any of them led to summit conferences. If he couldn't find any summit conferences that way, he might use information about world problems to infer possible topics for summit conferences and try again to retrieve them—this time with a better description of what must be retrieved.

IF the target concept's E-MOP specifies reasons why it could have been done

THEN

(1) Apply "Instantiate-Reasons" to infer reasons why the target concept could have happened.

(2) Search for them.

(3) If any are found, see if any of their resulting events or the events following them match the target concept.

(4) If reasons are found but their resulting events are not found, then use "Instantiate-Following-Events" to instantiate a result that matches the target concept. Search for it in memory. If a match is found, it will also match the target.

FIG. 6.8. Find-from-Reasons.

After finding the kinds of events that could cause the target event to happen, events resulting from the found event and events immediately following it are checked for a match to the target event.

Often, retrieving activities that might have preceded an event can aid in its retrieval. Since welcoming ceremonies normally come after flights during diplomatic trips, a particular welcoming ceremony might be retrieved by finding the flight that preceded it. For example, to retrieve "when the welcoming ceremony for Vance at the airport in Spain started three hours later than planned," it would probably be appropriate for a memory with events from Vance's point of view to attempt retrieval of a flight to Spain that was delayed for three hours. The strategy "Find-from-Preceding-Events" is used to retrieve an event based on events that preceded it. Enablement conditions, preconditions, and typical preceding events can be used similarly to causations to find a target concept. "Find-from-Preceding-Events" is similar to "Find-from-Reasons" except that "Instantiate-Preceding-Events" is called in step (1). Similarly, "Find-from-Preconditions" calls "Instantiate-Preconditions" in step (1). "Find-from-Enablements" calls "Instantiate-Enablements" in step (1). Both "Find-from-Enablements" and "Find-from-Preconditions" call "Instantiate-Following-Events" in step (4). Those strategies are presented below.

IF the target concept's E-MOP specifies typical preceding events

THEN

(1) Instantiate those preceding events using "Instantiate-Preceding-Events", and fill in the components using component instantiation strategies.

(2) Search memory for those events.

(3) If any are found, see if any of their resulting events or the events following them match the target concept.

(4) If preceding events are found but their resulting or following events are not, then use "Instantiate-Following-Events" to instantiate a result or succeeding event that matches the target concept. Search for it in memory. If a match is found, it will also match the target.

FIG. 6.9. Find-from-Preceding-Events.

IF the target concept's E-MOP specifies preconditions

THEN

(1) Instantiate those preconditions using "Instantiate-Preconditions" and fill in the components using component instantiation strategies.

(2) Search memory for the hypothetical preconditions.

(3) If any are found, see if any of their resulting events or the events following them match the target concept.

(4) If preconditions are found but their resulting or following events are not, then use "Instantiate-Following-Events" to instantiate a result that matches the target concept. Search for it in memory. If a match is found, it will also match the target.

FIG. 6.10. Find-from-Preconditions.

IF the target concept's E-MOP specifies enablement conditions

THEN

(1) Instantiate those enablement conditions using "Instantiate-Enablements", and fill in the components using component instantiation strategies.

(2) Search memory for the enablement conditions.

(3) If any are found, see if any of their resulting events or the events following them match the target concept.

(4) If enablements are found but their resulting events are not, then use "Instantiate-Following-Events" to instantiate a result that matches the target concept. Search for it in memory. If a match is found, it will also match the target.

FIG. 6.11. Find-from-Enablements.

2.5. Finding a Target from Resulting Events

The final set of executive strategies are those that guide search for events resulting from or following the target event. Resulting events include events enabled by the target event, and events and states caused by the target event. A student or ex-student might recall tests he's taken by remembering extraordinary results—the time he aced an exam or the one time he flunked, the time the results of an exam got him into a job he wanted, and so forth. It would be appropriate for CYRUS to recall individual negotiations episodes by remembering possible results of those episodes and the negotiations they belonged to. International negotiations can end successfully with the signing of a treaty or pact, can end unresolved but low-key, or can end unresolved and cause war. One way to find a meeting between Vance and Carter during which Carter told Vance to go to the Middle East would be to search for trips by Vance to the Middle East, the event that would result from the meeting.

IF the target concept's E-MOP specifies normal results

THEN

(1) Instantiate those results using "Instantiate-Results" and fill in the components using component instantiation strategies.

(2) Search memory for the hypothetical results.

(3) If any are found, see if any of the events preceding them or their reasons match the target concept.

(4) If resulting events are found but their reasons or preceding events are not, then use "Instantiate-Preceding-Events" to instantiate an event that matches the target concept. Search for it in memory. If a match is found, it will also match the target.

FIG. 6.12. Find-from-Results.

Thus, a target concept can sometimes be found by searching for its probable results and checking any results found to see if their preceding events or reasons match the target concept. The strategy that would direct that search is "Find-from-Results," described in Fig. 6.12.

Searching for events and states that could be enabled by the target event or that could have followed the target event can also aid retrieval. A good way to answer the question "Did Vance go to law school?" if it were not known, would be to recall whether he had ever been a lawyer. If so, then in the normal case, he would have gone to law school. The strategy to guide this search is "Find-from-Enabled Events." It guides instantiation and retrieval of events the target event could have enabled, then uses those events to find a match in memory to the target event by checking to see if the events that caused, enabled, or preceded those events match the target. Thus, step 3 of this strategy is similar to step 3 of Find-from-Results.

IF the target concept's E-MOP specifies events or states typically enabled by events in that E-MOP

THEN

(1) Instantiate those events or states using "Instantiate-Enabled-Events", and fill in the components using component instantiation strategies.

(2) Search memory for the hypothetical enabled events.

(3) If any are found, see if any of the events enabling them or events preceding them match the target concept.

(4) If enabled events are found but their enablements or preceding events are not, then use "Instantiate-Preceding-Events" to instantiate an event that matches the target concept. Search for it in memory. If a match is found, it will also match the target.

FIG. 6.13. Find-from-Enabled-Events.

IF the target concept's E-MOP specifies events that usually follow it in time

THEN

(1) Instantiate those events using "Instantiate-Results" and fill in the components using component instantiation strategies.

(2) Search memory for those hypothetical following events.

(3) If any are found, see if any of the events preceding them, enabling them, or causing them match the target concept.

(4) If following events are found but their reasons, enablements, or preceding events are not, then use "Instantiate-Preceding-Events" to instantiate a result that matches the target concept. Search for it in memory. If a match is found, it will also match the target.

FIG. 6.14. Find-from-Following-Events.

Events can follow other events in time but not be related causally. This often happens in scriptal situations (Schank & Abelson, 1977). In a restaurant, being seated usually precedes ordering, but does not actually enable ordering in the strict sense of the word. When events that could follow a target concept can be inferred, the strategy Find-from-Following-Events can be used to search memory for the target. Like Find-from-Enabled-Events and Find-from-Results, reasons, enabling events, and preceding events of the related event's episodic context are checked or reconstructed to see if they could match the target event.

3. WHEN IS ALTERNATE-CONTEXT SEARCH USEFUL?

Alternate-context search is helpful under two circumstances: (1) when the event being searched for is obscure, and (2) when many events corresponding to a general specification must be found.

To see what is meant by an "obscure event," consider the following question:

(Q2): Have you ever rented a Chevy?

Suppose a person who had rented cars many times were answering this question. People renting cars normally rent by size and not by manufacturer. Thus, unless a person once had a particularly bad or good experience renting a Chevrolet, he would probably not be able to retrieve an experience involving renting one without further specification. When he attempted retrieval, he might recall the following—"I've rented cars many times. I need more information to recall renting a Chevy." If he cannot elaborate on additional features of "Chevy renting," then he will have to answer "I don't know," although the event might be in memory. This is an example of an obscure event. It is one which might be present in memory, but for which there is not enough generalized information available to do the necessary elaboration to get it out.

When retrieval fails because of inability to produce a sufficient elaboration, executive strategies can be applied to search for alternate contexts which might be more easily retrieved. In one case, we observed a person doing the following reasoning in order to recall if she had ever rented a Chevy:

> I rent cars during trips when I need to be able to travel easily. In California, it is impossible to get around without a car. On my trip there last summer, I rented a Fairmont, and on my last trip there, I had a Toyota. Neither of them was a Chevy. What kinds of bad experiences have I had with rental cars? Was one of those cars a Chevy? I once missed a plane because I couldn't find the rental car place to return my car—that was a foreign car of some kind. Another time, I rented a car that was too big

> for me—I couldn't see over the steering wheel. It was the only car they had available. That might have been a Chevy, I have no idea if it was or not.

In giving this answer, the respondent recalled trips during which she might have rented cars, and rental car experiences during those trips. She then recalled bad experiences while renting a car to see if any of those involved Chevrolets. In other words, she searched memory for episodes related to renting cars.

In many ways, searching for an obscure event is similar to searching for instances of an event that has happened many times. In recalling "diplomatic meetings about SALT," CYRUS receives the message from memory "there have been many meetings about SALT. I need more information to retrieve individual ones." Meetings about SALT are elaborated as much as possible. When CYRUS has done as much elaboration as it can and has not retrieved all meetings, it continues its search by searching for diplomatic trips and summit conferences that could have been related to the meetings. Their recall allows recall of additional meetings.

The major difference between searching for an obscure event and searching for instances of an event is the certainty of knowing whether or not something will be found. There are definitely instances to be found of an episode that has happened many times and that has an E-MOP associated with it. There may or may not be episodes of an obscure event, one which seems to fit into an E-MOP in memory but which has no known E-MOP that corresponds to it.

4. HUMAN PROTOCOLS AND ALTERNATE CONTEXT SEARCH

Searching for alternate contexts is something that people seem to do in searching memory extensively. In answering the question "Name all the museums you have been to," we found that people often attempted to recall trips they had been on or visits from out-of-town friends to remember all of those experiences. The following protocol illustrates that type of search.

> Let me see. . . . What other museums have I been to? The last time I was in England, I went to a bunch of museums in London—the British Museum, some gallery whose name I can't remember, and Mme. Tussaud's Wax Museum. And I also went to some palaces there that were museums—the Royal Pavilion in Brighton and some other palace in London, um, . . . it was called Hampton Court. When I went on my first trip to France. . . . I once went on a trip around New York State, and I went to the photography museum in Rochester and the Corning Glass Museum. During my trip to California. . . .

This person seemed to be applying executive strategies to search for particular trips to Europe, searching the sequence of events of each trip for museum experiences, then doing the same for excursions around the United States.

Taking these strategies into account, we can predict how somebody like Cyrus Vance might answer the following question.

(Q3): Have you been sightseeing in Dubai?

We could imagine any of the following answers:

> "Why would I have been in Dubai? It must have been to talk about Mideast peace or to negotiate the oil situation."

> "Have I ever been to Dubai? Well, I've been to the Mideast a number of times, mostly to negotiate. Maybe I was in Dubai during one of those trips."

> "I know I've been to Dubai. Does it have any distinctive places where they might have taken me sightseeing? Perhaps the oil fields, or archaeological ruins, or a mosque."

In the first, we imagine him searching for reasons why he might have been in Dubai and gone sightseeing. In the second, we imagine search for trips the sightseeing could have been part of. In the third, we imagine enumeration of types of sightseeing experiences.

5. IMPLICATIONS OF EXECUTIVE STRATEGIES

One important implication of executive strategy application is that retrieval is fallible. There is no guarantee that all episodes requested from memory will be retrieved. If, during processing, a strategy that would yield an answer is neglected, episodes that would have been found by that strategy might not be found.

In a previous example, CYRUS was shown to be fallible in this regard in its inability to recall a ceremony commemorating the opening of air-traffic routes by flying between the two airports. If flying had been a standard sort of ceremony, that episode could have been recalled by recalling flying ceremonies. Flying, however, is not standard, so the ceremony could not be recalled in that way.

Failure to apply a relevant strategy can result in failure to retrieve relevant information from memory. Although "Find-from-Standardizations" is not successful in finding this ceremony, another strategy might work. In some cases, the reason for an event can be useful in recalling it. Since opening air routes is not a standard reason for a diplomatic ceremony, however, that would not work in this case. Alternatively, recalling ceremonies involved with negotiations (IMOPs) might aid retrieval of this particular ceremony.

In extensive memory search, strategies can be applied in succession until a satisfactory answer is retrieved from memory. When people attempted to recall museum experiences (see chapter 2), they seemed to do that. In their observations of people recalling persons in their high-school class, Williams and Hollan (1981) reported application of a succession of search strategies until a sufficient answer was found. In attempting to recall meetings with Gromyko, CYRUS recalls trips to Russia, negotiations episodes negotiating SALT, and summit conferences about SALT and arms limitations. Memory search can continue until strategies stop producing results or until a sufficient answer is found.

When CYRUS searches its memory extensively, it applies each appropriate strategy in succession until it has found a satisfactory answer. CYRUS knows it has found a satisfactory answer when it is asked for only one episode, and it finds one (as when trying to verify if something has happened); when it is asked for a specific number of episodes and it finds that many episodes; or when it is finished applying all the strategies it knows about. Thus, when searching for all of Vance's meetings with Gromyko, CYRUS first uses context instantiation strategies to infer that Vance and Gromyko must have talked at diplomatic meetings. Thus, it confines its search to diplomatic meetings. It then searches for diplomatic meetings with Gromyko and applies strategies to search for simple MOP instances and IMOP instances during which meetings with Gromyko could have occurred. Output from CYRUS follows:

```
Enter next question:

>What have you talked about with Gromyko?

The question is:
((ACTOR *VANCE* < = > (*MTRANS*) MOBJECT
   (*CONCEPTS* CONCERNING (*?*)) TO *GROMYKO*) TIME G1548)
The question type is "concept completion"
The question concept is:
((ACTOR *VANCE* < = > (*MTRANS*) MOBJECT
   (*CONCEPTS* CONCERNING (*?*)) TO *GROMYKO*) TIME G1548)
 applying INFER-FROM-PARTICIPANTS to *GROMYKO*
   inferring a diplomatic meeting
The inferred question concept is:
((< - > ($MEET ACTOR *VANCE* OTHERS *GROMYKO* TOPIC (*?*)))
 TIME G1548)
searching memory for question concept
 searching directly for input -- $MEET
   found (GN453)
applying strategies to search memory
 applying FIND-FROM-LARGER-EPISODES to search for
   episodes $MEET could have occurred in
      searching for sM-SUMMIT-CONFERENCE
      searching for sM-CONFERENCE
      searching for sM-VIPVISIT
         found (GN540 GN481)
```

```
        searching sM-VIPVISIT instance for input
          found (GN561 GN564 GN567)
        searching sM-VIPVISIT instance for input
          found (GN485 GN488 GN489)
    applying FIND-FROM-IMOPS to search for episodes
            $MEET could have occurred in
       searching for I-NEGOTIATE
          found (GN391A)
        searching I-NEGOTIATE instance for input
          found (GN542 GN594)
```

SALT and other arms limitations topics.

In searching memory to find out who Vance has discussed SALT with, CYRUS first decides those discussions were at political meetings and then applies Find-from-Standardizations, Find-from-Larger-Episodes, and Find-from-IMOPs to find them—the strategies it finds appropriate information for in its ''political meetings'' MOP.

Enter next question:

>Who have you talked to about SALT?

```
The question is:
((ACTOR *VANCE* < = > (*MTRANS*) MOBJECT
    (*CONCEPTS* CONCERNING *SALT*) TO (*?*)) TIME G1062)
The question type is "concept completion"
The question concept is:
((ACTOR *VANCE* < = > (*MTRANS*) MOBJECT
    (*CONCEPTS* CONCERNING *SALT*) TO (*?*)) TIME G1062)
    applying INFER-FROM-TOPIC to *SALT*
       inferring undifferentiated political meeting
The inferred question concept is:
((< = > (sM-MEETING ACTOR *VANCE* OTHERS (*?*) TOPIC *SALT*))
    TIME G1062
searching memory for question concept
    searching directly for input -- sM-MEETING
     found (GN545 GN525 GN517 GN486 GN453)
applying strategies to search memory
    checking locative preconditions of input
       could have happened during business trip to USSR
          searching for business trips to *RUSSIA*
           found (GN481 GN390)
              searching sM-VIPVISIT instance for input
               found(GN485 GN488 GN486 GN489)
              searching sM-VIPVISIT instance for input
    applying FIND-FROM-IMOPS to search for episodes
     sM-MEETING could have occurred in
       searching for I-NEGOTIATE
         found (GN391A GN486)
           searching I-NEGOTIATE for input
             found (GN525 GN545 GN488)
    applying FIND-FROM-LARGER-EPISODES to search for
      episodes sM-MEETING could have occurred in
       searching for sM-CONFERENCE
         found (GN448)
```

```
        searching sM-CONFERENCE instance for input
          found (GN450 GN453 GN456)
    applying FIND-FROM-STANDARDIZATIONS to search for
      standard types of sM-MEETINGS
        searching for $MEET
        searching for $CONSULT
        searching for $PUB-REL-MEET
          found (GN590 GN556 GN561)
```

Carter, Brezhnev, Gromyko, other American and Russian diplomats, and Egyptian vice president Mustafa Khalil.

Because CYRUS' memory organization provides multiple references to the same event, CYRUS often finds the same answer by following multiple paths. In the example above, some of the same meetings were retrieved by searching for trips that were retrieved by searching for negotiations.

6. SUMMARY

Executive strategies are used in searching memory extensively to find a target event. They guide search for event contexts related to the target—events that may have happened if the target event had happened, and that may refer to an instance of the target. After instantiating and retrieving an event that could contain the target event in its context, they search appropriate parts of its episodic context to find an instance of, or reference to, the target event.

Executive strategies have four steps. They call instantiation strategies to construct an alternate context for search from a target concept. They guide the traversal process by giving it a context specification to look for. If the alternate context for search is found, executive strategies guide search of its episodic context to find the target concept. If that does not produce a match to the target, they guide reconstruction of the appropriate aspect of the event's episodic context. Thus, they guide both application of instantiation strategies and search of an event's episodic context during extensive memory search.

Failure to apply a strategy will often result in failure to retrieve a relevant event from memory. In later chapters, we explore circumstances under which retrieval strategies are appropriate.

III MAINTAINING MEMORY ORGANIZATION

Up to now, we have been assuming that memory would be well organized for application of retrieval strategies. As new events are added to memory, therefore, it is necessary that good memory organization be maintained. Integrating unanticipated items into memory requires a memory capable of organizing itself. The reorganization process must maintain the memory's structure and also build up the knowledge retrieval strategies need to search that structure.

One interesting aspect of human memories is that they never seem to run out of space. Furthermore, the vast amount of knowledge people have does not interfere significantly with their memory capabilities (Smith, Adams, & Schorr, 1978). Experts, who know a lot about particular subjects, can remember facts in their domain of expertise much more easily than non-experts, who presumably have fewer facts to remember.

We can explain this by inferring that as people learn new facts, they integrate them with what they already know, reorganizing memory to make the important facts accessible. Previous knowledge aids in deciding where and how to place new inputs in memory.

The problem of keeping a memory organized is relevant to both psychologists (interested in human memory) and computer scientists (interested in computer memory). Computer science interest in this topic stems from the problem of organizing information in a computer memory. As new information is added to a computer memory, its retrieval processes should remain efficient. This requires automatic reorganization.

The two tasks a memory must do—(1) integrating new items into its framework (memory update) and (2) retrieving them, or "remembering"—cannot be decoupled from each other. When a new item is integrated into memory, not only must it be made accessible, but the accessibility of items already in memory must be maintained. The retrieval processes must continue to work efficiently as memory grows.

Memory update is also related to understanding. One aspect of understanding, for example, involves figuring out how a new item is similar to items already in memory. This is necessary in order to choose a frame (Charniak, 1977; Minsky, 1975) or knowledge structure (Schank & Abelson, 1977) for further processing the item. Choosing a frame for an item is also the first step in integrating a new item into memory. As in understanding, once a frame is chosen during memory update, it provides an appropriate point in memory from which to draw inferences and make assumptions. In fact, the end result of understanding and memory update is the same: The concepts that comprise and are related to an item have been specified, and the place for the item within memory's knowledge structures has been found.

To understand problems associated with memory update, then, we must look to both the retrieval and understanding processes. In understanding an event, previously made generalizations are used to infer aspects not explicit in the event and to make predictions about what will be true in the future. To make generalized information available for understanding, it must be built up as new items are added to memory. This requires noticing the similarities between a new item being added to memory and items that are already there. As similarities are noticed, generalizations are made based on those similarities. Those generalizations must then be integrated into memory along with the item itself, so that both can be used for later understanding.

In order for similarities to be noticed without enumerating a memory's contents, similar items must be directed to the same place in memory. When a second item is directed to a place in memory where another item resides, their similarities are noted, and generalizations are made based on those similarities. Once a generalization is made, it is used in understanding or predicting aspects of a later similar item. The same generalized knowledge is used by retrieval strategies.

Because noticing similarities is an important part of understanding, integration processes must allow similarities to be noticed and must make generalizations based on them. It would not be feasible, however, to have memory notice all similarities and differences. A person going to a meeting, for example, is not likely to connect the weather with the meeting unless it has some bearing on the meeting (e.g., how hard it is to get there). Generalization and noticing similarities must be directed and controlled.

Conceptual categories and generalized information by themselves will not allow the kinds of retrieval we see people doing. In order for retrieval to be directed, conceptual categories must have an internal organization that allows retrieval without sequential enumeration. We have already proposed an indexing scheme based on differences. We must now specify how to identify and choose indices for new items added to memory.

Indexing serves a number of functions. It is used to discriminate individual events and divide a category into reasonably sized subcategories. Indexing also allows similarities between events to be noticed and generalizations to be made. When two items are indexed in the same way, a subcategory can be formed, indexed in the parent. Relevant similarities between the two items can be extracted and stored as generalized information associated with the new subcategory. That generalized information can then be used during understanding, to guide memory search, and to limit later indexing.

Generalized information is not static, but changes with the addition of new items. Because later information might contradict a previous generalization, and because all generalizations cannot be made on the basis of only two items, memory update must provide for recovery from bad generalizations and control of later generalizations.

The following list summarizes some of the problems involved in creating and maintaining good memory organization:

1. How is a new item entered into a conceptual category, and how are its indices chosen?
2. What is the role of generalization in memory processing?
3. How can generalization be directed?
4. When is it appropriate to create a new subcategory (E-MOP)?
5. How are new subcategories created?
6. How can the generalized information associated with an E-MOP be derived?
7. How can memory recover from useless subcategories and generalizations?

In the next two chapters, these questions will be addressed and a process for automatically adding new items to memory while maintaining its organization will be described. Extending what we know about memory organization, we can lay out the following algorithm for adding new items to memory: When a new item is added to memory, conceptual categories must be chosen for it. Its differences from the norms of those categories must then be derived and features for indexing chosen. After that, the item must be indexed. As part of the process, indexing must be controlled to avoid combinatorial explosion of indices. In addition, as new conceptual categories are created through indexing, the generalized information that memory needs for understanding and retrieval must be added to each one.

7 Automatic Index Selection

1. INTRODUCTION

Index selection plays a crucial role both in adding a new event to a memory category and in retrieval. In attempting retrieval, strategies are employed to select plausible indices for traversal in the quest for a target event. Indices selected correspond to features of the target event. In adding a new event to a category in memory, it is important that it be indexed by features that will aid in any subsequent attempt to retrieve it. The same index selection process is used during both memory update and retrieval. This chapter motivates and presents that process with respect to E-MOPs.

In adding a new event to an E-MOP, the first step is to choose appropriate features for indexing. This means choosing features that differentiate it from other events indexed in the same E-MOP. Consider, for example, how the following event should be indexed in memory under each of the following circumstances:

EV1: Cyrus Vance has a meeting with Andrei Gromyko in Russia about the Afghanistan invasion.

Case 1: Vance has met many times before with Gromyko, but never in Russia, and never about the Afghanistan invasion.

Case 2: Vance has been in Russia for the past two weeks meeting with Gromyko every day about the Afghanistan situation.

Case 3: Vance has never met with Gromyko before, but has met with other foreign ministers before in their country of residence.

Case 4: It is Vance's first week on the job, and he has never been on a diplomatic trip before and never talked to Gromyko.

In the first case, the topic and location of EV1 can distinguish it from other meetings in memory. Therefore, both of those features would be reasonable indices for EV1 in a "diplomatic meetings" MOP. In the second case, however, its location and topic cannot distinguish this meeting from other meetings already indexed in that E-MOP. Indexing on those features will not be helpful in discriminating this meeting from others.

There are two major problems to be addressed in discussing index selection:

1. What characterizes a good E-MOP index?
2. How can E-MOP indices for an event be chosen?

In a memory where new categories are created as new items are added to the memory, it is not sufficient only to specify the types of indices initial categories should have. There must also be (a) a way of judging what would potentially be good indices in newly created categories, and (b) a procedure for choosing potentially good indices in new categories based on their parent categories. In CYRUS, different E-MOPs have different relevant features. The nationalities of participants in a diplomatic meeting can be good indices, but in a social setting, participants' nationalities are not as relevant. Indices appropriate to any particular E-MOP depend on its salient features. Important aspects of an E-MOP can be inferred from what is known to be important about its parent E-MOPs.

2. WHY INDEX BY DIFFERENCES?

In introducing E-MOPs, it was stated that indexing should be by differences from the E-MOP's norms. The reasons for this stem from the two major purposes of an indexing scheme. One purpose of most indexing schemes is to *subdivide categories* into smaller, more workable parts. If retrieval requires that each member of a category be enumerated during retrieval, then the larger the categories, the slower retrieval will be. While the most efficient way to search a category with a few members might be to check each member individually, when a category gets large, checking individual members is not efficient.

In addition to subdividing a category, indexing can serve to *make members of a category more accessible*. Through cross-indexing, the same item can be referenced in many different ways. Through subindexing, an item can be given a unique description. Thus, indexing should also make items *discriminable*, differentiating them from one another.

Indexing and subindexing should organize memory for efficient retrieval. In a well-indexed well-organized memory, retrieval should not have to slow down as new items are added. As in other large stores of information, indexing in an E-MOP should both (a) divide it into significantly smaller pieces, and (b) provide for discriminability of an E-MOP's events. In that way, retrieval efficiency can be maintained.

To see why this implies that indexing should be by differences, suppose indexing were not only by differences, but also included an E-MOP's norms. Since most events organized in any E-MOP have the E-MOP's norms as features, they would all have virtually the same indices. Thus, indexing by a norm would neither add to discriminability nor divide a memory category into smaller pieces. Instead, it would supply memory with unneeded redundancy and violate economy of storage.

Differences between events, on the other hand, differentiate them from each other, providing *discriminability*. Organizing events according to differences allows events to be recognized individually. If a unique difference from a norm is specified in a retrieval key, the event that corresponds to that specification can be retrieved.

Indexing by differences also serves to *subdivide* an E-MOP into smaller parts. A particular difference from an E-MOP's norm should distinguish only a small number of the E-MOP's items. Thus, only a small number of events in any E-MOP should have the same index and be stored in the same sub-MOP. Each time an index is traversed during retrieval, the number of events that will have to be considered for retrieval will decrease considerably. Thus, by dividing a memory category into smaller parts, an indexing scheme based on differences controls the size of the search space during retrieval.

Imagine, for example, somebody attempting to buy a house. Suppose he looks at numerous houses in one day and doesn't remember every detail of each one. Furthermore, most of the houses he sees are brick. One of those is very large, another small, one in bad shape, and so forth. Indexing these houses by their color will not aid his retrieval of them for two reasons. First, their color (brick red in most cases) cannot distinguish them from each other. All of the brick-red houses would be indexed the same way. Second, color is not a relevant feature in house buying. Imagine, however, that one house this person looked at was bright yellow with large purple dots painted on it. Would its color be a good index? In this case, the answer is "yes," despite the fact that color is normally irrelevant to house buying.

Discriminability is an important factor in indexing. Because a feature that is different from a norm provides discriminability, indexing an object with a weird color by its color will distinguish it from other similar objects. Indexing on a common color will not do that.

Let's return to the domain of political activities. Suppose Cyrus Vance was at a foreign-policy meeting with a few other people in a conference room at the White House. Unless there was something special about the room, the meeting's location would not be a good index for it in a meeting E-MOP, even if he had never been in that particular conference room before. It is too much like the locations of other meetings he's been to. Similarly, the number of people at this meeting would not serve as a good index. Because meetings normally happen in conference rooms and have a small number of people, indexing on those aspects would not aid in discriminating this particular meeting from others.

Suppose, however, that the meeting had taken place in Studio 54 (a discotheque). In this case, its location would be a good index in a "diplomatic meetings" MOP, despite the fact that the location probably has no bearing on the meeting or its results. Similarly to the way a yellow and purple house violates expectations of what houses normally look like, a discotheque violates expectations about the settings of foreign-policy meetings. A 600-person foreign-policy meeting would also violate normal expectations. Because it violates a norm, the size of the crowd would be a good index for a meeting with an unusually large number of people.

To take this example one step further, suppose that a meeting in Studio 54 had to be indexed in an E-MOP that organized the business meetings of the owner of Studio 54. Unlike the E-MOP for foreign-policy meetings, the "business meetings involving the owner of Studio 54" MOP might specify Studio 54 as one of its usual meeting locations. In that E-MOP, a meeting in Studio 54 would not be unusual, and its location would not be a good index.

The appropriateness of an index is determined by context. Since indices for events should be differences between an event and an E-MOP norm, index selection in a particular E-MOP depends on the norms the E-MOP has. To decide whether the locations of the two meetings above would be appropriate for indexing them, the location norms of the "diplomatic meetings" and "business meetings of the owner of Studio 54" MOPs must be consulted.

These examples point out two important indexing rules:

1. Normal aspects of a situation should not be indexed.
2. Weird and different aspects of a situation should be indexed.

Differences indexed in an E-MOP, then, are aspects of events that differ from corresponding E-MOP content frame information.

3. WHAT IS A DIFFERENCE FROM A NORM?

In order to index by differences, we must be able to define what a difference from a norm is and how one can be recognized. We identify four types of differences from norms:

1. a violation of the norm
2. a variation of a norm (e.g., the norm plus additional features)

3. a specialization of the norm
4. a generalization of the norm

In addition, extra aspects of an event not mentioned in an E-MOP's content frame can be treated as differences to be indexed.

If a meeting E-MOP specifies that its topics are usually contracts, and if the topic of a particular meeting is "SALT," then the topic can be treated as a specialization of the norm and be indexed. If a meeting is called to plan a summit conference, it too can be indexed by its topic because its topic violates the norm: It is not a contract.

In CYRUS, for example, the E-MOP "summit conference" has the following content frame:

norms:	topic is an international contract participants are heads of state of countries involved in contract and a group of their advisors location is a resort area in neutral country purpose is negotiations includes many diplomatic meetings duration is a few days

FIG. 7.1. 'summit conference' (sM-SUMMIT-CONFERENCE).

Taking these norms into consideration, consider how the "Camp David Summit" should be indexed in the "summit conference" E-MOP. Its purpose was to negotiate an accord between Israel and Egypt, an important international contract. Its participants were the heads of state of Israel, Egypt, and the United States, plus their advisors. Its location was the United States president's private resort complex in the United States (not quite a neutral country). It lasted almost two weeks. Figure 7.2 below illustrates a portion of CYRUS' "summit conference" MOP after adding the Camp David Summit and indexing it as just described.

Because the topic of the conference is *better specified* than the topic norm of the content frame, this conference is indexed according to its topic. The participants are *a more general case* than the E-MOP's norms for participants (there is an addition), and that difference must be indexed. The conference's location is indexed because it *violates* the norm. Because the purpose of the summit matches the norm (i.e., negotiation of its major topic), it does not get indexed. Finally, because this summit was longer than the norm (another violation), an index for its length is appropriate.

We shall see later how processing differs for each of these types of differences as events are added to E-MOPs. New specialized sub-MOPs can be created based

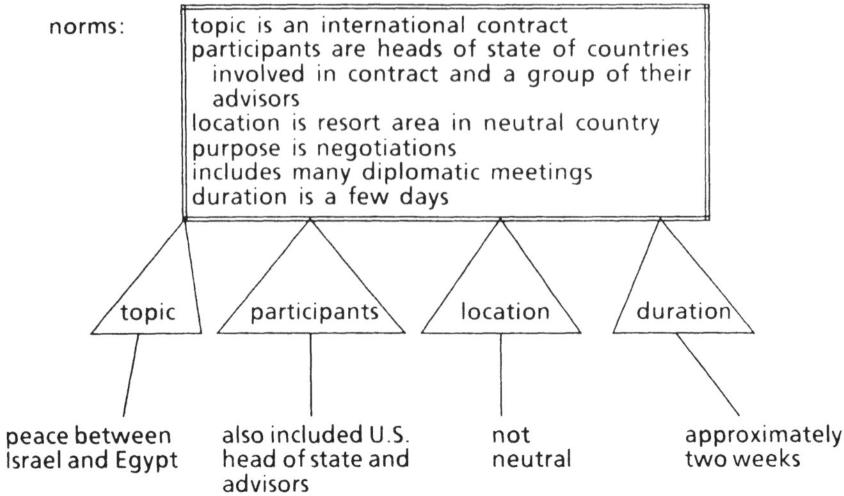

FIG. 7.2. 'summit conference' (sM-SUMMIT-CONFERENCE).

on specializations of the norm. Content frame aspects of an E-MOP can be refined and filled in based on violations and generalizations of the norm.

4. WHAT MAKES A GOOD INDEX?

Not all event properties make good indices. Because indexing is used in both adding to and retrieving from memory, retrievability and discriminability are very closely tied together. The better an index differentiates an event from other events in an E-MOP, the easier retrieval of the event will be. An event will be more retrievable if its indices are general rather than very specific.

In order to recognize that something is a good index, we need criteria for judgment. Not all differences from content frame properties should be indexed, not all should be indexed to the same level of detail, and the details appropriate for indexing in two seemingly similar situations might not be similar at all. Consider, for example, the following two situations:

> An employer is interviewing a prospective employee for a job as a computer programmer.
>
> An employer is interviewing a prospective employee for a job as a fashion model.

Because these are both interviews, it would be reasonable to index each in an employer's "interview" E-MOP using relevant features of the prospective employees. The features of the prospective employees that would make reasonable indices, however, differ greatly. It would be reasonable for the employer interviewing a prospective computer programmer to index the interview according to the interviewee's educational background. It would be less reasonable, however, for him to index the experience according to the color of the interviewee's hair (unless her hair is a strange color). On the other hand, it would be more reasonable for the employer interviewing a prospective model to index the experience according to the person's hair color and what he is wearing, rather than by his education.

The amount of detail that should be indexed for each feature of a situation depends upon the context in which the event is taking place. We must therefore explain what regulates how many and which details of an event are relevant for indexing.

4.1. Uniqueness

Because indices should divide a category into smaller pieces and differentiate events, *unique* features of events make good indices. A unique feature is one for which there is not already an index. If the only diplomatic meeting Vance has ever had with Dobrynin is indexed as a meeting with Dobrynin, then it will be retrievable through that unique feature.

Indexing Principle #1
Unique features of events make good indices.

All unique features of events, however, should not be indexed. Dobrynin is an important political dignitary whom Vance might want to talk to again. If he talks to Dobrynin again, it might be useful to remember the first time they met, so that predictions could be made from it, and so that similarities between "meetings with Dobrynin" could be computed. Thus, indexing the meeting above according to who its other participant was makes some sense. Suppose, however, that Vance had a public relations meeting with John Doe, president of the Nuke the Commies Organization. Although it is his first meeting with John Doe, indexing by actual meeting participants would not be the most reasonable participant index in this case.

A more general unique feature of John Doe is that he is a member of a radical anti-Communist organization. If Vance had never met before with a member of a radical anti-Communist organization, the fact that John Doe is a member of this type of organization would be a better index than his name.

Although both his name and his affiliation are unique, John Doe's affiliation is a better index than "John Doe" himself. Suppose Vance had another meeting with somebody from a radical anti-Communist organization. If the first meeting could be retrieved using the features of the second event, then the outcome and events of the earlier meeting could be used to predict the outcome and sequence of events of the later one.

Because "member of a radical anti-Communist organization" is also unique, but more general than "John Doe," it will be applicable as an index for retrieval in more cases. If Vance meets again with John Doe, this index can be traversed to retrieve his last meeting with John Doe. The same index will be traversable if he meets with somebody else from the organization, or if he meets with somebody from a similar organization. In each of these cases, the first meeting with John Doe could be retrieved and used for predictions.

All aspects of unique features of an event need not be indexed, then, but only the *most general* description of a unique feature. One description is more *general* than a second if it can be used to describe the second, i.e., if all of its aspects are also aspects of the second. A description of an event feature is *unique* to an E-MOP if there is no index for it and if it does not describe any other index (i.e., if no other event in the E-MOP has that feature).

In the example above, the two descriptions of the meeting participant—"John Doe" and "member of a radical anti-Communist organization"—are both unique descriptions of the participant. Because "member of a radical anti-Communist organization" describes "John Doe," it is more general and will be a more useful index.

Indexing Principle #2

The more general a unique feature used as an index, the more retrievable the event being indexed will be.

A more general description of a feature will make a better index because it will be accessible in more cases.

4.2. Predictive Power

What if John Doe had been scruffy and had needed a shower? Would those characteristics of John Doe be reasonable ones for indexing the event above in Vance's public relations meetings E-MOP? If predictions about future meetings with scruffy participants could be made from John Doe's appearance, then it would be a good index. If, however, no predictions about meetings could be made from his appearance, then it would not be appropriate.

Perhaps the most important property indices should have is *predictive power*. A feature that is predictive often co-occurs with some other event feature. It is one that a useful generalization can be based on. The nationality of participants in a diplomatic meeting, for example, is usually the same as one side of the contract being discussed. Thus, in a "diplomatic meetings" MOP, the nationality of participants is usually predictive of another feature, and actual nationalities of participants are good predictive features.

A predictive feature is one that, if it indexed an E-MOP instead of an event, would correlate with other E-MOP features. It is important to index individual events by features that are potentially predictive so that, if additional similar events are added to memory, a new E-MOP with useful generalizations can be formed based on the similarities between events with that feature.

Suppose, for example, that the nationality of participants is known to be predictive for meetings. The first time a meeting with a Russian is added to memory, one way it will be indexed uniquely is by the nationality of its participants—Russian. The second time a meeting with a Russian is added to memory, it also will be indexed as a meeting with a Russian, and if there are additional features in common, a new E-MOP can be formed and generalizations made about "meetings with Russians."

Predictions that a particular feature or set of features can make are used during retrieval and event reconstruction for elaboration. In reconstructing an event and in elaboration during traversal, specification of the value of a predictive property will allow inference of the properties it predicts. If the feature "participants are Russian" normally co-occurs with "meetings are rowdy," and if "participants are Russian" is an index in a "meetings" MOP, then knowing that a meeting was with Russians will allow the inference that "the meeting was probably rowdy" during retrieval. If the feature co-occurs with "topic is usually arms limitations," then knowing a meeting was with a Russian will allow inference that the "topic was arms limitations." During traversal/elaboration, that inference can be used to further elaborate aspects of arms limitations that would have been discussed.

The first time we see a particular feature, however, we cannot be sure whether or not it will be predictive later. One heuristic for judging feature predictiveness is to use previous experience. If a *type of index* (e.g., appearance of participants, nationality of participants, sides of a contract) has been useful previously for similar events, then there is a good chance it will be useful for the current event. If nationalities of participants has been predictive in indexing other "diplomatic meetings" or "diplomatic activities," then "nationality of participants is Canadian" will probably be predictive.

Indexing Principle #3
Indices should have predictive power or potential predictive power.

This principle implies that as new events are added to memory, the relative predictive power of different types of indices must be tracked. This tracking process is explained in the next chapter.

In the case of the meeting with John Doe, if no predictions for meetings have previously been made from the appearance of participants, then there is no reason to believe that appearance would be predictive in this case. There would be no reason, then, to index the event in the "public relations meeting" MOP according to the appearance of its participant. Furthermore, even if there are beliefs in the memory concerning the implications of a scruffy appearance, "scruffy appearance" would still not be a good index for this particular meeting in the "public relations meeting" MOP. That would be a prediction outside the realm of public relations meetings, i.e., a prediction about personality traits in general, but not about meetings.

E-MOP indices, then, should not only have potential predictive power, but they should make *context-related predictions*. A context-related prediction is one that predicts MOP-specific features. They should potentially correlate with some other content frame aspect of the E-MOP the event is being indexed in. Thus, if appearance will not correlate with other features *specific to* public relations meetings, then it will not have the predictive power to make it a good index for that context.

The fact that appearance is not a good index for participants of public relations meetings does not mean, however, that appearance is a bad index in general. Appearance of participants would probably be a good index for somebody running a modeling agency and interviewing a prospective model. The appearance of a model is a good indicator of how much money the model will bring into the agency (i.e., outcome) and thus would be predictive in that context.

Indexing Principle #4
The usefulness of an index depends on its context; a good index should make context-related predictions.

The heuristics presented for judging potential predictiveness of features is not foolproof. A feature that is judged to be a good index at one time might sometime later be judged not to be useful. "Nationalities of participants" might be predictive in general, but the particular index "nationality of participants is Canadian" might not be predictive of other features. Similarly, a nice appearance might turn out not to correlate with any other event-related features, whereas a scruffy appearance does correlate. After additional events are added to memory and it is discovered that a particular index does not correlate with other event features, the bad index should be marked as no longer useful and not be used anymore. Thus, the feature "nice appearance," though it might not be a norm of an E-MOP, could be marked as not useful for indexing, whereas the feature "scruffy appearance" might still be a good index for that E-MOP. In the next chapter, the process of refining the knowledge used for indexing is explained.

5. CHOOSING INDICES

In the last section, we questioned how much detail and which attributes of content frame aspects should be indexed. In beginning to answer this question, we defined criteria for judging whether an index is good. A good E-MOP index has predictive power, is contextually related, and is different from the E-MOP's norm. We can now judge potential indices according to these criteria and determine which particular indices are good in particular contextual domains. These criteria for discriminability suggest the following algorithm for index selection:

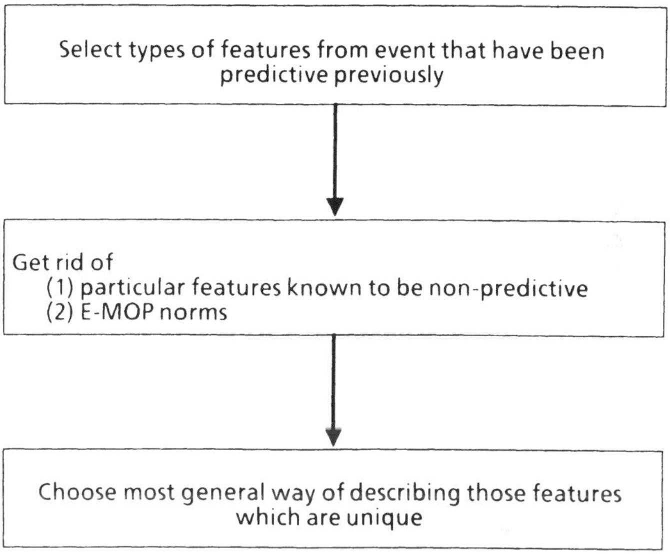

FIG. 7.3. Index selection.

Since only features with predictive power should be indexed, the actual process of choosing indices must first use information about predictability to select possible indices for an event. Each of those possibilities can then be checked to make sure (1) that it has not been marked as non-predictive, and (2) that it is not an E-MOP norm. In addition, each feature chosen as a potential index must be checked to see if there is a unique way of describing it. If so, the most general unique way of describing it should be used as an index.

In addition to presenting an algorithm, we must also describe the knowledge necessary to make the process work. In order for predictive power to be used in choosing indices, each E-MOP must keep track of types of indices that have been useful, and actual features that have not been useful and should no longer be used as indices. Thus, if "nationalities" have been useful previously in indexing "meetings," then the nationality of participants in a particular meeting will be chosen in the first step to index that meeting in a "meetings" MOP. If the

norms:
participants: diplomats of countries involved in contract being discussed
location: conference room in capital city of country of an important participant
topic: international contract
duration: one to two hours

predictive:
political roles of the participants
classes those roles fit into
nationalities of the participants
occupations of the participants
political leanings of participants
topic, place, participant
sides of the topic
issue underlying the topic (e.g., peace)

non-predictive features:
participants' occupation is foreign minister
participants' occupation is head of state

FIG. 7.4. diplomatic meetings ($MEET).

particular nationality of the meeting's participants has been marked as non-predictive, or if it is a norm, then it would be deleted from the set of possible indices in the second step. Similarly, in order to compute differences from a MOP's norms, its norms must be specified.

Consider, for example, CYRUS' "diplomatic meetings" MOP after enough meetings have been added to it for it to know some of its non-predictive features. Fig. 7.4 shows some of its predictive aspects, its norms, and the features it knows to be non-predictive at that point in time.

Suppose the following meeting with Gromyko were to be indexed in this E-MOP.

EV2: Cyrus Vance has a meeting with Andrei Gromyko in Russia about SALT.

Using predictive information in the E-MOP above, plus the knowledge that in general the place and participants in an activity are predictive, the following features would be chosen for indexing in the first step of the index selection process.

1. the meeting is with a foreign minister.
2. the meeting is with a diplomat.
3. the meeting is with a Russian.
4. the meeting is with a Communist.
5. the meeting is about SALT.
6. the topic concerns the United States and Russia.
7. the issue underlying the topic is arms limitations.

8. the meeting is with Gromyko.
9. the meeting is in Russia.

In the second step of the process, those features known to be non-predictive or norms of the E-MOP are deleted from the set of potential indices. Although in general, people's occupations can be predictive of other meeting aspects, the particular occupation "foreign minister" is not predictive for diplomatic meetings. Thus, feature (1) is deleted from the set of indices. Since participants in "diplomatic meetings" are normally diplomats, feature (2) is deleted from the set. Taking into account the norms and non-predictive aspects of the "diplomatic meetings" MOP above, the following features would remain as plausible indices for EV2 after step 2.

A. the meeting is with a Russian.
B. the meeting is with a Communist.
C. the meeting is about SALT.
D. the topic concerns the United States and Russia.
E. the issue underlying the topic is arms limitations.
F. the meeting is with Gromyko.
G. the meeting is in Russia.

One potential problem with indexing events in many different ways is combinatorial explosion of indices in memory. This problem can be controlled, however, by indexing only differences from an E-MOP's norms which are predictive of other features. In that way, indexing at lower levels of the memory structure is constrained. Knowledge about an E-MOP's norms, and about which of its features are predictive, then, is necessary in order to limit indexing. Keeping track of norms and non-predictive features is an important aspect of integrating new events into memory. The next chapter discusses the process of integrating a new event into memory, building up the norms of newly created E-MOPs. and using norms in controlling subsequent indexing and new E-MOP creation.

6. CLASSIFYING E-MOPs TO GUIDE INDEXING

Many of the features specified above for "diplomatic meetings" are true not only of meetings, but also of other classes of activities meetings fall into. "Diplomatic meetings," for example, are communicative activities, political and occupational. It seems likely that the topic of any communicative activity would be predictive of other aspects of the situation. Similarly, it seems likely that for any political activity, the polities involved in the activity would make good indices, and for any occupational activity, the occupations of other participants and the occupational role being played in an activity could be predictive.

The "diplomatic meetings" MOP, then, should not have to keep track of all indexing information for meetings. As a "communicative activity," "diplomatic meetings" share features with conferences, discussions, and consultations. The topic of any "communicative activity," for example, is probably appropriate as an index. If "communicative activity" specified its norms and which of its aspects were potentially good index types, then that information could be used by the "diplomatic meetings" MOP, the "conference" MOP, and so on, and would not have to be stored redundantly in each particular communicative MOP.

Classifying E-MOPs according to more general E-MOPs and E-MOP categories they are specializations of has two advantages. First, E-MOPs and E-MOP classifications for which the nature of good indices was already known could be used to guide choice of indices in more specialized E-MOPs. If the general nature of good indices for political events is known, for example, it can be used in deciding how to index events in "diplomatic meeting," "diplomatic trip," and other political E-MOPs. Second, generalized information common to a group of E-MOPs could be stored non-redundantly in one place, instead of in several different E-MOPs.

An important implication of this is that as new E-MOPs are created, knowledge about predictive features can be inherited from the E-MOPs it is created from, and knowledge about which features are appropriate for indexing does not have to be built up from scratch.

E-MOPs can be classified in "E-MOP classes" similarly to the way events are classified by E-MOPs. These categories should be, as E-MOPs are for events, memory structures that *organize the similarities between E-MOPs*. Formal "political activities," for example, always involve discussion of some political topic and always involve political dignitaries interested or involved in the topic of discussion.

"Occupational activities" are activities done for employment purposes and involve people related through employment. A low-level person does things because his higher-up asked him to or expects him to. In addition, occupational activities generally relate to other domains. While Vance was secretary of state, for example, almost all of his occupational activities were also political.

In CYRUS, the major E-MOP classifications we find useful are "international political activities," "occupational activities," and "social activities." Most of the things a secretary of state does that CYRUS knows about are related to his occupation and are both occupational and political. Some of the things he does, such as parties and state dinners, are also social.

Each classification groups together a packet of information common to a number of different E-MOPs. Thus, each E-MOP classification holds the same types of information E-MOPs hold. The major difference between an E-MOP and an E-MOP classification is that E-MOPs organize both memories and other E-MOPs, while an E-MOP classification organizes only other E-MOPs.

"Political activities," as a classification, keeps track of a large number of generalizations true of all political events. All political activities, for example, have as participants people with political occupations (i.e., political dignitaries), and the political affiliation of participants in a political event can be predictive of the topic of discussion. Their topics can be predictive, since they affect international relations. The topic of discussion of a political activity has sides, and representatives of each side take part in the discussion. Thus, the sides of a topic being discussed can be predictive. The topic usually has an underlying issue such as peace, arms control, aid of some sort, or international relations, which is also predictive of future international relations. These aspects of any political event are appropriate for indexing.

In addition to references to "political activities" and other classifications an E-MOP fits into, individual political E-MOPs need only specify their own MOP-specific information. In general, an E-MOP need only specify the E-MOP classifications and E-MOPs it is specialized from, plus its own MOP-specific information (i.e., differences between its own features and the feature descriptions in the E-MOP classes it belongs to). It can inherit the information stored in the classifications it belongs to.

Because the "diplomatic meetings" MOP in CYRUS is political and occupational, and a type of meeting, the types of features it indexes are chosen from among the types of indices marked as predictive for those types of activities. CYRUS chose the following indices for a diplomatic meeting between Vance and Dobrynin in Washington in which they discussed the MIG question.

1. participant was Dobrynin.
2. nationality of participant was Russian.
3. occupation of participant is Ambassador.
4. topic was the MIG question.
5. topic related to military issues.
6. sides of the contract discussed were Russia and the United States.

Because it is an "international political activity," its topic (4), the countries it involved (6), the issues underlying the topic (5), and the nationality (political leaning) of the participants (2) are indexed. Because it is an "occupational activity," the occupations of other participants are indexed (3). The event is indexed by its participant (1) because CYRUS has never seen a meeting with Dobrynin before (i.e., the meeting is unique in that way), and because CYRUS indexes all events by their participants.

Notice that the location of the meeting does not get indexed. There are two reasons for this. First, most diplomatic meetings occur in Washington. Thus, it is the norm. Second, if Washington were not the norm, the location would be indexed only if (a) meetings had happened there only a few times (i.e., if it was not known yet if "Washington" would be predictive), or (b) if meetings had happened there many times and there was some other meeting-specific feature that they had in common (i.e., if Washington as a meeting location was predictive of other features).

The following three sections explain CYRUS' context-based E-MOP classifications in detail and show how these classifications are used in CYRUS to choose indices.

6.1. Political Activities

CYRUS uses the classification "international political activity" to classify those E-MOPs in which people of other nationalities play a large role, or events that always take place in a foreign country. Thus, "diplomatic meeting," "diplomatic trip," "summit conference," and "negotiations" are all international political activities. Each of these E-MOPs has information peculiar to itself and inherits a packet of information shared by all international political activities. That packet of information includes descriptive features of "international political activities" plus knowledge that can be used for index selection.

Politically oriented activities can be differentiated, discriminated, or indexed by the political entities involved—either as participants, locations, or topics of discussion. Reasonable indices for political events include the following:

1. the political entities involved as participants
2. the political roles of the participants
3. the political relationship between the participants
4. the political aspects of the topic of discussion
5. the politics of the location of the activity
6. the appropriate political leanings of the participants
7. other related political events going on around this one

We choose features as reasonable indices if they can contribute to good predictability and discriminability. The topic of discussion during a political activity is usually an issue of importance to the political entities involved. Thus, the political entities involved as participants in a political event can help predict its topic of discussion. The political role of a participant may predict his behavior and visibility. A negotiator or arbitrator or a chief delegate will act differently in a political activity than will a lower level delegate.

Particular types of political activities can better constrain those indices. In "international political activities," it is international political entities that are predictive. Thus, the nationality of participants, their international political leaning (e.g., capitalist vs. communist), the area of the world they are from (e.g., eastern vs. western, Middle East,South American), and their political roles might all be good indices. During traversal/elaboration, each can predict another

content frame:
participants' occupations are political
participants are diplomats
topic is an international contract
included in other "international political activities"
includes other "international political activities"
initiated by international conflict

predictive aspects:
political roles of the participants (e.g., negotiator)
classes those roles fit into (e.g., diplomat, bureaucrat)
nationalities of the participants
polities on the sides of any dispute or contract being discussed
political leanings of participants

FIG. 7.5. International Political Activities.

aspect of a meeting—nationality predicts topic, while other aspects predict meeting outcome, sides in an argument, and so forth. A description of the location of an activity with respect to its topic and participants can also be a good index—Is it a politically neutral country? Is it in a country with the same leaning as the participants? Is it in a country with the same leaning as one side of a contract being discussed? If more concessions are made by a country hosting a meeting, then the meeting location will be a very good index. If the meeting is held in a neutral country, that would predict the explosiveness of the topic and make a good index by the criteria above.

CYRUS initially knows that the participants of international political activities have political occupations, are diplomats, and play political roles in these activities. It also knows that the topics of international political activities are usually international contracts, that political events are included in other political events, that they include other political events, and that they are often initiated by an international conflict.

CYRUS also knows that the political roles participants play in political activities (e.g., negotiation, arbitrator) might be predictive of other information, and therefore make good indices, and also that the classes those rules fit into (e.g., diplomat, bureaucrat), the nationalities of participants, the countries involved in any contract being discussed, and the political leanings of people and countries involved can be predictive indices. Fig. 7.5 shows CYRUS' knowledge about "international political activities." Each E-MOP classification has the same types of knowledge associated with it that E-MOPs have.

The predictive aspects of "international political activities" are used by CYRUS to choose features of an event as possible indices in the E-MOP it is being added to. The generalized information is used to narrow down the possible indices. Those features that are the same as content frame features will not be indexed.

Suppose, for example, that we wanted CYRUS to choose possible indices for the following event.

EV3: Cyrus Vance meets with Andrei Gromyko about SALT in Belgium.

Because this event describes a diplomatic meeting, CYRUS uses knowledge from its ''diplomatic meetings'' MOP to choose indices. A ''diplomatic meeting'' is a ''meeting,'' an ''international political activity,'' and an ''occupational activity.'' If Vance is involved in it, it is also a ''Vance activity'' (any activity Vance is involved in). ''Vance activities'' have as their norms that Vance is a participant and that they take place in Washington, in that way helping to limit indexing. All of these things must be taken into account in choosing indices.

CYRUS knows that meetings, in general, are a few hours long and are about contracts. It also knows that the underlying issue of the contract being discussed can be predictive, as can the sides of the contract, and the class the sides of the contract fall into. Thus, CYRUS uses its knowledge about meetings to choose the following features as possible indices for this event in the ''diplomatic meetings'' MOP.

(1) The contract is SALT.
(2) The contract is a military contract.
(3) The contract is international (i.e., between countries).
(4) The contract is between the United States and Russia.

In addition to being ''meetings,'' however, ''diplomatic meetings'' are also ''international political activities.'' Using only meeting information, the indices CYRUS can choose are incomplete. Because international political activities usually have an international contract as their topic, that feature should not be used as an index. In addition, some potentially good indices have not been chosen. The fact that the participant was Russian or Communist cannot be chosen as an index using only meeting information. Meeting specifications, by themselves, do not specify that participants' political leanings can be predictive.

Using the ''international political activity'' information illustrated above in Fig. 7.5, a more complete set of indices for the meeting can be chosen. The fact that the topic is an international contract would be deleted from the set of possible indices. Using the information that participants' nationalities and political leanings, the role of the participants, and the polities involved in a dispute can be predictive for international political activities, the following indices can be chosen in addition to the ones above:

(a) Participant is Russian.
(b) Participant is Communist.
(c) Participant is a diplomat.
(d) Participant is a negotiator.

Taking the norms of ''diplomatic meeting'' into account, however, the roles of the participants (c, d) would be deleted from the set of possible indices in this case, leaving the following:

(1) The contract is SALT.
(2) The contract is a military contract.
(3) The contract is between the United States and Russia.
(4) Participant is Russian.
(5) Participant is Communist.

This list of indices, however, is still not complete for event EV3, since it takes only ''meeting'' and ''political activity'' aspects of ''diplomatic meetings'' into account. ''Diplomatic meetings'' are also ''occupational activities'' and ''Vance activities,'' and features of each of those must also be taken into account in indexing. As ''Vance activities'' (all E-MOPs in CYRUS' Vance data base are ''Vance activities''), the participants and location of the event should be indexed. CYRUS always indexes events by their participants and location unless a particular index or location is marked as non-predictive. Thus, the following three indices would also be chosen for this event.

(6) Gromyko is a participant.
(7) The meeting is in Belgium.
(8) The meeting is in Europe.

In the next section, ''occupational activities'' are described, and choice of the remaining occupation-oriented indices for EV3 are shown.

6.2. Occupational Activities

Any event associated with the actor's occupation is an occupational event. The fact that an event is occupation-related means that it might have some employment-centered attributes which would make reasonable indices. The role of the actor within his occupational role may be a good index for occupational events, as will the occupations and occupational roles of the other participants. A professor, for example, acts as teacher, advisor, researcher, and committee member. His role during any activity determines his concerns and his relationship with other participants. Thus, if his situational role in an activity is not a norm, it will make a good index. Similarly, the roles and occupations of other people he interacts with in his job-related roles may make good indices. A meeting with the university president may be like a meeting with the department chairman in many ways, but the fact that it is the university president will add extra social constraints and considerations to a situation. Also related to the roles a person plays in this occupational role, the employment relationship between

content frame:
participants are in occupational roles
included in other "occupational activities"
includes other "occupational activities"

predictive aspects:
occupations of the participants
roles of the participants in the event
classes those roles fit into (e.g., diplomat, bureaucrat)

FIG. 7.6. Occupational activities.

participants in an event can be a good index. In occupational activities, the relationship of the event toward the progress of some job-related goal may also be a good index.

CYRUS uses the classification "occupational activity" for all of its E-MOPs that are usually done as part of the secretary of state's job. All of CYRUS' political E-MOPs are also occupational. In addition, "speeches," "state dinners," "consultations," and "briefings" are all occupational activities.

CYRUS knows that the participants of occupational activities are in job-related roles when they are participating in an occupational activity. It also knows that a participant's role in an activity could be predictive of other information, and therefore would be a good index. Fig. 7.6 shows CYRUS' knowledge about "occupational activities."

CYRUS uses this information to choose indices in the same way it uses its information about "political activities." It uses predictive aspects of "occupational activities" to choose possible features for indexing, and its content frame information (i.e., norms) is used to decide whether or not a possible feature should actually be used as an index.

In the previous section, we showed index selection for a meeting between Vance and Gromyko (EV3, repeated below) using "international political activity" and "meeting" information.

EV3: Cyrus Vance meets with Andrei Gromyko about SALT in Belgium.

Occupational aspects of the meeting must also be taken into account in choosing its indices. In choosing indices for this meeting, the predictive aspects specified for occupational activities can be used to choose the following features as possible indices for EV3 in the "diplomatic meetings" MOP.

(a) The actor is acting as negotiator.
(b) The actor is acting as a diplomat.
(c) The participant is a foreign minister.

Because the actor (Vance) in Vance's "diplomatic meetings" MOP normally acts as negotiator and diplomat, (a) and (b) must be deleted from the set of possible indices. Because the fact that the other participant is a foreign minister (c) is non-predictive for "diplomatic meetings," it too is deleted. Thus, using "meeting," "political activity," and "occupational activity," the following eight indices for the meeting with Gromyko in Belgium would be chosen:

(1) The contract is SALT.
(2) The contract is a military contract.
(3) The contract is between the United States and Russia.
(4) Participant is Russian.
(5) Participant is Communist.
(6) Gromyko is a participant.
(7) The meeting is in Belgium.
(8) The meeting is in Europe.

Occupations normally have some relation to some other aspect of one's life. Because of that, particular occupations and occupational events can take on predictive aspects of those other contextual domains. Most of CYRUS' occupational E-MOPs, for example, are also political E-MOPs, and aspects of both are taken into account in indexing. Any indices for events that could be provided through looking at them as political activities would also be good occupational indices. Vance's work as secretary of state involved him in international political activities. Thus, political aspects cannot be separated from occupational aspects of his activities in many cases.

Good occupational indices, then, must take into account attributes of an actor's occupation. A particular occupation must contribute its norms and information to produce good predictive and discriminating indices. Thus, good indices for Vance's activities as a lawyer would include his various roles as a lawyer, the kinds of relationships lawyers have with clients and other lawyers, and case-related features. Similarly, occupational activities in the life of a minister should be indexed according to both occupational and religious aspects of his job.

6.3. Social Occasions

Like political and occupational activities, "social activities" have a number of predictive aspects appropriate for indexing. In social activities, the social relationship of the participants will be appropriate for indexing. So will the social group (e.g., which clique) the participants belong to and the social organization, if any, the participants are affiliated with. In real life, personality characteristics of the participants in a particular social setting may also be good predictive indices, since it seems likely that people monitor whether or not they would like to do any activity again with the people or groups of people involved.

In CYRUS' domain, social occasions are all occupational activities as well. Social occasions CYRUS knows about are "state dinners," "dining," and "parties." CYRUS knows that social activities often have hosts, and that it is important to index those activities according to who the host was. If CYRUS were to be used to make plans, this would be in keeping with social protocol—it is appropriate to reciprocate social invitations.

The following is the generalized information CYRUS has about "social activities":

```
content frame:
        participants include a host -- the inviter, guests -- the invited


predictive aspects:
        the host
        the other participants
        the relationship of the host to the actor
```

FIG. 7.7. Social activities.

As for the other E-MOP classifications, "social activities" contains predictive and normative information which CYRUS uses to choose indices for social events. Consider, for example, the following event:

EV4: Vance has dinner with Moshe Dayan and Ezer Weizmann in Israel. Weizmann is the host.

Using "social activities" information, the following features are possible indices for this event in the "dining" MOP:

(1) Weizmann is the host.
(2) Dayan is a participant.
(3) The host is related through employment.

Because this is also an occupational and political activity (since the host is related through political employment), indices for political and occupational activities must also be chosen. Using those specifications, plus knowledge about "Vance activities" in general, CYRUS chooses the following additional indices for this event.

(4) The host is Israeli.
(5) The host is a foreign minister.
(6) The other participants are Israeli.

(7) The dinner took place in Israel.
(8) The dinner took place in the Middle East.

The dinner is indexed in the "dining" MOP ($DINE) using these eight features as indices.

7. SUMMARY OF INDEXING

The process for choosing indices uses predictive information on E-MOPs and E-MOP classes to guide its selection. Features to be indexed are chosen based on possible predictive power. Each is then checked to make sure (1) that it is not an event norm, and (2) that it has not been marked as non-predictive. The feature should also be checked to see if it has a unique description, and if so, its most general unique description should be indexed.

Thus, for any content frame aspect being indexed, its level of detail will depend on how similar other indices and other fillers of the same aspect are. The first time a person dines out during a job interview, for example, that dining experience can be indexed as having been during a job interview. After he has dined out during job interviews a number of times, however, indices for larger episodes the event was part of will have to be more detailed and will start to look like "during an interview at a small company" or "during an interview in Atlanta." After many such experiences, we might expect more detailed indices such as "during an interview at IBM in Atlanta."

Detail does not have to be added to indices forever, however. Non-predictive features of activities should not be indexed. Thus, information about predictive power must be maintained. When an aspect of a potential index fails to have predictive power, that aspect of the description of the feature being indexed should no longer be indexed or included in indices. Thus, if after many experiences dining out during job interviews, the size of the company does not predict anything about the meal, the size of the company will not be used in indexing larger episodes the meal was part of. Thus, indices such as "during an interview at a small (large, medium-sized) company" will no longer be made.

Predictive power is an important criterion for choosing indices. Since any feature marked as non predictive will not be indexed, predictive power, along with norms, helps limit the number of indices and level of detail that have to go into an index. Maintenance of predictive power information is discussed in the next chapter.

E-MOPs can be classified in contextually related E-MOP categories that can be used to help determine which features of the content frame might have predictive power. For international political events, that includes the sides of an international conflict and the political leanings of the sides. For occupational activities, it includes the occupational roles being played by the actor, occupational roles played by other participants, and relationships between those roles. Classifying E-MOPs in categories such as these constrains the number of features relevant for indexing. In political activities, politically significant attributes of role fillers make good indices. Non-political attributes, such as hair color of the participants, do not have to be considered for indexing except when they are relevant to a particular political E-MOP.

8 Generalization and Memory Reorganization

1. INTRODUCTION

As new events are added to memory, its organization must be maintained. Because it is impossible to anticipate beforehand the events that will be added to memory, memory's organization must be able to change to accommodate new, unexpected events. A current events data base whose categories are tuned to today's current events and issues, for example, must be able to integrate new events into its memory. Although unexpected, a memory that knows about "war," for example, should be able to accommodate a sudden brushfire war in the Middle East. In this chapter, the process of integrating a new event into memory is explained.

2. ADDING A NEW EVENT TO AN E-MOP

The first step in adding a new event to an E-MOP is extraction of its MOP-relevant features. This process, the process of index selection, was explained in the last chapter. After choosing features for indexing, events are indexed in E-MOPs by the chosen features. The actual processing when an event is added to an E-MOP depends on the relationship of each of the selected features to events already indexed in the E-MOP. A feature chosen for indexing can have one of three relationships to the E-MOP:

1. There is nothing yet indexed in the E-MOP with that feature.
2. There is one other item with that feature indexed in the E-MOP.
3. There is an E-MOP indexed by that feature.

The first of these relationships is easy to handle. If a feature has not been indexed before (1), an index is built for it. This event will then be indexed uniquely in that E-MOP. The second and third cases are more interesting. They trigger generalization processes that build up content frame information. All three cases are discussed below.

2.1. Initial Indexing

If there is not already an index for a feature (case 1), then one is created for it. Any time an event is indexed by a feature unique to an E-MOP, it can be retrieved from that E-MOP by specifying that feature. Thus, the more features an event has that are unique to an E-MOP, the more ways there will be of retrieving it uniquely. The rule below summarizes the process of creating a new index:

> IF there is no prior index for a relevant feature of an event
>
> THEN
>
> (1) construct an index
> (2) index the event's description there

FIG. 8.1. Index creation.

One of the discriminations CYRUS makes on meetings is the underlying topic of the contract being discussed. A meeting about the Camp David Accords is indexed as a meeting whose underlying topic is "peace," and a meeting about military aid to Pakistan is indexed as a meeting with underlying topic "military aid." The first time CYRUS hears about a meeting in which Vance discusses military aid, it will index that meeting uniquely in the "diplomatic meetings" MOP under the property "underlying topic is military aid." From past experience, it knows that the underlying topic can be predictive of other event aspects in political events. Another aspect of "diplomatic meetings" that CYRUS knows can be predictive is the occupation of the participants. Thus, if this meeting were also the first meeting Vance had had with a defense minister, then CYRUS would also index it uniquely under the occupation of its participants. Later, in answering questions, if a meeting's unique aspect is mentioned in a question, it will be directly retrievable without elaboration.

Suppose the memory organization of CYRUS' meetings looked like Fig. 8.2 before adding any meetings about military aid to memory. In this "diplomatic meetings" MOP, there are indices for the underlying topic of the contracts being discussed, the occupations and nationalities of the participants, and the larger episodes the meeting is included in. Each index indexes either an E-MOP (labeled MOPn) or an event description (labeled EVn). Suppose a meeting between Vance and the defense minister of Pakistan about military aid were added to this E-MOP. The event description includes the information that the meeting was with a defense minister, a Pakistani, and that its topic was military aid. If we call

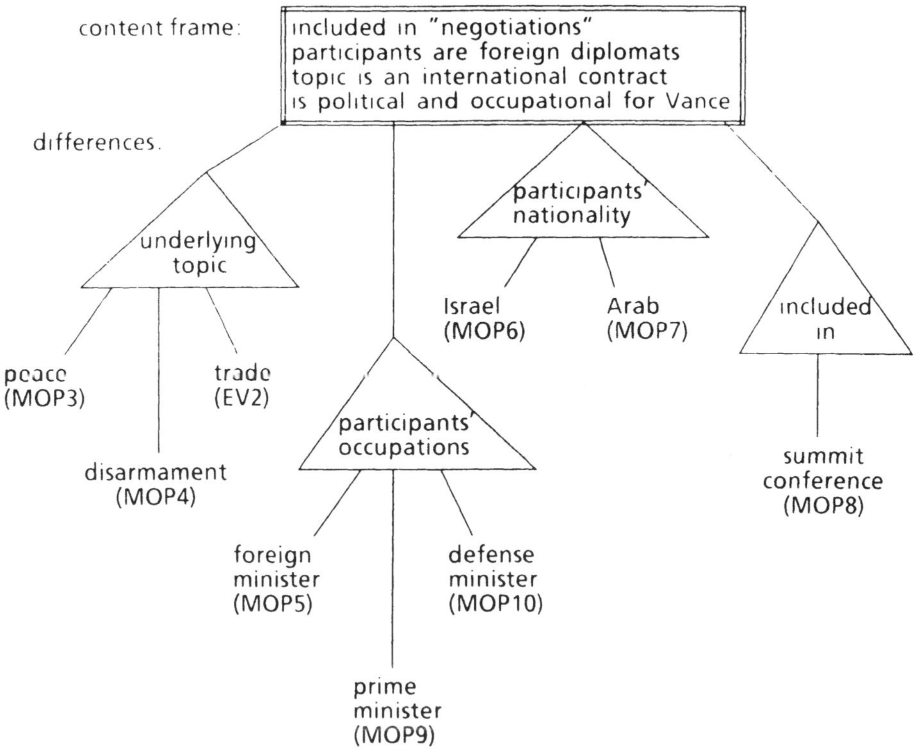

FIG. 8.2. 'diplomatic meetings'—$MEET.

this meeting EV7 and add it to the E-MOP illustrated above, that E-MOP would have the structure in Fig. 8.3. Two new indices, one for the underlying topic of the meeting and one for the nationality of the participants are added to the diplomatic meetings MOP, and this new event, EV7, is indexed uniquely at those points. In addition, it is added to the E-MOP "diplomatic meetings with defense ministers" (MOP10 above, not shown in detail) and indexed in that E-MOP according to its differences from that E-MOP's content frame. Because there is only one "diplomatic meeting about military aid" in memory at this point, if we asked CYRUS to recall a "diplomatic meeting about military aid," it would retrieve EV7 without the use of retrieval strategies.

2.2. E-MOP Creation

The second time an event with a particular feature is added to an E-MOP (case 2), a new sub-MOP is created. When a second event is indexed at a point where there is just one other event, the previous event is remembered. This is called *reminding* (Schank, 1980). Suppose, for example, that one of Vance's meetings had included a meal at a very fancy restaurant, and that it was his first working

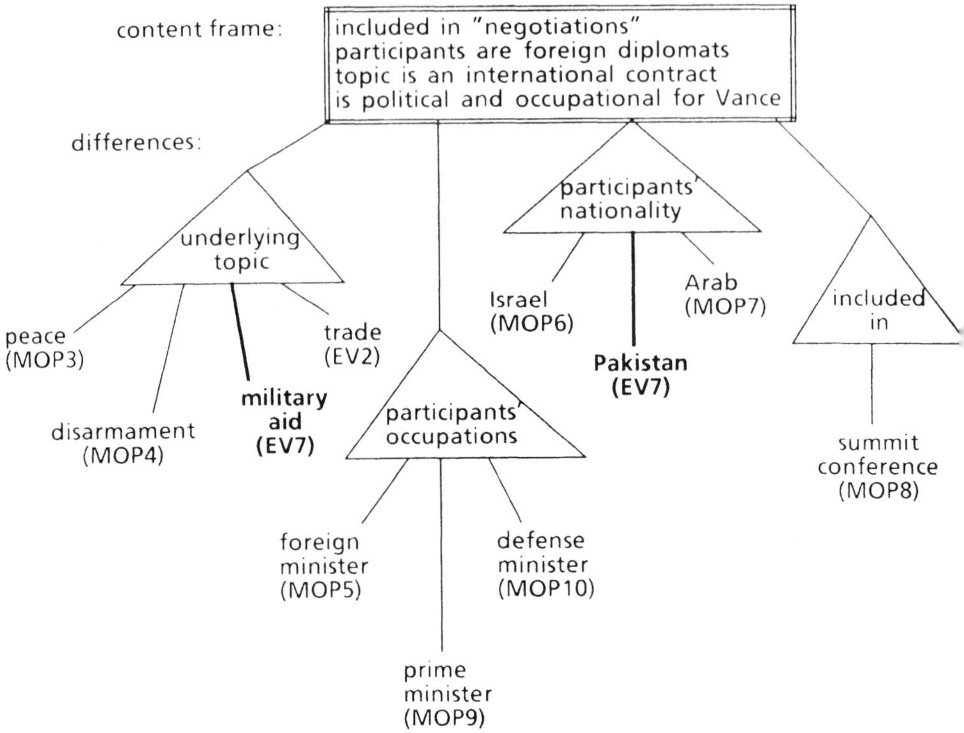

FIG. 8.3. 'Diplomatic meetings'.

lunch that had been at a restaurant. A second working lunch at a restaurant would be indexed in memory in the same way as the first one. Upon indexing the second one, the first one would be found.

Reminding triggers the creation of new E-MOPs. When reminding occurs, the current and previous events are compared for common features. Similarities between the two events are extracted, and a new E-MOP with generalized information based on those two occurrences is created. In the example above, a new E-MOP "working lunches in restaurants" would be created from the two events, and their similarities would make up its content frame. Features compared for similarity are chosen by applying the index selection process. E-MOPs are created as follows:

IF there is one event indexed at an index point for a new event
THEN
(1) create a new E-MOP at that point
(2) extract the similarities of the two events and add those as content frame features of the new E-MOP
(3) index the two events in that E-MOP according to their differences from its norms

FIG. 8.4. E-MOP Creation.

To see that this reminding and generalization process mimics the human process, imagine a person who has been to a French restaurant once in his life. According to the rules for indexing a first event, we imagine it is indexed under "serves French food" in his "restaurant" MOP. When he goes to a French restaurant a second time, we expect him to remember the first time so that he can use that experience to predict the sequence of events of the second one. Thus, he will be reminded of the first experience in a French restaurant. If there are other similarities between the experiences, we expect him to make generalizations based on those similarities. Thus, if both restaurants were fancy, and if in both there was good quiche as an appetizer, then he might make the generalizations that French restaurants are fancy and that they are a good place to have quiche. He would have to store that generalization somewhere, and the likely place to store it would be on a newly created E-MOP "restaurant that serves French food," an E-MOP created from the two experiences.

When CYRUS indexes a second event where a first is already indexed, it examines the first episode, notices similarities between the two episodes, and creates a new E-MOP. The second time Vance met about military aid, for example, CYRUS was reminded of the prior meeting because both have the same topic. It checks the descriptions of both to see what other similarities they have. Since both were with defense ministers, CYRUS concluded that "meetings about military aid are usually with defense ministers." It also created a new "meetings about military aid" MOP and indexed the two meetings within that E-MOP. Below is CYRUS' response to a second meeting about military aid, this one with the defense minister of Israel in Jerusalem.

```
Adding        $MEET  actor (Vance)
                     others (defense minister of Israel)
                     topic (Military aid to Israel)
                     place (Jerusalem)
to memory...

Reminded of   $MEET  actor (Vance)
                     others (defense minister of Pakistan)
                     topic (Military aid to Pakistan)
                     place (Washington)

because both are "diplomatic meetings"
        both have contract topic "military aid"

    creating new MOP. meetings about military aid
       generalizing that when
    Vance meets about military aid, often he meets with a defense minister
```

FIG. 8.5.

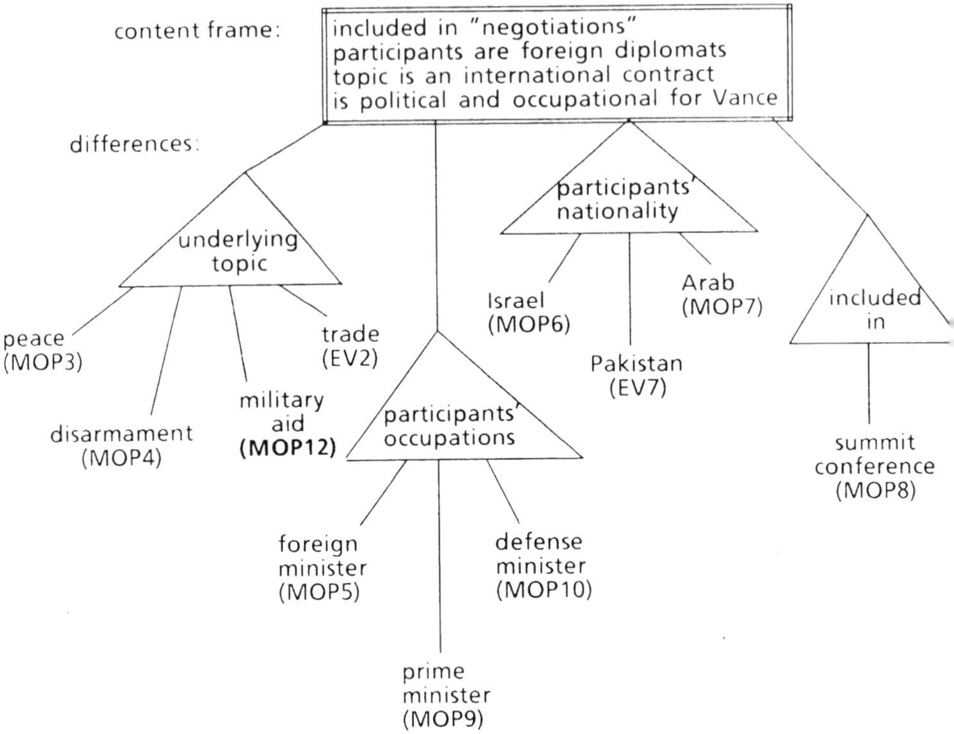

FIG. 8.6. Diplomatic meetings.

After adding this event to memory, the "diplomatic meetings" MOP, which started out as in Fig. 8.3, will look like Fig. 8.6. This event, EV9, will be indexed as an event with underlying topic military aid, just as event EV7 with the Pakistani defense minister was indexed. That will cause reminding of EV7, and a new E-MOP "diplomatic meetings about military aid" will be created at that point (MOP12 in Fig. 8.6). Event EV9 will also be indexed in MOP10, "diplomatic meetings with defense ministers," and also in MOP6 as a meeting with an Israeli.

The "diplomatic meetings" MOP, then, looks the same as before adding this meeting except that a new E-MOP has been created at its index for "underlying topic is military aid." Other changes in organization will occur in the new E-MOP and in other E-MOPs this event was added to—"diplomatic meetings with Israelis" (MOP6) and "diplomatic meetings with defense ministers" (MOP10).

The newly created E-MOP, "diplomatic meetings about military aid" (MOP12), has a content frame and indexes its episodes according to their differences from those norms. It is a *specialization* of "diplomatic meetings," and its content frame includes only those features that are more specialized or differ-

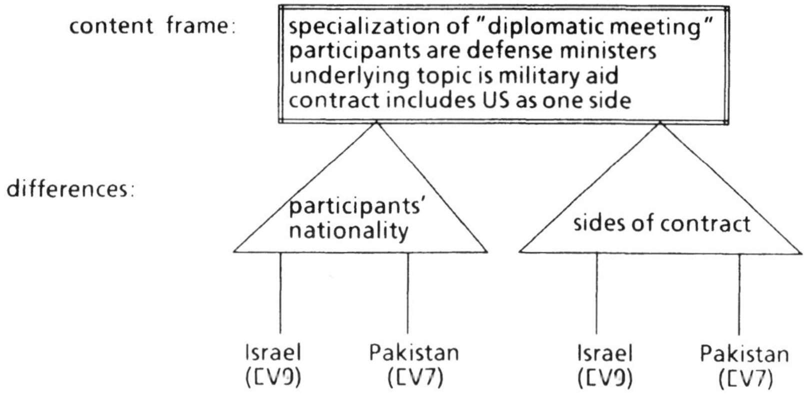

FIG. 8.7. diplomatic meetings about military aid—MOP12.

ent from those in the parent MOP. Thus, it contains the information that these meetings are about military aid and are usually with defense ministers, two aspects its meetings (EV7 and EV9) have in common that are not specific to diplomatic meetings. The two events are indexed in this E-MOP according to their differences from these norms. One of those is the nationalities of the participants. Another is the sides involved in the contract under discussion. Thus, the new E-MOP has the content frame and indices shown in Fig. 8.7.

Later, if CYRUS hears about a third meeting whose topic is military aid, it will assume that the meeting is with the defense minister of the country requesting aid unless given contrary information. If asked for the participants of that third event, it will be able to answer "probably the defense minister."

2.3. E-MOP Refinement

When an aspect of an event's description is common to many past events, there will already be a sub-MOP indexed by that feature (case 3). In that case, the new event is indexed in the sub-MOP by the same procedure used to index it in the more general E-MOP. In addition, features of the new event are compared against the generalized information of both the parent E-MOP and the sub-MOP, and the validity of previous generalizations is checked and refined:

IF there is an E-MOP at an index point for a new event

THEN

(1) index the event in that E-MOP
(2) check the validity of its generalizations
(3) update its generalizations as necessary

FIG. 8.8. E-MOP Refinement.

To see that this is consistent with people, imagine a person going a third time to a French restaurant. The third and subsequent times a person goes to a French restaurant, the discrimination "serves French food" will direct the episode to the "restaurants which serve French food" sub-MOP of the "going to a restaurant" MOP (the one we imagined being created in the section above). If the first two French restaurants a person went to were fancy, for example, then we would have expected him to make the generalization that "restaurants that serve French food are fancy." If the third one was also fancy, it would serve to strengthen that generalization. If, however, it was not fancy, it would weaken the generalization. The person would no longer automatically expect a French restaurant to be fancy. If later visits to French restaurants proved that most French restaurants are fancy, the generalization would be strengthened again, and the non-fancy restaurant could be stored as an exception.

CYRUS, also, confirms and disconfirms generalizations as new events are added to its memory. On entering another meeting about military aid to memory, CYRUS indexes it among other events already indexed there. Thus, a new meeting about military aid will be entered into the "meetings about military aid" sub-MOP of "diplomatic meetings" and will be indexed within that E-MOP.

In this way, reminding, generalization, and new E-MOP creation occur within newly created E-MOPs. If a new meeting about military aid to Pakistan is added to the E-MOP "meetings about military aid" illustrated in Fig. 8.7, CYRUS will be reminded of the first because both will be indexed as "Pakistan was one side of the contract discussed," and a new E-MOP, "diplomatic meetings about military aid to Pakistan" will be formed, a specialization of "diplomatic meetings about military aid."

Notice that the choice of an index and the choice of a sub-MOP to put an event into are the same. When a second event is indexed in the same way as a previous event, reminding happens and a new E-MOP is formed. In a sense, then, adding a new event to an E-MOP is like reminding, except that "reminding" is of a generalized group of events as opposed to a particular event. Another difference is that upon "event reminding," a new E-MOP and new generalization are added to memory; upon "E-MOP reminding," those generalizations are checked. The processes that go into confirming and disconfirming generalizations are explained in the next section.

3. GENERALIZATION

CYRUS does two types of generalization: initial generalization and generalization refinement. Initial generalization happens when the second event with a particular feature is added to an E-MOP. It is triggered by reminding and has been described as a process of feature extraction and comparison. Common features of the current event and the one already in memory are extracted and added to the norms of the new E-MOP. The events are then indexed in that MOP by their differences.

Generalization refinement is triggered as a result of monitoring E-MOP indices and content frame features. Because initial generalizations made in creating an E-MOP might be incomplete, inaccurate, or wrong, the update process must be able to monitor the correctness of generalized information in newly created E-MOPs. Checking the correctness of generalizations requires monitoring both the norms and indices in an E-MOP. Undergeneralization or incomplete generalization is recognized when a particular feature indexes most of the events in an E-MOP. In that case, the corresponding sub-MOP is collapsed and its norms are added to those of the parent MOP. A feature is overgeneralized if it is an E-MOP norm but does not correspond to later events added to the E-MOP. When an E-MOP's norm fails to correspond to new events, that norm must be removed and an E-MOP built for it.

Index monitoring is also necessary as a way of keeping track of a feature's predictive power. If a particular feature does not correlate with other features, it should be marked as non-predictive so it will no longer be indexed. In this section, the processes of recovery from over-generalization or false generalization, generalization beyond the initial ones, and recovery from non-predictive indices are discussed in detail.

3.1. Initial Generalization

When event reminding occurs, there are two events available for comparison, creation of a new E-MOP, and generalization—the current one and the previous one it is similar to. Each of those events has a set of features that describe it. Those features are compared to each other, and any that are in common are initially added to the content frame or norms of the new E-MOP.

Consider, for example, two trips that Vance might go on to the Middle East, one to Israel, and one to Egypt, both to negotiate Arab-Israeli peace. Suppose that in both he talked to the head of state of the country he was visiting, and in both, he was invited to a state dinner. Suppose both of those events were indexed as "trips to the Middle East" in the "diplomatic trips" MOP. What would the new "trips to the Middle East" MOP look like if these two trips were its initial two events?

Consider the generalized information we have available about "diplomatic trips." They are usually for the purpose of negotiations, include diplomatic meetings with diplomats of the foreign country, and are political and occupational. Consider, now, the specifications we have of the two trips:

```
TRIP1: destination: Israel
       purpose: negotiate Arab-Israeli peace
       seq of events: included meeting with Begin
                      included state dinner
```

TRIP2: destination: Egypt
purpose: negotiate Arab-Israeli peace
seq of events: included meeting with Sadat
included state dinner

The trips are similar in that both were to the Middle East, both had the same purpose, both included meetings with the head of state, and both included state dinners. Their differences were that each was to a different country, and each meeting was with a different head of state.

In creating a new E-MOP ''diplomatic trips to the Middle East'' from these two trips, the content frame of the new E-MOP should contain all of the similarities between the two events that are not true of diplomatic trips in general. Diplomatic trips generally include meetings with diplomats and are for the purpose of negotiating. However, because the negotiations and diplomatic meetings associated with these two trips are specializations of those ''diplomatic trip'' content frame properties, they will be good content frame norms for ''diplomatic trips to the Middle East.'' Because their sequences of events both included state dinners, not true of all trips, that too, can be added to the content frame of the new E-MOP.

Thus, a new ''diplomatic trips to the Middle East'' MOP created from these two trips would have the following structure:

FIG. 8.9. diplomatic trips to the Middle East.

Some generalizations produced by extracting the similarities between these two events are more reasonable than others. The Middle East will be the location for all meetings indexed in this E-MOP., since that is the index for this sub-MOP in ''diplomatic trips.'' Probably, these trips will continue to have the purpose of negotiating Arab-Israeli peace, at least as long as there is no peace there. We would not, however, expect that every trip to the Middle East will include a state dinner. There may also be attributes of trips to the Middle East not common to these first two trips. As additional meetings are added to the E-MOP, the unreasonable generalizations will be disconfirmed and removed from the content frame and missed generalizations will be added.

3.2. Generalization Refinement

The first two events added to an E-MOP are special. They initiate the set of generalizations that will be used in future indexing and retrieval. There are two possible problems with this method of generalization. First, some similarities between the first two events might be purely coincidental. In the example above, it is only coincidental that both trips included state dinners. In that case, the program (and probably a person too) jumps to a wrong conclusion. The feature does not really belong in the content frame of the E-MOP. It is not a real generalization.

The second problem that could occur in using the first two events to build the content frame of an E-MOP is that one or both of the events might be lacking a feature that events of their type normally have. Perhaps later "trips to the Middle East" will always include a meeting with the head of the opposition party, a feature that the first two events did not have for some reason. In that case, the later generalization must be added to the E-MOP's content frame at a later time.

As additional items are added to an E-MOP, the unreasonable generalizations must be discovered and deleted. In addition, new events must be monitored to see if additional generalized information can be extracted from them. One way to do that is to check each new event as it is processed to see if it conforms to the E-MOP's generalizations. If a feature of a new event conforms to a generalization, the certainty of that norm will increase. The certainty of each content frame feature that has a conflicting value in a new event will decrease. When the certainty of an aspect reaches a certain threshold, it can then be considered an actual norm for the E-MOP, or a real generalization. When a low threshold is reached, that aspect of the E-MOP's description need no longer be considered active for comparison.

We can think, then, of three classes of E-MOP features:

1. norms or actual generalizations
2. potential generalizations or active possibilities
3. E-MOP indices—not potential or active possibilities for generalization

When an aspect is an active possibility or potential generalization (2), each new event added must be checked for confirming or disconfirming evidence of that aspect. Eventually, the aspect will become a norm (1) or a more general index (3), and not an active generalization possibility. At that point it will no longer have to be monitored.

In CYRUS, the certainty of a generalization is a function of the number of events indexed in an E-MOP and the number of events with features that conflict with that generalization. Until the E-MOP organizes a reasonable number of events, however (6 in CYRUS), generalization certainty is not considered. This is an implementation detail that lends stability to an E-MOP until it can stabilize itself. As soon as an E-MOP reaches a reasonable size, the certainties of the generalizations are evaluated and those that fall below a threshold are removed, while all others remain.

All features that index an E-MOP in its parent MOP are considered norms (1) of the E-MOP immediately upon E-MOP creation. Since these features index the E-MOP, there will never be an event indexed in the E-MOP that does not have that feature. The E-MOP "diplomatic trips to the Middle East," for example, is indexed in the E-MOP "diplomatic trips" by its destination (the Middle East). Any event indexed in the E-MOP "diplomatic trips to the Middle East" will have to have that feature. Thus, it was a norm for the E-MOP "diplomatic trips to the Middle East" as soon as the E-MOP was created.

Other similarities between the first two events are considered potential content frame properties (2) until the E-MOP has grown to a reasonable size. At that time, norms that do not fit other E-MOP events are removed, and features that are true of a majority of events, but were not true of the first two, are added to the content frame. Thus, if later trips to the Middle East do not include state dinners, that will be removed from the E-MOP's content frame. If all trips to the Middle East following the two initial ones include a parade immediately after arrival, that would be added to the content frame. The next sections explain how that is done.

3.3. Making Additional Generalizations

Often, the first two events indexed in an E-MOP do not contain all of the features common to events of that type. In that case, additional generalizations must be made later and added to the E-MOP's norms. For an example of this, suppose that in the first two museums a person went to, the exhibits were paintings. One was what we know of as a typical museum, where he walked around looking at the exhibits. The other was an avant-garde museum where he sat in a chair and the exhibits came by on a belt.

What kind of generalizations could he make? If he had not been to other museums before, then we could not expect him to know that the second museum was weird. Thus, the only generalization we could expect him to make would be that "museums are places to see paintings." We would also expect him to recall his first experience as "walking around to see the paintings" and his second as "exhibits were brought around to me." Suppose, further, that on later museum trips, he went to a number of typical museums, but with exhibits more varied than paintings. He would have to give up his generalization that "museums are places to see paintings" in favor of "museums are places to see art work." We would also expect him to update his generalizations about the sequence of events in a museum to include "walking around to see the exhibits," realizing at some point that his second museum experience with the conveyor belt was weird, and from then on recalling it that way.

How can the generalization that "normally in a museum one walks around to see the exhibits" be made? The reason this is problematic is that it was not a common aspect of the first two visits to museums. We would expect the next museum trip in which he went to a museum and walked around to remind him of his first museum trip. In CYRUS, that would trigger creation of a "going to a museum" sub-MOP specified as "going to a museum and walking around seeing exhibits." Subsequent museum trips would fall into that sub-MOP, and eventually it would grow to contain almost all museum trips. Because it would contain almost all trips, its indexing structure would be practically the same as that of "going to a museum."

In order to automatically produce a more economical memory organization, indexing has to be monitored. Upon monitoring the indexing, it would be possible to notice that almost all museum experiences were falling into that sub-MOP and that it and its generalizations must therefore be the norms for museum trips. If that were done, the generalizations for "going to a museum and walking around" could be moved to the "going to a museum" MOP as its norms, and it and its sub-MOPs could be collapsed. Nothing would be lost since each museum trip in the "going to a museum and walking around seeing exhibits" sub-MOP would have been indexed in other ways in the more general "going to a museum" MOP. A lot would be gained, because as more generalizations were added to the more general E-MOP, less indexing would have to be done in it. Thus, there would be savings in both space and time.

Constant monitoring of an E-MOP's norms and indices will enable processing of this sort. Unless we want to consider all sub-MOPs of an E-MOP as potential generalizations, however, we need a rule for determining when sub-MOPs should be collapsed and their generalizations merged with those of their parent E-MOPs. The rule we might consider is the following:

IF a sub-MOP indexes a large majority of the events in its parent E-MOP,
and if the parent E-MOP is a reasonable size

THEN

(1) collapse the sub-MOP
(2) get rid of its index
(3) add the indexed feature plus other content frame features of the sub-MOP to the content frame of the parent E-MOP

FIG. 8.10. Collapsing sub-MOPs.

This rule necessitates a way either of measuring the size of an E-MOP or of keeping track of relative sizes of E-MOPs and their sub-MOPs as updating is done. In CYRUS, the sizes of E-MOPs and their sub-MOPs are kept until the E-MOPs become large, at which time they are marked as "large."

CYRUS uses this rule to decide when to collapse specialized E-MOPs and move their generalizations to the parent E-MOP. After an E-MOP reaches a stable size (6), CYRUS checks each sub-MOP referred to by an incoming event to see if any index a large majority (two-thirds) of the events in the E-MOP. If so, the generalizations corresponding to that set of items will also be good generalizations for the entire set of events in the parent E-MOP. CYRUS thus collapses the sub-MOP and merges its generalizations with those of the parent.

3.4. Recovery from Bad Generalizations

The rules for making and adding generalizations are heuristics. As a result, every generalization made using these rules is not guaranteed to be good. When new information and events contradict a previously made generalization, there must be a way of recovering. In a previous example, we illustrated how CYRUS would make the generalization that "trips to the Middle East include a state dinner." We also stated that after processing additional trips to the Middle East, CYRUS might discover that "generalization" does not fit the majority of episodes indexed in the E-MOP.

Recovery from bad generalizations is more complex than adding new generalizations. When new information and events contradict a previously made generalization, that generalization must be removed from the E-MOP's norms.

Sometimes a bad generalization will result from the process of collapsing sub-MOPs. This happens if the sub-MOP contains a generalization that contradicts a previous generalization associated with the parent E-MOP. Because the sub-MOP holds a large majority of the events in the parent E-MOP, its generalizations should be believed, and those associated with the parent should be doubted and removed if they are different.

Removing a bad generalization raises a special problem. While a feature is in the content frame of an E-MOP, events are not indexed by that feature. On the other hand, if a feature is included among an E-MOP's norms, then many of the events already in the E-MOP have it as a feature. Because events were not indexed by that feature, however, it would be expensive, and perhaps impossible, to go back and find all events supporting the generalization.

Generalization removal, then, can have grave implications in retrieval. If a retrieval key specified a feature that had been removed as a generalization, but which had not yet been indexed, then the retrieval processes would not be able to find any trace in memory of an event with that feature. It would have to conclude that there had never been such an event in memory.

To correct this problem, an index to an empty sub-MOP is created each time a feature is removed from a MOP's content frame. This allows retrieval processes to return a message saying they could not find a specific event, but there have been some. Clearly, this is preferable to returning nothing.

Old generalizations, then, must be indexed—even if there are no distinctly known events that correspond to them. A sub-MOP indexed by the old generalization must be created with as much generalized knowledge as possible. That generalized knowledge can come from other generalizations removed at the same time. This makes sense, since it is often the case that all generalizations removed at the same time are associated with each other. When CYRUS, for example, recovers from its generalization that "diplomatic meetings are about Arab-Israeli peace," it is recovering at the same time from generalizations that diplomatic meetings involve Israelis and Egyptians. These two generalizations go together. When an E-MOP for "diplomatic meetings about Arab-Israeli peace" is created, the other falsely generalized information can be associated with it as its generalized information.

Taking this "fix" into account, consider the retrieval process. Suppose, after recovering from the generalization that diplomatic meetings are about Arab-Israeli peace, memory is asked to retrieve "a meeting about Arab-Israeli peace with Begin in Jerusalem." While "diplomatic meetings" was marked as having topic Arab-Israeli peace, sub-MOPs of "diplomatic meetings" did not index that feature. Although there may be an E-MOP, then, for "diplomatic meetings with Begin," it will have no index for "topic is Arab-Israeli peace," nor will it have that feature marked as one of its norms (since it was a norm of a parent MOP). Thus, this target event will not be retrievable from the E-MOP "diplomatic meetings with Begin," or from any other sub-MOP of "diplomatic meetings" indexed while "topic is Arab-Israeli peace" was in its content frame.

The meeting with Begin will also not be retrievable from the newly created "diplomatic meetings about Arab-Israeli peace" MOP, since that E-MOP will not yet have any individual events indexed in it. Thus, although there will be a "diplomatic meetings about Arab-Israeli peace" MOP, the retrieval strategies will find no evidence that any of those meetings were with Begin, or that any meetings with Begin were about Arab-Israeli peace. It will have to return with the message that there never was any such meeting.

One more procedure must happen, then, during recovery from bad generalizations. Empty sub-MOPs created from old generalizations must be marked as having been "once generalized." In that way, the retrieval functions will be able to come back with the message "there may be events with this description, but I can't find particular ones," instead of failing completely if no distinct event could be found.

The following rule summarizes the process of recovery from false generalization:

IF a content frame feature has been disconfirmed

THEN

(1) remove it from the E-MOP
(2) create an empty sub-MOP for it indexed by that feature
(3) add other features removed from the E-MOP's content frame at the same time to the content frame of the new sub-MOP
(4) mark the new E-MOP as "once generalized"

FIG. 8.11. Recovery from false Generalization.

After a sub-MOP has been created from a recovered generalization, later events fitting that sub-MOP will be indexed there as in any other MOP. Those that had not been indexed while it was a generalization, however, are not directly retrievable using that index.

Considering the implications of memory reorganization on retrievability, we can now point out an important need for executive search strategies as part of the retrieval process. Although false generalization on one E-MOP might keep a particular event from being well indexed, events it was related to might have been more richly indexed. If that is the case, they will be easier to retrieve than the event whose features had been falsely generalized. Finding a ''once-generalized'' E-MOP during traversal, then, should signal that executive strategies will be particularly appropriate.

3.5. Maintenance of Predictive Power Judgments

The last kind of monitoring that must be done during memory update is monitoring for predictive power of features. The predictiveness of a particular type of feature is inherited from the E-MOP classifications and more general E-MOPs a MOP belongs to. Particular values of some type of feature, however, might turn out not to be predictive. In CYRUS, for example, ''occupations of event participants'' is marked as a predictive feature for all occupational events. Some occupations, however, are better than others at predicting additional event features. ''Defense ministers'' in ''diplomatic meetings,'' for example, normally meet about military aid, making that occupation predictive for diplomatic meetings. ''Foreign ministers'' and ''heads of state,'' however, are not predictive of any other meeting features.

In CYRUS, after a feature has occurred a reasonable number of times (6 in CYRUS), the MOP indexed by the feature is checked for generalizations. If there are no norms in addition to the feature that indexes the E-MOP, then the feature is judged to be non-predictive in the parent MOP and is marked as such. After being marked as non-predictive, that feature is no longer used as an index in that MOP.

In order to constrain later indexing, similarities between events in newly created E-MOPs must be maintained. An E-MOP indexed by a feature that is non-predictive will have no generalized information to keep track of, and it will not be able to constrain indexing and new E-MOP creation. Thus, its indices will duplicate the indices in its parent MOP without keeping track of useful generalized information. It will waste space without contributing to the organization of generalized information.

3.6. Why Generalize?

Indexing and subindexing could certainly be done without the use of generalized information. Why, then, should new E-MOPs be created and generalized knowledge be built up? There are four reasons. First, in retrieving events from memory, elaboration is often necessary. Elaboration uses generalized information associated with E-MOPs. If that information were not added to newly created E-MOPs, elaboration could not be guided. Suppose, for example, that a "diplomatic meetings about military aid" MOP did not hold the information that their participants are usually defense ministers. In that case, the following question would be hard to answer.

(Q1): Who has Vance talked to about military aid?

In answering this question, the question "What countries have been in need of military aid recently?" might first be answered. Once those countries have been enumerated, however, it must be deduced which representatives of those countries would probably have been at meetings. Using the information that they usually include defense ministers, meeting participants can be found easily by recalling the defense ministers of each enumerated country and checking for meetings with each. Without the information that these meetings are usually with defense ministers, processing would have to proceed differently. Retrieval might have to include enumeration of the top officials of the enumerated countries, instead of simple defense minister look-up.

This question probably could be answered without the specific generalization about defense ministers. There are two important points to make, however. First, retrieval is easier using the information about defense ministers. Second, if the generalization about defense ministers was not made, other generalizations would also not have been made. Without generalized information, elaboration cannot be done. Since there are cases when elaboration is necessary for retrieval, and elaboration cannot be done without generalized information, retrieval would have to fail in many cases.

There is a second important reason why generalized information on new E-MOPs is necessary. Features in the content frame of an E-MOP are not indexed. By making generalizations and building up content frame information on new E-MOPs, later indexing in those E-MOPs is constrained. Suppose again that the E-MOP "meetings about military aid" did not have the generalized information that its participants are usually defense ministers. Each time a new meeting about military aid was indexed at that point in memory, it would be further subindexed as a "meeting about military aid with a defense minister." If, in fact, all or most meetings about military aid were with defense ministers, then all of the events indexed as "meetings about military aid" would also be indexed as "meetings about military aid with defense ministers," and the indexing under each of those points would be the same. Memory would have a lot of unneeded redundancy.

Third, generalized information can be used in generating default answers to questions. Suppose the particular participants of a certain meeting were not known, but that their nationalities were, as in the following example.

EV1: Vance met with a Jordanian about military aid.

This meeting would be indexed in the "meetings about military aid" MOP. Suppose the following question was later asked of the memory.

(Q2): Which Jordanian has Vance met with about military aid?

Retrieving EV1 would not answer this question since an actual person was being asked for. Using generalized information on the "meetings about military aid" MOP, however, the answer "probably the Jordanian defense minister" could be given.

A fourth way generalization is important is in understanding. Understanding requires "world knowledge" to resolve ambiguities and fill in implicit information. It seems logical that the same structures in memory are used both in storing and retrieving knowledge, and in processing.[7] An implication of this claim is that the generalized knowledge created in adding a new item to memory is later used in understanding. A further implication is that if generalizations were not made, then understanding could not take place in the sense that we know it.

4. HOW CYRUS' MEMORY GROWS

To see how these processes work in practice, we will examine growth of CYRUS' "diplomatic meetings" MOP. Initially, CYRUS' "diplomatic meetings" MOP has no indices, but does have a content frame with generalized information about diplomatic meetings. It knows that diplomatic meetings are generally instrumental to negotiations, that their participants are foreign diplomats, that their topic of discussion is usually some international contract or dispute, and that they are political and occupational activities for Vance. Political activities for Vance are activities involving diplomats, whose topics of discussion are usually international relations of some sort. "Diplomatic meetings," then, is initialized with the following content frame:

content frame:	included in "negotiations" participants are foreign diplomats topic is an international contract topic involves the United States is political and occupational for Vance is a meeting

FIG. 8.12. diplomatic meetings—$MEET.

[7]Support of this claim is beyond the scope of this book. For support, see Schank (1980) or Schank (1982).

After adding two "diplomatic meetings" to CYRUS, one concerning SALT with Gromyko (EV2) and one concerning Arab-Israeli peace with Begin (EV1), both part of negotiations, CYRUS' "diplomatic meetings" MOP includes the following structure:

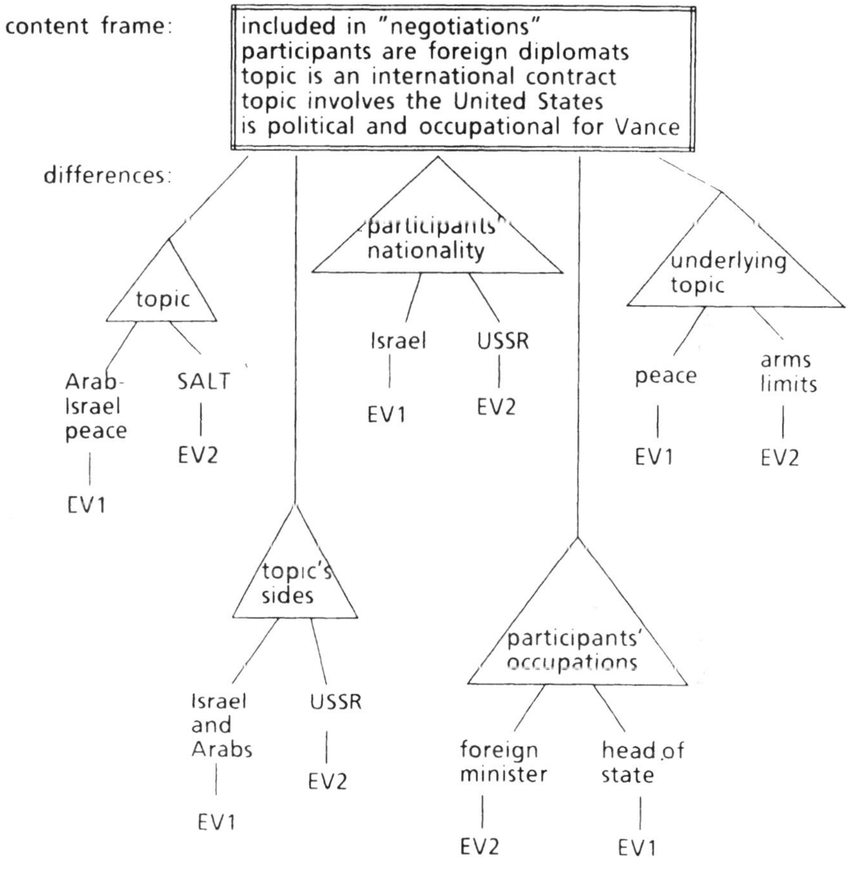

FIG. 8.13. diplomatic meetings—$MEET.

These two meetings are indexed by their topics, the issue underlying those topics, the sides involved, and the nationalities and occupations of the participants. Because both are part of negotiations standard to the topic they are discussing, neither is indexed by its purpose or larger episodes it is part of. Because these two meetings have nothing in common except generalized information already known about meetings, they are each indexed uniquely by their differences, and "diplomatic meeting" content frame information does not change.

At this point, all indices in this E-MOP index event descriptions. In CYRUS, and in the E-MOP pictured above, those event descriptions are pointers to events themselves. In a more reconstructive memory, each event description would be the set of features of the meeting that were different from or in addition to the E-MOP's norms. Other unspecified features could be inferred through E-MOP content frame information. The event description indexed under "meeting with a head of state" would include the information that the meeting was about Arab-Israeli peace, and that it was with Begin, an Israeli. The event description indexed under "meeting about Arab-Israeli peace" would include the information that the meeting was with Begin, the Israeli prime minister.

Both of the meetings just indexed in this MOP happened in August, 1978. If we continue adding meetings to CYRUS in the order in which they happened, we can illustrate how the structure of the "diplomatic meeting" MOP changes over time. The next meeting processed by CYRUS was another meeting about Arab-Israeli peace, this time with Sadat. Because this meeting had features in common with Vance's meeting with Begin, reminding occurred, new E-MOPs were created, and generalized information was added to those E-MOPs. The content frame of "diplomatic meetings" remained the same, since there were no additional overwhelming similarities between the three meetings indexed up to that point. After adding this meeting to memory, CYRUS' "diplomatic meetings" MOP had the following structure:

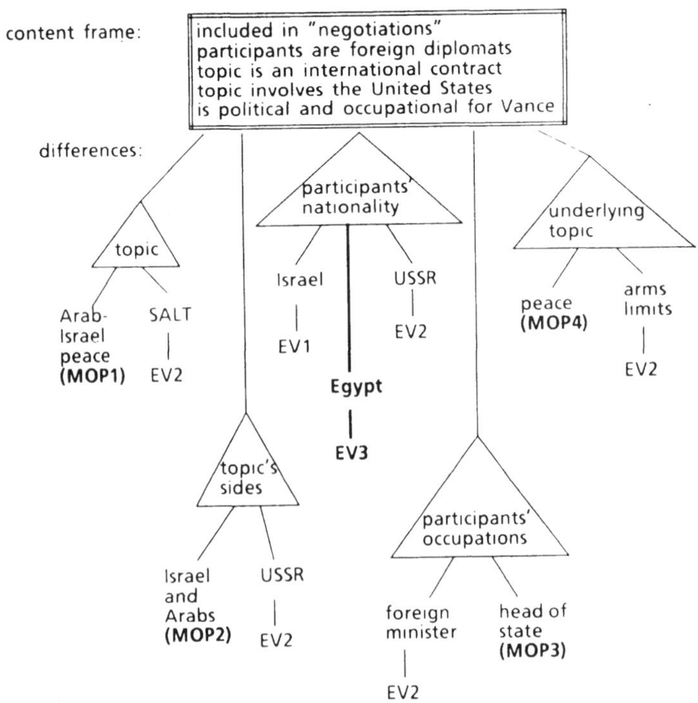

FIG. 8.14. diplomatic meetings—$MEET.

Because this meeting, too, was with a head of state and was about Arab-Israeli peace, new E-MOPs were created at those index points (MOP1, MOP2, MOP3, and MOP4). Those E-MOPs each contain as norms the information common to the two meetings that initiated their creation—in each of these cases, that both were about Arab-Israeli peace, involved Israel and the Arabs, and were with a head of state. Each one also is marked as a specialization of "diplomatic meeting." The newly created E-MOP "diplomatic meetings about Arab-Israeli peace" (MOP1), for example, has the following structure:

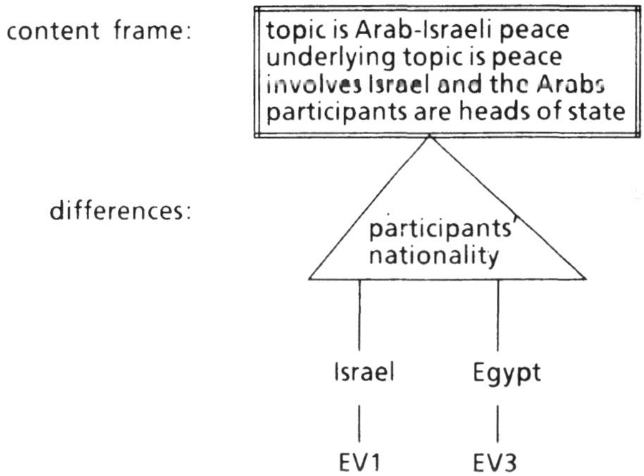

FIG. 8.15. diplomatic meetings about Arab-Israeli peace—MOP1.

4.1. CYRUS Overgeneralizes

When CYRUS finds an index that indexes nearly all the events in the E-MOP, it predicts that that feature should actually be one of the E-MOP's norms and updates the content frame appropriately. As additional diplomatic meetings were added to CYRUS' memory, its "diplomatic meetings" MOP continued to grow. The next eight meetings Vance had were meetings concerning Arab-Israeli peace. Some were part of the Camp David Summit. Because so many of the diplomatic meetings CYRUS knew about were about Arab-Israeli peace, and because there was only one meeting that had been about anything else at that point, CYRUS made the generalization that "Vance's diplomatic meetings are generally about Arab-Israeli peace." Thus, after adding those eight meetings to memory, CYRUS' "diplomatic meetings" MOP had the content frame and structure shown in Fig. 8.16.

As a result of this overgeneralization, CYRUS removed some of the sub-MOPs it had created previously. Thus, its E-MOPs "diplomatic meetings about Arab-Israeli peace," "diplomatic meetings about a topic involving the Arabs

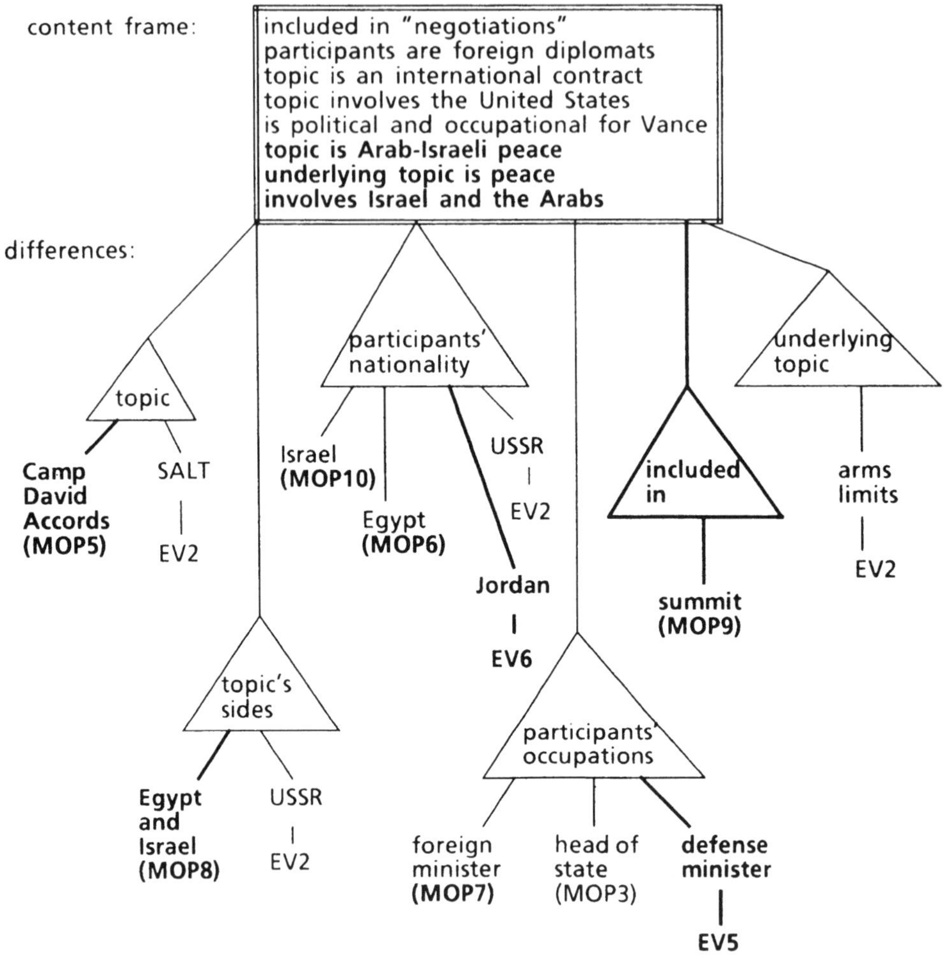

FIG. 8.16. diplomatic meetings—$MEET.

and Israel,'' and ''diplomatic meetings about peace'' (MOPS 1, 2, and 4 in Fig. 8.14) were collapsed. They were subsumed by the generalizations made about ''diplomatic meetings'' in general. CYRUS later recovered from this overgeneralization. Notice, however, that at this point in memory's growth, there were specialized E-MOPs with features specialized from those content frame features. New E-MOPs for ''diplomatic meetings about a topic involving Egypt and Israel'' (MOP8) and ''diplomatic meetings about the Camp David Accords'' (MOP5) specialize the content frame property ''topic involves Arab-Israeli peace.'' In addition, the E-MOPs ''meetings with Israelis'' (MOP10) and ''meetings with Egyptians'' (MOP6) were created.

At this point, CYRUS had made a number of erroneous generalizations about diplomatic meetings. It generalized that diplomatic meetings usually involve Arab and Israeli concerns and are normally about peace between the Arabs and Israel. As people, we recognize that the meetings CYRUS had seen up to this point were not a good sampling of Vance's meetings. As far as CYRUS knew, however, the meetings it had seen were typical. To it, then, these were valid generalizations, and CYRUS used them to constrain further index and new E-MOP creation, and to guide elaboration during retrieval.

4.2. Implications of CYRUS' Mistake

To see how these generalizations guide retrieval, and how erroneous generalizations can cause forgetting, consider how CYRUS would answer the following question based on the MOP above:

(Q3): What have you talked about at diplomatic meetings?

In answering this question, CYRUS would first check generalized information about topics of "diplomatic meetings" in order to direct its search. It would find that meetings are generally about Arab-Israeli peace. At that point, it would recall the most important specific Arab-Israeli topics it knew about—the Camp David Accords. It would thus attempt retrieval of "diplomatic meetings about the Camp David Accords." Since there could have been other topics involving Arab-Israeli peace that it could not retrieve in that way, it continues its search of memory. Using this topic information, it would also infer that participants were from the Middle East (since nationalities of participants and sides of the topic under consideration generally correspond) and search the E-MOP for meetings with people from each of the Middle Eastern countries. It would thus do a good job of elaborating on and retrieving meetings about Arab-Israeli peace, but as a result of its overgeneralization, it would forget the SALT meeting entirely.

Suppose, however, that it was asked the following question:

(Q4): Who have you talked to about SALT?

Although elaboration at this point does not allow retrieval of a meeting about SALT, specification of a unique characteristic of such a meeting does allow its retrieval. Because an indexed feature unique to one event in the "diplomatic meetings" MOP is specified in the question, CYRUS can retrieve the appropriate meeting by simply traversing the E-MOP.

There is an important observation to be made about retrieval of events that are different from an E-MOP's norms. Because the E-MOP's norms will not aid in inferring their features, they may not be retrievable through elaboration. They will, however, be easily retrievable if their differentiating features are specified.

This example illustrates the difference between recall and recognition found in people. Because recall may require reconstruction and elaboration, a person freely recalling a list of items is likely to forget some. On the other hand, when presented with a well-specified item forgotten during recall, he may recognize it.

4.3. Getting CYRUS Back on the Right Track

CYRUS' memory at this point was, at best, confused. It is not always possible to know when there is a good sampling. As a result, indices and norms must constantly be monitored to keep memory's generalized information up to date with the events it organizes.

When a content frame feature is no longer true of most events indexed in an E-MOP, CYRUS updates both its content frame and indices, removing that feature from its content frame and adding indices for it to the E-MOP. Those indices will not be able to point to actual events, but they will point to the fact that there are events in memory with that feature. In that way, it recovers from false generalizations.

As additional meetings were added to CYRUS' memory, it began to notice that very few of them matched the content frame that it had generalized. After approximately 20 meetings had been added to CYRUS' "diplomatic meetings" MOP, its content frame became more stable. At that point, it had a good sampling, and the meetings balanced each other in all relevant ways. It recovered and readjusted its generalizations to fit reality. It removed the bad generalizations from the content frame, created E-MOPs indexed by each of those features, and used those features to index later meetings.

After CYRUS had processed approximately 60 diplomatic meetings, its "diplomatic meetings" MOP had the structure in Fig. 8.17. The entire structure of CYRUS' "diplomatic meetings" MOP after 60 meetings is not illustrated here. The interesting features to note, however, are that its content frame had recovered from the erroneous generalizations that were made, and it again had indices and corresponding E-MOPs for the features "topic involving Arabs and Israel," "topic is peace," and "topic is Arab-Israeli peace." Those were the E-MOPs that had been removed when CYRUS made the previous overgeneralization.

4.4. Maintaining Predictive Power Information

When CYRUS finds an index with no predictive power, it marks that index as useless and no longer uses it. When CYRUS began adding new meetings to memory, it indexed all events according to the occupations of their participants. By the time it had added 60 meetings to memory, however, it knew that the occupation "foreign minister" was not predictive of other features, and it therefore no longer used that feature to index meetings in its "diplomatic meetings"

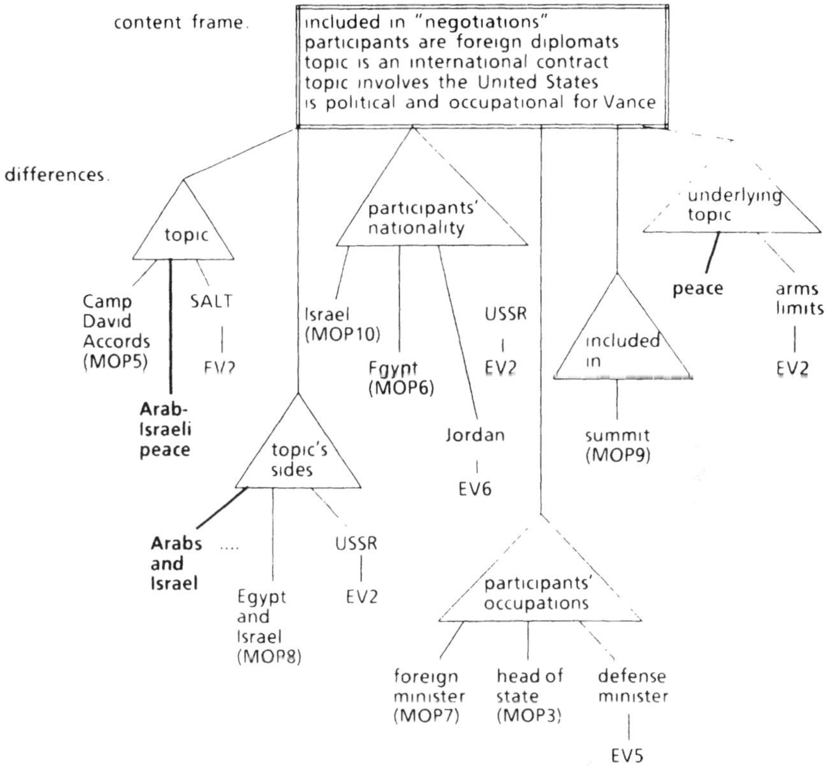

FIG. 8.17. diplomatic meetings—$MEET.

MOP. Some of the sub-MOPs to "diplomatic meetings" also have features marked as non-predictive or useless.

As CYRUS is adding new events to memory, it monitors both its indices and its content frame, keeping its content frame up-to-date, and attempting to ascertain which indices are predictive and which are not useful. As a result of this monitoring, recovery from over-generalization or false generalization, generalizations beyond the initial ones, and recovery from non-predictive indices are possible.

5. FURTHER IMPLICATIONS OF MEMORY REORGANIZATION—FORGETTING

In order to evaluate the implications of memory reorganization, we must recall the internal structure of episodes in memory. An episode is composed of many events and episodes related to each other through containment, causality, and time. Every event in memory points to all of the episodes it is related to by specifying those features of each episode that can retrieve it from its MOPs. The set of features that describe an event are derived at the time the event is entered into memory. Because memory's organization changes over time, however, a reference that was unique at input time may not be unique at retrieval time. During retrieval, if the available specification of a contextually related event is no longer unique, then elaboration must be applied to reconstruct additional details of the related event and enable its retrieval.

Consider, for example, the following event:

EV2: On his recent visit to the Philadelphia, Vance was welcomed by a marching band playing "Stars and Stripes Forever."

Suppose this particular welcoming ceremony was the first that had included a band. In that case, the trip would refer to the welcoming ceremony as "welcomed by a band." Since the welcoming ceremony itself would be stored in its own E-MOP, that specification would be a unique reference to the welcoming ceremony. Suppose, however, that during later trips around the United States, Vance was again greeted by bands, sometimes high-school marching bands, sometimes college bands, sometimes military bands. The specification "welcomed by a band" associated with his visit to Philadelphia would no longer be unique. It would describe an E-MOP rather than an individual event. To retrieve the particular welcoming ceremony, the specification "welcomed by a band" would have to be elaborated until it described a unique event that could be retrieved from the "welcoming ceremony" MOP.

Elaboration, as a process of inferring plausible features, can be faulty. In that case, the wrong event might be retrieved from memory. If a recalled event is consistent with the information that is known, its differences will not be noticed, and false reconstruction will occur. Faulty retrieval of this kind corresponds to what psychologists refer to as *recall intrusion* (Crowder, 1976, Owens, Bower, & Black, 1979) and *recognition confusion* (Bower, Black & Turner, 1979, Gibbs & Tenny, 1980). Mistakes of this sort happen in the retrieval process we have described when some aspect of the reconstruction directs retrieval to the wrong episode, which is then substituted for what actually happened.

Retrieval interferences occur because of the constantly changing memory structure. The features specified for related events depend on the memory organization at the time the event is entered into memory. They will be features that discriminate the related event in its E-MOP at that time. If memory changes before retrieval time, then what was once a unique specification of an event may no longer be unique. Faulty or unsuccessful elaboration can then cause forgetting.

6. SUMMARY

When new events are added to memory, they must be added in such a way that memory's organization is maintained. Adding a new event to an E-MOP is a process of integrating it into memory. The event is indexed in the E-MOP so that it can later be retrieved, and generalized information necessary to aid its retrieval is built up.

The first step in adding a new event to an E-MOP is to choose appropriate features of the event for indexing. Each feature chosen can have one of three relationships to the E-MOP:

1. There is nothing yet indexed in the E-MOP with that feature.
2. There is one other item with that feature indexed in the E-MOP.
3. There is an E-MOP indexed by that feature.

When there is not already an index for a feature (1), a new index is built, and the event is indexed at that point. When there is one other event with a particular feature (2), a new E-MOP is formed based on the similarities between the new event and the previous one with that feature, and the two events are indexed in that E-MOP. When there is already an E-MOP indexed by a particular feature (3), the new event is integrated into that E-MOP. That integration includes refining the E-MOP's generalized information and indexing the event in the E-MOP. Refining an E-MOP's generalizations involves both collapsing sub-MOPs and adding their generalized knowledge to that of the parent E-MOP, and removing a false generalization from the content frame of an E-MOP and creating an E-MOP for it.

The memory organization that is built up in adding new events to memory is a hierarchical organization of categories and their subcategories. As new events are added to memory, they are multiply indexed in each of the categories or subcategories they fit into. In many cases, this results in the creation of specializations of the subcategories. The event being added to memory must then be indexed in those sub-subcategories. In a system that creates multiple new indices for each new event as it is added to memory, and that creates new subcategories automatically, the number of indices and categories in memory would quickly reach astronomical proportions if it were not controlled.

Two ways of controlling creation of new indices and sub-MOPs have been presented. Because only differences from norms with predictive power are indexed, maintaining both generalized knowledge and knowledge about the potential predictive power of indices is necessary to prevent combinatorial explosion of indices and subcategories, In this chapter, maintenance of both of those kinds of information has been explained.

Generalization maintenance is important to both the retrieval and updating processes. During retrieval, generalized information is needed to apply retrieval strategies. During memory update, generalized information constrains later indexing and new E-MOP creation.

IV STATE OF THE PROGRAM, STATE OF THE ART

9 How CYRUS Works

1. INTRODUCTION

At CYRUS' completion, it had two data bases. The more detailed data base contains information about former United States Secretary of State Cyrus Vance. He was chosen because he was in the news often enough to generate a large number of news updates, but he did few enough types of events to make the initial specification of E-MOPs feasible. When Vance resigned, CYRUS began organizing information about Vance's successor, Edmund Muskie, into a second data base. The initial memory organization CYRUS started with for each man was the same. However, because of their differing experiences, the new E-MOPs built by the system for Muskie's events are somewhat different than those built for Vance.

In one mode of operation, CYRUS is hooked up with FRUMP (DeJong, 1979a) to form a complete fact retrieval system called CyFr. FRUMP reads stories from the UPI news wire and sends conceptual summaries of stories about Muskie and Vance to CYRUS. CYRUS then adds the new events to its memory and answers questions about them. CYRUS' Muskie memory has been built up entirely from FRUMP-processed stories. Its Vance memory is built partially of FRUMP-processed stories and partially of stories encoded by hand.

2. CYRUS' E-MOPs

CYRUS' E-MOPs correlate with the kinds of activities a secretary of state does. Below is a complete list of CYRUS' E-MOPs:

Scripts:

$MEET -- diplomatic meetings with foreign dignitaries
$CONSULT -- consultations with American officials
$PUB-REL-MEET -- political meetings with non-diplomats
$STATE-DINNER -- state dinners
$FLY -- flights
$REPORT -- press conferences
$SPEECH -- speeches
$PARTY -- parties
$DINE -- dinner with associates

Simple MOPs:

sM-MEETING -- political meetings
sM-CONFERENCE -- political conferences
sM-SUMMIT-CONFERENCE -- specialized political conferences
sM-TRAVEL -- traveling
sM-TRIP -- generalized trip
sM-VIPVISIT -- diplomatic trip
sM-SIGHTSEE -- sightseeing
sM-CEREMONY --ceremonies
sM-SOCIAL-POL-ACTIVITY -- social political activities
sM-DIPLOMATIC-ACTIVITY -- diplomatic activities

IMOPs:

I-NEGOTIATE -- negotiations
I-DIPLOMACY -- diplomacy
I-SOCIALIZE -- socializing
I-CELEBRATE -- celebration

FIG. 9.1. CYRUS' E-MOPs.

CYRUS' E-MOPs fall into three MOP classes—scripts, simple MOPs, and IMOPs. Scripts have a highly stereotypical sequence of events. Simple MOPs are less stereotypical. IMOPs (Intentional MOPs) have a less stereotypical sequence of events, but their goals are stereotypical. For a better description of the distinction between these three categories, see chapter 2.

Within CYRUS, the information associated with E-MOPs is represented using Conceptual Dependency (CD) notation (Schank, 1975). CYRUS' representations of some of the content frame properties for $MEET (''diplomatic meetings'') and sM-VIPVISIT (''diplomatic trips'') are presented in Figs. 9.2 and 9.3.

The FRAME property on any E-MOP specifies its slots and names variables for those slots. The atoms beginning with ''&'' are variables. The atoms before those are the names of the slots. Thus, $MEET has slots for ACTOR (the person from whose point of view the episode is stored), OTHERS (other participants), TOPIC, PLACE, TIME, and DURATION. Together, the ACTOR and OTHERS make up the PARTICIPANTS. Default values for each of those slots can be found as content frame properties on the E-MOP. The content frame property has

```
MOP-type: script

FRAME:
   ((< = > ($MEET ACTOR &ACTOR OTHERS &OTHERS TOPIC &TOPIC))
    PLACE &PLACE TIME &TIME DURATION &DUR))

&OTHERS: (CLASS (#PERSON) OCCUPATION (RT-DIPLOMAT))
&TOPIC:    (CLASS (#CONTRACT #EVENT))
&DUR:  (*ORDERHOURS*)


MOP-categories: (sM-MEETING)

SMOPs:
   ((< = > (sM-CONFERENCE ACTOR &ACTOR OTHERS &OTHERS
                          TOPIC   &TOPIC))
    PLACE &PLACE TIME &TIME)
   ((< = > (sM-VIPVISIT ACTOR &ACTOR DESTINATION &PLACE))
    TIME &TIME)

IMOPS:
   ((< = > (I-NEGOTIATE ACTOR &ACTOR OTHERS &OTHERS
                                    TOPIC &TOPIC)))

MAINCON:
   ((ACTOR &ACTOR < = > (*MTRANS*)
                  MOBJECT (*CONCEPTS* CONCERNING &TOPIC)
                  FROM &ACTOR TO &OTHERS)
    PLACE &PLACE MANNER (*BILATERAL*))

MOST-RECENT:
   ((< = > ($MEET ACTOR *VANCE* OTHERS *SADAT* TOPIC *CDA*))
    TIME TIM342 PLACE *EGYPT*)
```

FIG. 9.2. $MEET

the same name as the variable. The specification on $MEET for &OTHERS is that they are persons who are diplomats. The topic (&TOPIC) is either a contract or an event, and the default duration (&DUR) is a small number of hours (*ORDERHOURS*).

"MOP-categories" are more general categories the E-MOP falls into. $MEET is a "political meeting" (sM-MEETING) and thus inherits the properties of "political meeting." Because "political meeting" is both an occupational and a political activity, $MEET does not have to specify that it falls into those categories.

The "SMOPs" and "IMOPs" properties specify larger episodes diplomatic meetings are normally part of. These two properties are used during retrieval to direct memory search. The variable names in each of those specifications denote the correspondence between the slot fillers of those related episodes and those of a typical diplomatic meeting. As in Cullingford's (1978) scripts, the "MAINCON" gives the main activity in the sequence of events of the script. The main activity of $MEET is bilateral communication of information between the participants.

In addition, each E-MOP in CYRUS keeps track of the last episode that was added to the E-MOP (specified by MOST-RECENT in the E-MOP above). Thus, most-recent events are treated specially and are more accessible than other events in the E-MOP. In this way, CYRUS can always retrieve at least one event from an E-MOP even if appropriate indices cannot be proposed by elaboration processes.

Information in the E-MOP sM-VIPVISIT (''diplomatic trips'') is represented as follows:

```
MOP-type: simple MOP

FRAME:
   ((< = > (sM-VIPVISIT ACTOR &ACTOR DESTINATION &DEST
                        ORIGIN &ORIG OTHERS &OTHERS))
    TIME &TIME PLACE &DEST DURATION &DUR)

&OTHERS: (CLASS (#PERSON) OCCUPATION (RT-DIPLOMAT)
          NATIONALITY *USA*)              ~ (i.e., American diplomats)
&DEST: (CLASS (#LOCALE #POLITY))
&ORIG: *WASH-DC*
&DUR: (*ORDERDAYS*)

MOP-categories: (sM-TRIP)

IMOPs:
   ((< = > (I-NEGOTIATE ACTOR &ACTOR OTHERS &NEG-OTHERS
                                          TOPIC &TOPIC)))

SEQ-OF-EVENTS:
   ((< = > ($FLY ACTOR &ACTOR DESTINATION &DEST ORIGIN &ORIG
                 PARTY &OTHERS)))
   ((< = > ($WELCOME ACTOR &WELCOMER GUEST &ACTOR))
    PLACE &WEL-PLACE)
   ((< = > (sM-DIP-ACTIVITY ACTOR &ACTOR OTHERS &PARTY))
    PLACE &DEST)
       repeat: indefinitely
   ((< = > ($FLY ACTOR &ACTOR DESTINATION &ORIG ORIGIN &DEST
                 PARTY &OTHERS)))

MAINCON:
   ((< = > (sM-DIP-ACTIVITY ACTOR &ACTOR OTHERS &PARTY))
    PLACE &DEST)

&NEG-OTHERS: (CLASS (#PERSON) NATIONALITY &DEST
                   OCCUPATION (RT-DIPLOMAT))
&TOPIC: (CLASS (#CONTRACT) SIDES (&DEST))
&WELCOMER: (CLASS (#PERSON) NATIONALITY &DEST
                  OCCUPATION (RT-DIPLOMAT))
&WEL-PLACE: (CLASS (#LOCALE) TYPE (*AIRPORT*)
                   LOCATION &DEST)
&PARTY: (CLASS (#GROUP)
         MEMBERS (&ACTOR &OTHERS &NEG-OTHERS))

MOST-RECENT:
   ((< = > (sM-VIPVISIT ACTOR *VANCE* DESTINATION *ISRAEL*
                        ORIGIN *WASH-DC*))
    TIME TIM547 PLACE *ISRAEL*)
```

FIG. 9.3. sM-VIPVISIT

The FRAME, MAINCON, MOP-categories, IMOPs, and MOST-RECENT properties hold the same information explained above for $MEET. In addition, the SEQ-OF-EVENTS feature holds the normal sequence of events for a diplomatic trip. A trip includes flying to the destination, being welcomed at the airport, repeatedly doing diplomatic activities, and then flying home. The role filler specifications at the bottom of the diagram (after the MAINCON) are specifications of the role fillers for episodes related to trips. &WEL-PLACE, for example, is used in the $WELCOME scene of a sM-VIPVISIT and holds the information that the place of a welcome is the airport of the country being visited.

3. RETRIEVAL IN CYRUS

CYRUS retrieves answers to questions posed to it in English. Although the retrieval process described in previous chapters is the primary part of CYRUS' question-answering procedure, it is only one part of it. CYRUS' question-answering loop is based on Lehnert's (1978) description of the question-answering process. In order to answer a question, it must be parsed and its conceptual category (i.e., question type)[8] and question concept extracted. The *question concept* (Lehnert, 1978) of a question is the the part of the question that must be searched for, i.e., its target event. The target event is searched for, using the retrieval process already described, and when it is found, processes corresponding to the question category are applied to it to formulate an answer. If the question asks "why," for example, the causes of the retrieved event are extracted. An English language generator outputs an answer. The entire question-answering process can be described by the algorithm in Fig. 9.4. In this section, parts of the question-answering cycle are explained and illustrated.

3.1. Searching CYRUS' Memory

CYRUS' memory is searched using the retrieval process described in chapters 3 through 6. Given a target concept, a context for search is constructed, the appropriate E-MOPs are traversed, and the target event is elaborated as necessary. If an appropriate answer has not been found, executive strategies are applied to search for alternate related events. Because strategy application has been described in detail in previous chapters, the application of strategies themselves are not described in this chapter. Rather, the subset of strategies implemented in CYRUS are pointed out.

---

[8]Examples: yes/no, concept completion, causal antecedent. These will be discussed in more detail in section 3.7.

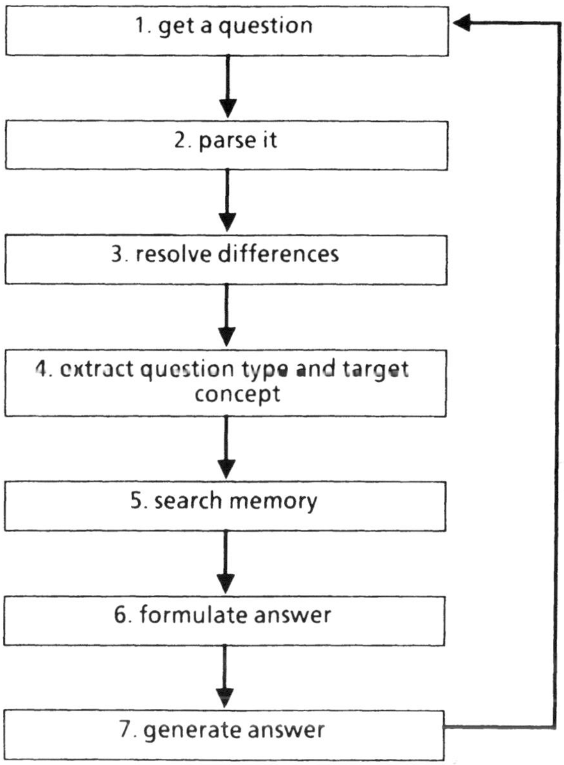

FIG. 9.4. Question Answering in CYRUS.

E-MOPs keep track of their causal, containment, and temporal relations to other E-MOPs. CYRUS' E-MOPs implement the containment and temporal relations, but do not keep track of causal information. Thus, CYRUS' E-MOPs specify larger episodes they usually occur in, and their normal sequence events, standard methods of achievement, and temporal relationships within the event sequence of another E-MOP. An implication of this is that only those strategies associated with containment relationships are implemented and applied within CYRUS. Those strategies include "Find-from-Seq-of-Events," "Find-from-Larger-Episodes," "Find-from-IMOPs," and "Find-from-Standardizations."

Initial context construction involves using contextual information associated with components of the target concept to infer an E-MOP for traversal. CYRUS' context instantiation strategies include those associated with topics, participants, and places.

The traversal/elaboration procedure and most of the retrieval strategies that have been presented are implemented in CYRUS. When an E-MOP is reached during traversal, CYRUS applies component instantiation rules to elaborate on the target concept and then continues its traversal. Calls to component instantiation rules are embedded in CYRUS' traversal procedure. When elaboration is necessary, choice of component instantiation rules is driven by the types of indices the E-MOP to be traversed has. If it has "participant" indices, for example, the procedure INFER-PARTICIPANTS is applied to infer participants. Thus, CYRUS' component instantiation rules are driven by the memory's organization.

When CYRUS applies search strategies, it applies those associated with the type of E-MOP being searched for. Thus, for scripts, it applies "Find-from-IMOPs" and "Find-from-Larger-Episodes." It continues applying search strategies until sufficient matches to the target event are found. A satisfactory answer has been found when CYRUS is asked for one example and finds one (as in verifying if something has happened), when it is asked for a particular number of episodes and finds that many, or after it has applied all the strategies it knows.

3.2. Parsing Questions

CYRUS' question parser is based on CA (Birnbaum & Selfridge, 1981). Martin Korsin extended that parser for CYRUS and added necessary word definitions. The parser takes an English question as input and produces a conceptual dependency representation of the meaning of the question. The parser has definitions for approximately 300 words and can parse one- and two-clause questions. The following is an example of parser output:

>Has Vance talked to Gromyko about SALT recently?

```
parsing...
((ACTOR *VANCE* < = > (*MTRANS*)
                MOBJECT (*CONCEPTS* CONCERNING *SALT*)
                TO *GROMYKO*)
 TIME (#TIME TENSE (PAST))
 MODE (*?*))
```

FIG. 9.5. Parser output.

After parsing a question, CYRUS searches memory to retrieve an answer as explained in previous chapters. Because Gromyko is a foreign dignitary, CYRUS chooses $MEET ("diplomatic meetings") as its context for search in answering the question above and searches for a recent meeting between Vance and Gromyko. It finds one, gives an answer, asks for the next question, and parses it as in Fig. 9.6.

When people ask questions, they often reference aspects of the previous context using pronouns. CYRUS' parser does not resolve those references, but marks pronominal references for the reference resolver to resolve (see Fig. 9.4). The question "Did he talk to him about SALT?" has two references which must be resolved.

```
The question is:
((ACTOR *VANCE* < = > (*MTRANS*)
                  MOBJECT (*CONCEPTS* CONCERNING *SALT*
                  TO *GROMYKO*)
 TIME G0852 MODE (*?*))
 The question type is "verification"
 The question concept is:
 ((ACTOR *VANCE* < = > (*MTRANS*)
                  MOBJECT (*CONCEPTS* CONCERNING *SALT*
                  TO *GROMYKO*) TIME G0852)

    inferring a diplomatic meeting

 The answer is:
 ((< = > ($MEET ACTOR *VANCE* OTHERS *GROMYKO* TOPIC *SALT*))
  TIME G1058 PLACE *GENEVA* DURATION G1061)
  Modality YES

 yes, most recently in Geneva in December.


 >Did he talk to him about SALT?

 parsing...
 ((ACTOR (*PP* PPCLASS (#PERSON) GENDER (*MASC*) REF (DEF))
     < = > (*MTRANS*)
     MOBJECT (*CONCEPTS* CONCERNING *SALT*)
     TO (*PP* PPCLASS (#PERSON) GENDER (*MASC*) REF (DEF)))
  MODE (*?*) TIME (#TIME TENSE (PAST)))
```

FIG. 9.6.

3.3. Reference Resolution in CYRUS

CYRUS' reference resolution processes combine pattern matching with a process of matching individual pronouns to references made in the previous question and answer. Any time a pronominal reference in a question can refer to only one component of the conceptual representation underlying the previous answer, CYRUS resolves the reference to that component.

Unfortunately, references do not always uniquely specify a component of a previous answer, as exemplified in the dialog above (repeated below):

Q1: Has Vance met with Gromyko recently?

A1: Yes, most recently in Geneva in December.

Q2: Did he talk to him about SALT?

Because the answer to A1 implicitly specifies two men (Vance and Gromyko), the "he" and the "him" in the second question cannot be resolved by choosing the male person in the answer that came before it. The way CYRUS resolves the reference is to match the representation of the question with the representation of the answer that came before it. The following are the representations for A1 and Q2, repeated from above:

```
A1: ((< = > ($MEET ACTOR *VANCE* OTHERS *GROMYKO* TOPIC *SALT*))
    TIME G1058
    PLACE *GENEVA*
    DURATION G1061)


Q2:
   ((ACTOR (*PP* PPCLASS (#PERSON) GENDER (*MASC*) REF (DEF))
       < = > (*MTRANS*)
       MOBJECT (*CONCEPTS* CONCERNING *SALT*)
       TO (*PP* PPCLASS (#PERSON) GENDER (*MASC*) REF (DEF)))
    MODE (*?*) TIME (#TIME TENSE (PAST)))
```

FIG. 9.7. Reference resolution.

The pronominal references in the question must be resolved by pattern matching. Sometimes, however, the two patterns do not match each other, as in Fig. 9.7. A1 specifies a "diplomatic meeting," while Q2 refers to an MTRANS. In order to resolve the reference in this case, the MAINCON (primary action) of $MEET is instantiated. It is also an MTRANS, and the two MTRANSs are matched against each other. Following is an instantiation of the MAINCON of A1:

```
((ACTOR *VANCE* < = > (*MTRANS*)
               MOBJECT (*CONCEPTS* CONCERNING *SALT*)
               TO *GROMYKO*)
 TIME G1058
 PLACE *GENEVA*)
```

Matching this to Q2, CYRUS can now resolve the references in Q2. The actor is understood to be *VANCE* and the TO slot is filled by *GROMYKO*. Q2 can be understood as "Did Vance talk to Gromyko about SALT?" CYRUS' resolution of the references is illustrated below:

```
resolving references...
The question is:
((ACTOR *VANCE* < = > (*MTRANS*)
               MOBJECT (*CONCEPTS* CONCERNING *SALT*)
               TO *GROMYKO*)
 MODE (*?*) TIME G0906)
```

FIG. 9.8. Reference resolved.

The emphasis in designing CYRUS was on its memory organization and search. As a result, its other components are not as well developed. CYRUS' reference resolution procedure works for the sets of questions that have been given to CYRUS, but a general solution to reference handling awaits further research.

3.4. To Search or Not to Search?

In previous chapters, CYRUS' strategies for extensive search of memory have been described. Memory search, however, does not always need to be extensive. When a question references the answer to a previous question, it can be answered by searching the episodic context of the previous answer instead of searching all of memory. In the dialog above, A1 should be used to attempt to answer Q2 before searching memory for another episode.

The reference resolution process in CYRUS is instrumental in deciding whether the episodic context of a previous answer should be searched or whether memory should be searched extensively. If a question's references are all to components of the last answer, then the episodic context of that event should be searched to answer the question. Thus, in the example above, A1 is chosen for search because all of the references made in Q2 were to components of A1.

```
answering question using previous context:
 directly


The answer is:
((< = > ($MEET ACTOR *VANCE* OTHERS *GROMYKO* TOPIC *SALT*))
 TIME G0943 PLACE *GENEVA* DURATION G0946)
Modality YES


yes, for 5 hours.
```

FIG. 9.9.

Reference resolution processes are also used to aid in choosing a context for search in CYRUS, as illustrated by this last question. Although Q2 does not specify a context for search, context instantiation strategies did not have to be applied to infer an E-MOP. Rather, a context for search can be inferred directly from the previous answer during the reference resolution process because its MAINCON matches the question concept. Thus, CYRUS infers that the "talking" (MTRANS) referred to in the question is a reference to a "diplomatic meeting" without applying context instantiation strategies.

3.5. Search of Episodic Context

Once reference is used to decide that a question should be answered using the previous context, that episode must be searched for the target event. CYRUS uses the algorithm in Fig. 9.10 to search that context.

In answering Q2, the first test in this procedure is satisfied, and the question is answered using the meeting context from the previous question. Consider, for example, the following continuation of the dialog:

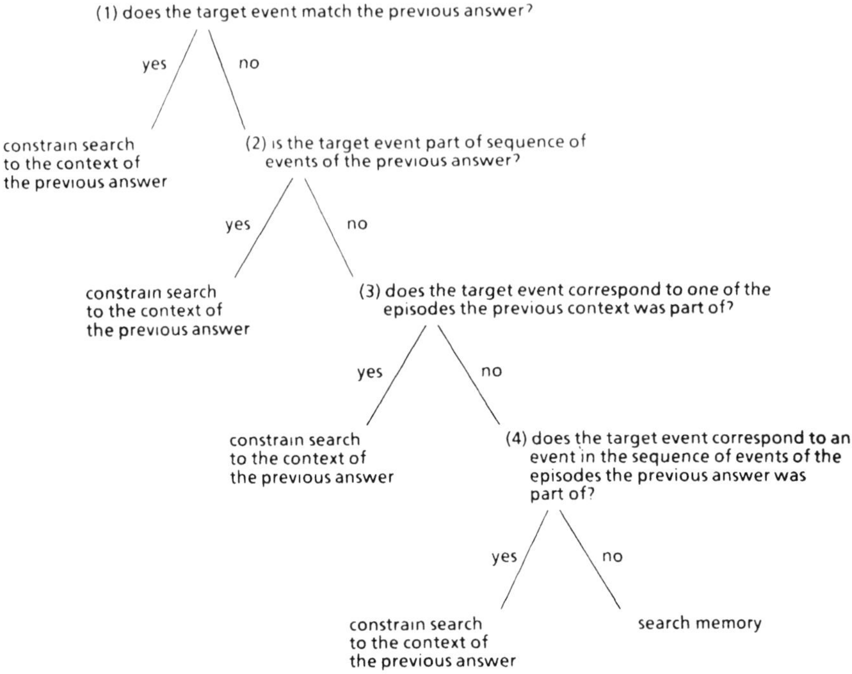

FIG. 9.10. Episodic context search in CYRUS

Q2: Did he talk to him about SALT?

A2: Yes, for 5 hours.

Q3: When did he leave Geneva?

In answering Q3, the first test fails. The second one is applied. Because $MEET (the previous answer's E-MOP) is a script, however, its sequence of events is not appropriate for search, and CYRUS applies the third test to check whether Vance's leaving Geneva is a larger event the meeting was part of. That test also fails, and it applies the last test, checking to see if "leaving Geneva" is part of the sequence of events that the meeting from A2 was part of. This test is successful, and CYRUS answers the question.

>When did he leave Geneva?

```
parsing...
((ACTOR (*PP* PPCLASS (#PERSON) GENDER (*MASC*) REF (DEF))
        < = > (*PTRANS)
        FROM *GENEVA*
 TIME (*?*))
resolving references...
The question is:
((ACTOR *VANCE* < = > (*PTRANS*) FROM *GENEVA*) TIME (*?*))
```

```
The question type is "time"
The question concept is.
((ACTOR *VANCE* < = > (*PTRANS*) FROM *GENEVA*))

answering question using previous context
 directly
 using top-level events

The answer is:
((< = > ($FLY ACTOR *VANCE* ORIGIN *GENEVA* DESTINATION *WASH-DC*))
 TIME G1021)
```

on December 24.

3.6. Using Time as a Context for Retrieval

CYRUS also uses the above process to answer questions with embedded time specifications. It first searches for the embedded time specification, treats the event it finds as the context for retrieval, and applies the algorithm above to find the target. Consider, for example, the following question:

>Last time Vance was in Saudi Arabia, did he go sightseeing?

```
parsing...
((< = > (sM-SIGHTSEE ACTOR *VANCE*))
 MODE (*?*)
 TIME (#TIME EVENT ((ACTOR *VANCE* IS (*LOC* VAL *SAUDI-A*))
                    TIME (#TIME TENSE (PAST))
        NUMBER (-1)
        TENSE (PAST)))
```

This question is composed of a time specification, "last time you were in Saudi Arabia," and a target event—sightseeing. The representation the parser produces for this question embeds the time specification in the time slot of the target sightseeing event. The event representation in the time slot is the representation for "Vance was in Saudi Arabia." The NUMBER slot of the TIME representation specifies that it is the last time that event happened that is of interest.

CYRUS answers this question by first finding Vance's last trip to Saudi Arabia, and then applying the algorithm above to its context to find a sightseeing event.

```
resolving references...
The question is:
((< = > (sM-SIGHTSEE ACTOR *VANCE*)) MODE (*?*) TIME G0699)

The question type is "verification"
The question concept is:
((< = > (sM-SIGHTSEE ACTOR *VANCE*)))

   inferring a diplomatic trip
```

```
answering question using time context
 directly

The answer is:
((< = > (sM-SIGHTSEE ACTOR *VANCE* SIGHT LOC23))
 PLACE *DHARAN* TIME G0748)
Modality YES
```

yes, at an oilfield in Dharan.

3.7. Formulating an Answer

After retrieving a target event from memory, additional processing must often be done to formulate an answer. Consider, for example, the following question:

(Q4): Why did Vance meet with Gromyko yesterday?

In answering this question, it is necessary to first retrieve the target event ''Vance's meeting with Gromyko yesterday,'' and then to figure out why it took place.

The processing after retrieving a target event from memory depends on the conceptual question category the original question fit into. The conceptual categories CYRUS uses are listed below. They are based on those proposed by Lehnert (1978).

1. Identification
2. Feature specification
3. Enablement
4. Instrumental / Procedural
5. Concept completion
6. Time
7. Place
8. Verification
9. Duration
10. Motivational
11. Result orientation

FIG. 9.11. CYRUS' question categories.

To answer an enablement question, for example, the enablement conditions are extracted from the events retrieved from memory. If there are no specific enablement conditions found, the instantiation strategy ''Instantiate-Enablements'' is used to infer the enabling conditions. CYRUS does that to answer the following question:

>How did Vance become Secretary of State?

```
The question is:
((CON (*?*) ENABLE
    ((ACTOR *VANCE* IS (OCCUPATION VAL (RT-SEC-OF-STATE))))))
The question type is "enablement"
The question concept is:
((ACTOR *VANCE* IS (OCCUPATION VAL (RT-SEC-OF-STATE))))

    applying Instantiate-Enablements to RT-SEC-OF-STATE
```

```
The answer is:
((ACTOR *VANCE* IS (OCCUPATION VAL (RT-SEC-OF-STATE))))
Enablements:
((< = > ($APPOINT ACTOR *CARTER* APPOINTEE *VANCE*)))
```

He was appointed by President Carter.

In general, those questions that ask about content frame properties can be answered by applying associated context instantiation rules if actual answers are not available. "Result orientation" questions can be answered by applying "Instantiate-Results," and motivational questions can be answered by applying "Instantiate-Reasons."

Questions that ask about role fillers or slots of an episode can be answered by extracting the appropriate role filler from the retrieved events, or by using component instantiation strategies to infer what its value would plausibly have been. "Time," "place," "duration," and "concept completion" questions are the question types that require extraction of slot-filler information. When CYRUS answers the question "Where is Vance today?" a "place" question, it uses a component instantiation strategy to infer that Vance's location must be his place of residence if it does not know of a trip he is on today.

After formulating an answer to a question, an English-language generator called PHLUENT (McGuire, 1980) generates an answer in English. The generator, written by Rod McGuire, transforms conceptual dependency representations of events into English. The generator was designed so that when the same event is used to answer more than one question, information given previously is not repeated in the later answer unless it is necessary to form a coherent sentence.

4. MEMORY UPDATE IN CYRUS

CYRUS takes as input conceptual representations of episodes. Thus, stories must be analyzed and a conceptual representation built before sending them to CYRUS. CYRUS has two modes of receiving representations of stories. In one mode, the stories are analyzed and their representations are coded by a human reader. The representations encoded by the human reader are automatically integrated into CYRUS' memory by CYRUS.

In its second input mode, CYRUS is hooked up to FRUMP (DeJong, 1979a, 1979b), a computer program that reads and summarizes news stories from the UPI wire. The complete FRUMP-CYRUS hookup is called CyFr. FRUMP and CYRUS were run together each morning for approximately 6 months picking up stories about Vance and Muskie that came in over the UPI wire. After analyzing a story, FRUMP sent its conceptual representation to CYRECV, a program that interfaces between FRUMP and CYRUS.

CYRECV was built to convert FRUMP's representations into representations CYRUS can deal with and to fill in contextual details. If, for example, FRUMP reports that Vance attended a meeting with Begin in Israel, then CYRECV will infer that Vance was on a diplomatic trip to Israel, that there were negotiations going on involving Israel and the United States, and that those negotiations were the goal of Vance's trip. CYRECV then sends its filled-out event representations to CYRUS, which integrates them into memory as described in chapters 7 and 8. CYRUS can then answer questions about the new data. CyFr has processed approximately 50 stories about Vance and approximately 30 more about Muskie.

4.1. The FRUMP-CYRUS Interface

In order to hook FRUMP and CYRUS together, there were a number of augmentations that had to go into both programs. FRUMP uses a knowledge structure called a *sketchy script* to hold the knowledge it needs to understand stories. While FRUMP originally had a sketchy script for meetings and diplomatic trips, it had no scripts corresponding to any of the other activities a secretary of state does. Thus, the knowledge necessary for reading stories about press conferences, speeches, summit conferences, state dinners, welcomes, and so forth, had to be added. In addition, because information about Vance and Muskie was usually buried deep within stories about other topics, and because FRUMP was designed only to skim stories, FRUMP's story processing had to be augmented to allow it to read stories in more detail than it had previously been doing.

Before FRUMP and CYRUS were hooked up, CYRUS had been accepting hand-coded input. There were additional problems that had not been encountered in that mode that had to be taken care of when CYRUS began using FRUMP's summaries. The hand-coded representations for events that CYRUS had been receiving had two characteristics that the FRUMP-coded stories did not have. First, they always specified the E-MOPs an event was an instance of. If a story stated that "Vance and Gromyko talked yesterday," the story was coded as "a diplomatic meeting between Vance and Gromyko." FRUMP, however, does not make inferences such as that. FRUMP's representations are of low-level events and use conceptual dependency primitives rather than specifying scripts or E-MOPs.

The second difference between the people-coded and FRUMP-coded representations of stories was that FRUMP does not make all the inferences about related events that people make while reading stories. When a person reads that "Vance and Gromyko met yesterday in Moscow to discuss SALT," he infers that Vance was on a diplomatic trip to Russia and that this meeting was part of the SALT negotiations. FRUMP does not make those inferences.

A program had to be written to make these two types of inferences. FRUMP's conceptual dependency representations had to be turned into references to E-MOPs, and other related episodes had to be inferred. Although it is CYRECV, the program that interfaces CYRUS and FRUMP, that makes these inferences, it uses the same knowledge that CYRUS uses to construct contexts for search. Thus, CYRECV includes both types of context instantiation rules: those that construct contexts from components, and those that construct related contexts.

Another problem taken care of in the FRUMP-CYRUS interface was identification of new persons and places mentioned in news stories that CYRUS did not already know about. When CYRECV encounters a person or place that CYRUS does not already know, it queries FRUMP requesting its knowledge about that entity and creates a set of new structures, which are added to CYRUS' memory. It is a set of structures that are created, rather than just one, since a description of a person or a place may refer to another entity unknown by CYRUS, and that entity will also have to be described to CYRUS' memory. CYRECV also sets up parser definitions for new persons and places it encounters. Thus, the parser's lexicon is extended along with CYRUS' memory.

The following is an example of CyFr's operation.

```
@FRUMP

FILE (JUN069.J1) SKIMMED AT 8:52 AM ON 6-13-1980

INPUT: a085 r i ss czc ryr wyd
   Pm-vance 6-1------------By Anthony Luke---madrid, spain
(upi)-secretary of State Cyrus Vance arrived today for talks with Spanish leaders
aimed at keeping this strategic Mediterranean nation in the Western defense orbit.
   Vance flew to Madrid from the Netherlands where he reported on the Salt ii
agreement to a meeting of foreign ministers of the North Atlantic Treaty
Organization. Foreign Minister Marcelino Oreja Aguirre left a cabinet meeting to
greet Vance at Barajas airport where the secretary of state's plane landed at
12:30 p.m. (6:30 a.m. Edt), a half hour behind schedule.
   Vance greeted Oreja warmly. After a brief welcoming ceremony he left with his
wife in a 14-car motorcade for the U.s. embassy. ...
     ----Upi 6-1 10 000 aed----***

SELECTED SKETCHY SCRIPT $MEET

REQUESTS.
 RQ154
  SATISFIED = T
     ((ACTOR (*VANCE*) < = > (*PTRANS*) OBJECT (*VANCE*)
                          TO (*MADRID*)
      TIME (*TODAY*) TENSE (*PAST*) GOAL &GOAL1)
  GOAL1
     ((ACTOR (*VANCE*) < = > (*MTRANS*) TO GROUP1)
      MANNER (*BILATERAL*) MEET-TYPE (*TALKS*))
 RQ155
  SATISFIED = T
     ((ACTOR (*VANCE*) < = > (*PTRANS*) OBJECT (*VANCE*)
                          TO (*MADRID*) FROM (*NETHERLANDS*))
      INST (*PLANE*) TENSE (*PAST*))
 RQ158
  SATISFIED = T
     ((ACTOR (*OREJA*) < = > (*MTRANS*)
                          MOBJECT (*CONCEPT* TYPE (*GREETING*))
                          TO (*VANCE*))
       LOC (*MADRID*) TENSE (*PAST*))

CPU TIME FOR UNDERSTANDING = 91472 MILLISECONDS

**Generating ENGLISH:
   Vance went to Madrid today to talk with Spanish leaders. Vance went on a plane
from the Netherlands to Madrid. Foreign Minister Marcelino Oreja Aguirre
welcomed Vance in Madrid.

Sending to CYRUS (DUMPS: (JUN069.C1))
```

FRUMP's representations of these events are conceptual dependency representations and do not specify the E-MOPs they fall into. Thus, the first thing CYRECV does is to infer the E-MOPs these events would be part of. CYRUS knows that a *PTRANS* on a plane is a $FLY and constructs that context. FRUMP's MEET-TYPE in the MTRANS representation above specifies the context for the MTRANS. FRUMP's "*TALKS*" corresponds to CYRUS' $MEET script. An MTRANS of a concept of type "*GREETING*" is recognized by CYRUS as a $WELCOME. CYRECV constructs those contexts also, as below:

```
@CYRECV

reading in file ((CYRUS UPDATES) (JUN069.C1)) from FRUMP
converting file to CYRUS format
inferring scenes from primitive acts
    inferring fly from *PTRANS*
    constructing $WELCOME from *MTRANS*
    constructing $MEET from *MTRANS*
```

CYRECV goes on to infer that if Vance flew from the Netherlands to Madrid, then he must have been on diplomatic trips to both places. It constructs representations for both of those diplomatic trip episodes and puts the flight into their sequence of events. It also infers that Vance's talks with Spanish leaders must have been part of negotiations of some sort, that they must have been part of the diplomatic trip to Madrid, and that the welcome must have also been part of the trip.

```
inferring higher level episodes from scenes
  inferring sM-VIPVISIT from $FLY
    adding $FLY to its sequence of events
  inferring sM-VIPVISIT from $FLY
    adding $FLY to its sequence of events
  inferring I-NEGOTIATE from $MEET
  adding $WELCOME to the sequence of events of sM-VIPVISIT
  adding $MEET to the sequence of events of sM-VIPVISIT
Conversion complete.
Sending file ((CYRUS UPDATES) (JUN069.F1)) to CYRUS
```

The following event representations are what CYRECV constructed for the story above. Representations constructed by CYRECV are sent to CYRUS for integration into memory.

```
CY84:  ((< = > (sM-VIPVISIT ACTOR *VANCE* DESTINATION *HOLLAND*))
        TIME TIM100129)
   sequence of events:  (CY79)
CY82:  ((< = > (sM-VIPVISIT ACTOR *VANCE* DESTINATION POLN13
                          ORIGIN *HOLLAND* GOAL CY78))
        TIME TIM100127)
   sequence of events:  (CY79 CY81 CY78)
CY91:  ((< = > (I-NEGOTIATE ACTOR *VANCE* OTHERS GROUPN45))
        TIME TIM100126)
CY78:  ((< = > ($MEET ACTOR *VANCE* OTHER GROUPN45))
        TIME TIM10026)
   contained in:  (CY82 CY91)
```

```
CY79: ((< = > ($FLY ACTOR *VANCE* DESTINATION POLN13 ORIGIN *HOLLAND*))
        TIME TIM100122)
   contained in: (CY84 CY82)
CY81: ((< = > ($WELCOME ACTOR HUMN26 GUEST *VANCE*))
        PLACE POLN13 TIME TIM100120)
   contained in: (CY82)
```

Some of the entities referred to in the representation were previously unknown by CYRUS, and "tokens" describing them were created by CYRECV. POLN13, for example, refers to Madrid. Its definition refers to POLN3, Spain, a structure that had been defined for CYRUS in a previous story. Similarly, GROUPN45 is defined for CYRUS as a group of Spanish officials, i.e., diplomats with nationality Spanish.

The following is a story CyFr has processed about Muskie.

```
@FRUMP

FILE (JUN030.M06) SKIMMED AT 4:1AM ON 6-13-1980

INPUT: 6-3
   Washington (Upi)-The State Department announced that Secretary of State
Edmund Muskie will travel to Asia this month to attend a meeting of the Asean
nations.
   The announcement said that Muskie, who will attend a Nato Council meeting in
Ankara June 24-25 will then fly to Kuala Lumpur, Malaysia, to meet with other
foreign ministers of the alliance of non-communist Southeast Asian nations.
   Muskie is beginning the trip by accompanying President Carter to Italy and
Yugoslavia for state visits and to Venice for the annual economic summit meeting of
major Western nations.
   Muskie is scheduled to return to Washington on June 29.

SELECTED SKETCHY SCRIPT $MEET

REQUESTS:
RQ215
  SATISFIED = T
    ((ACTOR (*CARTER*) < = > (*PTRANS*) OBJECT (*CARTER*)
                             TO (*ITALY* *YUGOSLAVIA*)
                             FROM (*USA*))
     GOAL GOAL1)
  GOAL1 ((ACTOR (*CARTER*) < = > (*MTRANS*))
          MEET-TYPE (*TALKS*))

RQ217
  SATISFIED = T
    ((ACTOR (*MUSKIE*) < = > (*PTRANS*) OBJECT (*MUSKIE*)
                             TO (*ASIA*) FROM (*USA*))
     TIME (*JUNE*) TENSE (*FUTURE*) GOAL GOAL2
  GOAL2 ((ACTOR (*MUSKIE*) < = > (*MTRANS*) TO (*ASEAN*))
          MANNER (*BILATERAL*) MEET-TYPE (*TALKS*))
***BUNDLES: |CYRUS
REQUESTS:
RQ325
  SATISFIED = T
    ((ACTOR (*MUSKIE*) < = > (*MTRANS*) TO (*NATO*))
     MANNER (*BILATERAL*) MEET-TYPE (*TALKS*) TIME (*JUNE*)
     LOC (*ANKARA*) TENSE (*FUTURE*))
CPU TIME FOR UNDERSTANDING = 63776 MILLISECONDS
**Generating...
```

```
ENGLISH:
   Carter begins going from the United States to Italy and Yugoslavia to talk.
Secretary of State Edmund Muskie will go from the United States to Asia this month
to have talks with ASEAN. Muskie will have talks with NATO in Ankara in June.

Sending to CYRUS (DUMPS: (JUN030.M06))
***************

@CYRECV

reading in file ((CYRUS UPDATES) (JUN030.E06)) from FRUMP
converting file to CYRUS format
inferring scenes from primitive acts
  inferring travel from *PTRANS*
  inferring travel from *PTRANS*
  constructing $MEET from *MTRANS*
  constructing $MEET from *MTRANS*

inferring higher level episodes from scenes
  inferring I-NEGOTIATE from $MEET
    adding $MEET to its sequence of events
  inferring sM-VIPVISIT from sM-TRAVEL
    adding sM-TRAVEL to its sequence of events
  inferring sM-VIPVISIT from sM-TRAVEL
    adding sM-TRAVEL to its sequence of events
  inferring sM-VIPVISIT from $MEET
    adding $MEET to its sequence of events
Conversion complete.
Sending file ((CYRUS UPDATES) (JUN030.E06)) to CYRUS
```

4.2. Integrating New Events From FRUMP Into Memory

In CYRUS' normal mode of operation, it integrates new events into its memory as described in chapters 7 and 8, with one variation. CYRUS does not index in newly created sub-MOPs until the E-MOP contains six events. There are two reasons for this. First, it keeps memory from growing too fast. Second, it seems to take that many events before an E-MOP's generalized information stabilizes. Waiting until that time to index events in the E-MOP means that better generalizations can be made the first time, thereby minimizing the problems of ''bad'' generalizations discussed in chapter 8.

Some additional updating problems had to be taken care of in integrating stories processed by FRUMP into memory. CYRUS did not have the capability of recognizing whether an event was already in memory. Before FRUMP and CYRUS were hooked together, all of CYRUS' inputs had been hand-processed. Because of that, the same event was never presented to CYRUS more than once. Had that occurred, CYRUS would have stored the event as two (or more) separate events. In automatically processed stories, however, events are often repeated. Thus, there is a need to recognize whether or not an event is already in memory.

This problem is not a simple one. A description of an event from a news story might have additional or different information from an event already in memory, but still refer to the same event. As a result, application of the traversal procedure to the new event is not sufficient for identifying the two as the same event. Consider, for example, the following two descriptions of the same event:

EV1: Vance went to Russia last week.

EV2: Vance went to Russia last week to negotiate SALT.

Because the second event has more information than the first, it cannot be used as a target event to retrieve EV1. Thus, if EV1 were already in memory and EV2 were presented later, EV2 would be added as a separate event. What CYRUS does to get around that problem is to query memory with the smallest amount of information that will describe an event.

In the case of events that take place over a long period of time, that includes the actor, the time period, and those of its features that are marked as identifying features. Since its place identifies a trip, CYRUS would search memory using the specification "Vance went to Russia last week" to see if EV2 were already in memory. If EV1 had previously been added to memory, CYRUS would find it and merge the information in the two events.

For events that normally take place over a small period of time (a few hours or less), CYRUS uses the entire given specification to search memory. This method is not foolproof. If the following two descriptions were of the same event, CYRUS would not recognize that fact and would add each one to memory separately.

EV3: Vance met with Gromyko in Moscow yesterday.

EV4: Vance attended a meeting about SALT yesterday.

5. A VANCE EXAMPLE

Upon receiving representations of events to be added to memory, CYRUS checks to see if an event is already in memory and if not, it integrates the event into memory. The following output is CYRUS' integration into memory of the Vance story presented in section 4.2. FRUMP's summary of that story is repeated below.

Vance went to Madrid today to talk with Spanish leaders. Vance went on a plane from the Netherlands to Madrid. Foreigh Minister Marcelino Oreja Aguirre welcomed Vance in Madrid.

FIG. 9.12.

When CYRUS adds this episode to its memory, it adds each of the individual events to the E-MOPs it belongs in. Thus, it adds two trips—one to Madrid and one to the Netherlands, a diplomatic meeting, a welcome, a flight, and a negotiations episode. It first checks to see if any of the events are already in memory. If so, it updates the information it has about those events.

```
Are you interested in Muskie or Vance? (M or V): *VANCE

*(PROCESS-FILES)

reading in file (JUN069.F1)
updating memory with new events

searching memory for CY84 -- sM-VIPVISIT ... not found
searching memory for CY79 -- $FLY ... not found
searching memory for CY82 -- sM-VIPVISIT ... not found
searching memory for CY81 -- $WELCOME ... not found
searching memory for CY78 --$MEET ... not found
searching memory for CY91 -- I-NEGOTIATE ... not found
```

In this case, CYRUS did not have previous knowledge about any of the events in this story. It goes on to add each event to memory.

```
Adding item ((< = > (I-NEGOTIATE ACTOR *VANCE* OTHERS GROUPN45))
            TIME TIM100126
    creating index for (PARTICIPANTS NATIONALITY) = POLN3
                                   in I-NEGOTIATE
    creating index for PARTICIPANTS = GROUPN45
                                   in I-NEGOTIATE
13022 msec CPU (1714 msec GC), 20000 msec clock, 25593 conses
NODES = 2226 ALISTS = 576
```

The first event added to memory was the negotiating episode that had previously been inferred. CYRUS creates indices for the participants—a group of Spanish leaders (GROUPN45), and for the nationality of the participants—Spanish (POLN3). Because it had no other events with either of those features, this negotiating episode is now uniquely specified in memory in two ways. CYRUS goes on to add the next event.

```
Adding item ((< = > ($MEET ACTOR *VANCE* OTHERS GROUPN45))
             TIME TIM100126)
  it is part of (sM-VIPVISIT I-NEGOTIATE) episodes
    creating index for
        (PARTICIPANTS NATIONALITY) = POLN3 in $MEET
    creating index for PARTICIPANTS = GROUPN45 in $MEET
    creating index for PLACES = POLN3 in $MEET
    creating index for PLACES = POLN13 in $MEET
11616 msec CPU (1895 msec GC), 33000 msec clock, 54688 conses
NODES = 2231 ALISTS = 576
```

In adding the meeting with Spanish leaders to memory, CYRUS indexes it in the "diplomatic meetings" MOP ($MEET) according to the nationality of its participants, the participants themselves, the country it took place in, and the city. Again, none of these features correspond to features of other events in memory, so the meeting is indexed uniquely by each of these indices.

```
Adding time ((< = > ($WELCOME ACTOR HUMN26 GUEST *VANCE*))
               PLACE POLN13 TIME TIM100120)
  it is part of (sM-VIPVISIT) episodes
Reminded of ((< = > ($WELCOME ACTOR *DAYAN* GUEST *VANCE*))
              PLACE LOC20 TIME TIM403)
  because in both Vance does $WELCOME with
       (TIME SEASON) = SUMMER
     creating new MOP
       no additional similarities to generalize on
     creating index for ACTOR = HUMN26 in $WELCOME
     creating index for PLACES = POLN3 in $WELCOME
     creating index for PLACES = POLN13 in $WELCOME
844 msec CPU (0 msec GC), 1000 msec clock, 2494 conses
NODES = 2234 ALISTS = 576
```

When CYRUS adds the "welcome" to its memory, it is reminded of a previous welcoming ceremony that also happened in the summer. This reminding happens because the feature "time is summer" already indexes another event. CYRUS thus creates a new E-MOP indexed by that feature and attempts to make generalizations about "welcoming ceremonies that take place during the summer." In fact, it can find no domain-relevant similarities between them. If, after other summer welcoming ceremonies are added to memory. it can find no similarities between them, it will mark "time is summer" as a non-predictive index, and it will no longer index welcomes by that feature. The other indices CYRUS creates for this welcoming ceremony correspond to the person who did the welcoming—Oreja (HUMN26)—and its location.

```
Adding item ((< = > (sM-VIPVISIT ACTOR *VANCE* DESTINATION POLN13
                                  ORIGIN *HOLLAND*))
               TIME TIM100127 )
  it is part of (I-NEGOTIATE) episodes
  its seq of events includes ($FLY $WELCOME $MEET)
   Putting this event into MOP with specifications
     Vance does sM-VIPVISIT with (TIME SEASON) = SUMMER
     assuming that
       GOALS = I-NEGOTIATE
   creating index for ORIGIN = *HOLLAND* in sM-VIPVISIT
   creating index for PLACES = POLN3 in sM-VIPVISIT
   creating index for PLACES = POLN13 in sM-VIPVISIT
   Putting this event into MOP with specifications
    Vance does sM-VIPVISIT with PLACES = *EUROPE*
     assuming that
       (EVENTS MOP) = $REPORT
      GOALS = I-NEGOTIATE
   creating index for
         (EVENTS PARTICIPANTS) = GROUPN45 in sM-VIPVISIT
11825 msec CPU (2012 msec GC), 50000 msec clock, 47891 conses
NODES = 2240 ALISTS = 576
```

CYRUS next adds the trip to Madrid (POLN13) to its memory. The first feature it chooses for indexing is the time—summer. In this case, CYRUS already has an E-MOP for "diplomatic trips in the summer," and it adds the trip to that E-MOP. Apparently, that E-MOP holds the generalized information that "diplomatic trips in the summer have the goal of negotiations." It thus infers that this trip was also for that purpose. CYRUS then goes on to index this trip as a "trip from the Netherlands," a "trip to Spain," a "trip to Madrid," a "trip to Europe," and a "trip whose events had Spanish leaders as participants." In indexing the trip as a "trip to Europe," CYRUS finds that it already has an E-MOP for "trips to Europe," and it adds this event to that E-MOP. It makes the generalization that the trip was for the purpose of negotiations, and that it included a press conference ($REPORT), since those are features it has generalized about "trips to Europe." The other indexed features caused no reminding, nor did they retrieve E-MOPs. Those features, then, uniquely index this trip. The flight to Madrid is added to memory similarly.

```
Adding item ((< = > ($FLY ACTOR *VANCE* DESTINATION POLN13
                                         ORIGIN *HOLLAND*))
             TIME TIM100122)
  it is part of (sM-VIPVISIT sM-VIPVISIT) episodes
    creating index for (TIME SEASON) = SUMMER in $FLY
    creating index for ORIGIN = *HOLLAND* in $FLY
    creating index for (ORIGIN PLACE) = *EUROPE* in $FLY
    creating index for PLACES = POLN3 in $FLY
    creating index for PLACES = POLN13 in $FLY
1709 msec CPU (0 msec GC), 5000 msec clock, 6634 conses
NODES = 2245 ALISTS = 576
```

In adding the last event from this story to memory (the trip to the Netherlands [*HOLLAND*]), the size of its E-MOP "trips to Europe" reaches its critical size (6). CYRUS thus refines the generalizations it has for that E-MOP and begins indexing its events.

```
Adding item ((< = > (sM-VIPVISIT ACTOR *VANCE* DESTINATION *HOLLAND*))
             TIME TIM100129)
  its seq of events includes ($WELCOME $FLY)
  Putting this event into MOP with specifications
      Vance does sM-VIPVISIT with (TIME SEASON) = SUMMER
     assuming that
      GOALS = I-NEGOTIATE
  Putting this event into MOP with specifications
      Vance does sM-VIPVISIT with PLACES = *EUROPE*
     assuming that
      (EVENTS MOP) = $REPORT
      GOALS = I-NEGOTIATE
     no additional similarities to generalize on
     removing generalizations
         (EVENTS MOP) = $REPORT
     from MOP Vance does sM-VIPVISIT with PLACES = *EUROPE*
  creating index for (TIME SEASON) = SUMMER in
      MOP Vance does sM-VIPVISIT with PLACES = *EUROPE*
  creating index for PLACES = *HOLLAND* in
      MOP Vance does sM-VIPVISIT with PLACES = *EUROPE*
14948 msec CPU (2059 msec GC), 29000 msec clock, 34836 conses
NODES = 2283 ALISTS = 584

updating complete
```

The first index CYRUS chooses is an index for time—summer. It adds this event to the E-MOP "diplomatic trips in the summer" similarly to the way it added the trip to Madrid to that E-MOP. It then adds this trip to its E-MOP "trips to Europe." As in adding the trip to Spain, it makes the generalizations that the trip to the Netherlands included a press conference and had the goals of negotiations.

Now that it has a reasonable number of trips to Europe indexed, it refines the generalizations it has made about "trips to Europe" and also starts indexing within that E-MOP. It can make no additional generalizations beyond the ones it already has. After examining the generalizations it does have, it decides that the fact that there was a press conference during the trip was a bad generalization. It thus deletes that from its generalizations and builds an index for it. It indexes this trip in the "diplomatic trips to Europe" MOP as a "trip in the summer" and as a "trip to the Netherlands."

After integrating these events into memory, CYRUS answers the following questions. Note that CYRUS' parser can parse questions asked of it in the second person or third person. When the Vance data base is being queried, the word "you" is equivalent to "Vance." In the questions below, Vance is referred to as "you."

*(DIALOG2)

Enter next question

>WERE YOU IN EUROPE LAST YEAR?

The question is:
((ACTOR *VANCE* IS (*LOC* VAL *EUROPE*)) TIME G0717 MODE (*?*))

searching memory for question concept
  searching directly for input -- $M-VIPVISIT
   found (CY82)

yes, most recently in Madrid.

Enter next question

>WERE YOU WELCOMED THERE?

The question is:
((< = > ($WELCOME GUEST *VANCE*) MODE (*?*)
 TIME G1831 PLACE POLN3)

answering question using previous context:
 directly

yes, by Foreign Minister Marcelino Oreja Aguirre.

Enter next question

```
>WHO DID YOU TALK TO THERE?

The question is:
((ACTOR *VANCE* < = > (*MTRANS*) TO (*?*))
 TIME G1519 PLACE POLN3)

    inferring undifferentiated political meeting

answering question using previous context:
 directly

  a group of Spanish officials.

Enter next question

>DID YOU ALSO GO TO HOLLAND?

The question is:
((ACTOR *VANCE* < = > (*PTRANS*) OBJECT *VANCE* TO *HOLLAND*)
 TIME G1607 MODE (*?*))

answering question using previous context:
 directly
 using top-level events
 using co-occuring events
 current context not applicable
 searching memory for question concept
    searching directly for sM-VIPVISIT
      found (CY84)

  yes.
```

6. A MUSKIE EXAMPLE

The entire Muskie data base was built up from stories processed by FRUMP. The events that were added to the Vance data base in the example above were added to a detailed data base that already had a lot of events in it. The Muskie data base, on the other hand, has many fewer events in it, and those that it has are more sparse. Because of the sparseness of the data, CYRUS often cannot make any generalizations when it is reminded.

The following is the output when the Muskie story from section 4.2 is added to the Muskie data base. Recall that FRUMP produced the following summary:

> Carter begins going from the United States to Italy and Yugoslavia to talk. Secretary of State Edmund Muskie will go from the United States to Asia this month to have talks with ASEAN. Muskie will have talks with NATO in Ankara in June.

The indices CYRUS creates as the new events are added have not been output in this run. However, all of the reminding and subsequent generalization that CYRUS does in adding this episode are illustrated.

```
Are you interested in Muskie or Vance? (M or V) : *MUSKIE

*(PROCESS-FILES)

reading in file (JUN030.F06)
updating memory with new events

searching memory for CY77 -- sM-VIPVISIT ... not found
searching memory for CY71 -- sM-TRAVEL ... not found
searching memory for CY73 --$MEET ... not found
searching memory for CY70 -- sM-TRAVEL ... not found
searching memory for CY76 -- sM-VIPVISIT ... not found
searching memory for CY74 -- I-NEGOTIATE ... not found

Adding item ((< = > (I-NEGOTIATE ACTOR *MUSKIE* OTHERS *NATO*))
              PLACE POLN12 TIME TIM100115)
   its seq of events includes ($MEET)
181 msec CPU (0 msec GC), 0 msec clock, 662 conses
NODES = 108 ALISTS = 48

Adding item
    ((< = > (sM-VIPVISIT ACTOR *MUSKIE* DESTINATION LOCN6
                   ORIGIN *USA* GOAL
                   ((< = > ($MEET ACTOR *MUSKIE* OTHERS ORGN9))
                    TIME TIM100114)))
      TIME TIM100117)
 to memory
   its seq of events includes (sM-TRAVEL sM-TRAVEL $MEET)
Reminded of
    ((< = > (sM-VIPVISIT ACTOR *MUSKIE* DESTINATION *EUROPE*
                   ORIGIN *WASH-DC* GOAL
                   ((< = > ($MEET ACTOR *MUSKIE* OTHERS *GROMYKO*))
                    TIME TIM10028)))
      TIME TIM1003)
because in both Muskie does sM-VIPVISIT with
    GOALS = ($MEET)
   creating new MOP
   no additional similarities to generalize on
Reminded of
    ((< = > (sM-VIPVISIT ACTOR *MUSKIE* DESTINATION *EUROPE*
                   ORIGIN *WASH-DC* GOAL
                   ((< = > ($MEET ACTOR *MUSKIE* OTHERS *GROMYKO*))
                    TIME TIM10028)))
      TIME TIM1003)
because in both Muskie does sM-VIPVISIT with
    ORIGIN = *USA*
    creating new MOP
generalizing that when Muskie does sM-VIPVISIT with
    ORIGIN = *USA*
often
    GOALS = ($MEET)
1150 msec CPU (0 msec GC), 2000 msec clock, 3675 conses
NODES = 109 ALISTS = 48

Adding item ((< = > (sM-TRAVEL ACTOR *MUSKIE* DESTINATION LOCN6
                          ORIGIN *USA*)) TIME TIM100102)
   it is part of (sM-VIPVISIT) episodes
Reminded of ((< = > (sM-TRAVEL ACTOR *MUSKIE* DESTINATION *EUROPE*
                          ORIGIN *USA*)) TIME TIM1002)
```

```
      because in both Muskie does sM-TRAVEL with
      ORIGIN = *USA*
    creating new MOP
      no additional similarities to generalize on
712 msec CPU (0 msec GC), 1000 msec clock, 2482 conses
NODES = 110  ALISTS = 48

Adding item ((< = > ($MEET ACTOR *MUSKIE* OTHERS *NATO*))
               TIME TIM100110 PLACE POLN12)
   it is part of (I-NEGOTIATE sM-VIPVISIT) episodes
217 msec CPU (0 msec GC), 0 msec clock, 810 conses
NODES = 113  ALISTS = 48

Adding item ((< = > (sM-VIPVISIT ACTOR *MUSKIE* DESTINATION POLN12))
               TIME TIM100118)
   its seq of events includes (sM-TRAVEL $MEET sM-TRAVEL)
   it co-occurs with (sM-VIPVISIT I-NEGOTIATE)
132 msec CPU (0 msec GC), 1000 msec clock, 521 conses
NODES = 115  ALISTS = 48

updating complete
```

After adding this episode to memory, CYRUS answers the following questions about it and a previous story. As in the Vance examples above, the data base is queried in the second person. When the Muskie data base is being queried, CYRUS knows that the word "you" refers to "Muskie."

```
*(DIALOG2)

Enter next question
```

>Have you been to Europe recently?

```
The question is:
((ACTOR *MUSKIE* IS (*LOC* VAL *EUROPE*)) TIME G0668 MODE (*?*))
searching memory for question concept
    searching directly for sM-VIPVISIT
      found (CY2)
```

yes, most recently last month.

```
Enter next question
```

>Why did you go there?

```
The question is:
((CON (*?*) REASON
   ((ACTOR *MUSKIE* < = > (*PTRANS*) OBJECT *MUSKIE* TO *EUROPE*)
   TIME G0790)))
answering question using previous context:
   directly
```

to talk to Andrei Gromyko.

```
Enter next question
```

>Who did you talk to there?

The question is:
((ACTOR *MUSKIE* < = > (*MTRANS*) TO (*?*))
TIME G0896 PLACE *EUROPE*)

inferring undifferentiated political meeting

answering question using previous context
directly

to NATO in Brussels on MAY 14 1980 and to Andrei Gromyko in Vienna.

Enter next question

>Are you going to Asia?

The question is:
((ACTOR *MUSKIE* < = > (*PTRANS*) OBJECT *MUSKIE* TO LOCN6)
MODE (*?*))

searching memory for question concept
searching directly for sM-VIPVISIT
found (CY76)

yes, this month.

Enter next question

>Who will you talk to?

The question is:
((ACTOR *MUSKIE* < = > (*MTRANS*) TO (*?*)) TIME G1136)

inferring undifferentiated political meeting

answering question using previous context:
directly

with NATO in Ankara, Turkey.

7. DIFFERENCES BETWEEN THE VANCE AND MUSKIE MEMORIES

Although the Vance and the Muskie memories started out the same, after adding events to the two data bases, their organizations were quite different. The two E-MOPs in Figs. 9.13 and 9.14, for example, are the Vance and Muskie "diplomatic meetings" MOPs, each with 10 meetings.

Each of these E-MOPs shows all of the indices in "diplomatic meetings" ($MEET), except those for actual participants and location.

There are four differences between these two E-MOPs, representative of the differences between other E-MOPs in the two memories:

1. The indices are different.
2. The types of indices are different. The Vance E-MOP has topic indices and larger episode indices, while the Muskie E-MOP has neither of those.

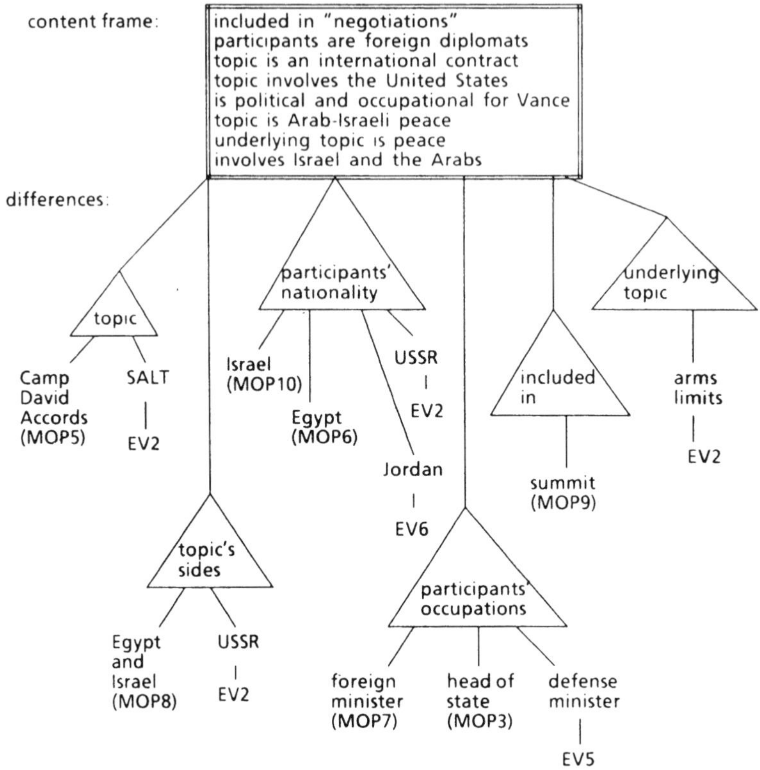

FIG. 9.13. Vance's diplomatic meetings E-MOP—$MEET.

3. The content frames of the two E-MOPs are different (i.e., different generalizations have been made).
4. The Vance E-MOP indexes mostly sub-MOPs, and the Muskie E-MOP indexes mostly individual events.

Three factors contribute to these differences. First, the experiences the two men have had are different. This is the reason for the differences between the indices in the two E-MOPs. The events entered into the Vance memory included meetings with Egyptians, while those entered into the Muskie data base did not. Thus, the E-MOP from the Vance data base has indices for "participants are Egyptian," while the Muskie E-MOP does not. On the other hand, Muskie met with Thai representatives, and Vance did not. Thus, there is an index corresponding to "participants are Thai" in the Muskie E-MOP but not in the Vance one.

Second, the events entered into the Vance data base contain much more detail than those entered into the Muskie memory. The Vance data base holds mostly hand-coded stories, while the Muskie memory has FRUMP-coded stories. Be-

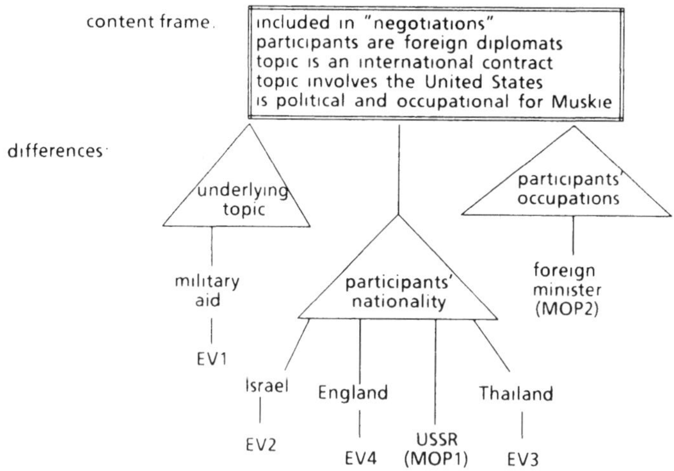

FIG. 9.14. Muskie's diplomatic meetings E-MOP—$MEET.

cause the topics of meetings are so unconstrained, FRUMP has difficulty picking up meeting topics. Thus, while a typical Vance meeting has a detailed topic specification, Muskie's meetings do not. A typical meeting description entered into the Vance data base would be "a meeting with Begin about the Camp David Accords in Jerusalem," while a typical meeting Muskie had with Begin would be entered as a "diplomatic meeting with Begin in Jerusalem." This factor accounts for the differences in the types of indices in the two E-MOPs. Because the Muskie memory is not usually aware of the topics of Muskie's meetings, it cannot index them by aspects of their topics.

The third, and most important, factor that accounts for differences between the two E-MOPs is the degree of similarity between the events entered into the E-MOPs. The first ten events added to the Vance E-MOP were very similar to each other. Eight of them were meetings about the Camp David Accords. On the other hand, except for three meetings with Gromyko, the meetings entered into the Muskie data base had very different participants and locations.

This factor accounts for differences (3) and (4). The Vance "diplomatic meetings" MOP has a more filled-out content frame because the meetings entered into it had so many similarities. The Vance E-MOP indexes more sub-MOPs than individual events for the same reason. The Muskie E-MOP indexes mostly individual events and not sub-MOPs because most of its events were dissimilar. The more similarities between events in an E-MOP. the more filled-out the MOP's generalized information can be. In addition, the more similar events in an E-MOP are, the more sub-MOPs will be indexed in the MOP rather than individual events. The extent of new category creation, then, is a function of the degree of similarity between the items added to an E-MOP, and not the number of items it organizes.

7.1. CYRUS' Generalizations

There is a fifth difference between the two memories, which does not show in the illustrations above. That difference is in the generalizations made by the two memories. When new categories are created, generalizations are abstracted from the similarities between events. Thus, each sub-MOP represents a set of generalizations. The extent of generalization in memory is dependent on the similarities between the items in memory.

Consider first, the Muskie "diplomatic meetings" MOP illustrated above. Its sub-MOPs include "meetings with Russians" and "meetings with foreign ministers." Its "meetings with Russians" MOP has three events indexed in it and has the following content frame.

content frame:	participants are Russian participant is a foreign minister participants include Gromyko

FIG. 9.15. Muskie's meetings with Russians E-MOP.

One can read off the generalizations an E-MOP organizes as "when ⟨E-MOP descriptions⟩ then ⟨other content frame features⟩." Thus, this E-MOP organizes the following generalization:

> When meetings are with Russians, they are with foreign ministers and they include Gromyko.

Another sub-MOP that the Muskie "diplomatic meetings" MOP indexes is "meetings with foreign ministers." That E-MOP organizes three meetings with Gromyko and a meeting with the foreign minister of Israel, Itzhak Shamir. The meetings with Gromyko have similarities, but the only similarities between them and the meeting with Shamir are the meeting format. CYRUS thus does not have any generalizations associated with "meetings with foreign ministers," but is waiting until it has six meetings before it decides what they have in common. The generalizations it is considering are those in the content frame of "meetings with Russians" (i.e., the similarities between the majority of its meetings). After an additional two meetings are added to that E-MOP, CYRUS either will find similarities between them and fill in its content frame, or it will find no similarities and mark "participant is a foreign minister" as a non-predictive feature of "diplomatic meetings" and will no longer index it.

The Vance "diplomatic meetings" MOP has many more sub-MOPs and thus many more generalizations. After ten meetings were added to that E-MOP, only one of them had been with a Russian. Thus, it did not have a sub-MOP for "meetings with Russians." After additional meetings with Gromyko were added to its memory, however, it did create that E-MOP. The following figure illustrates the Vance memory's "meetings with Russians."

content frame:	participants are Russian participant is a foreign minister participants include Gromyko topic is SALT topic is arms limitations topic involves Russia location is Moscow

FIG. 9.16. Vance's 'meetings with Russians' E-MOP.

Contrast this E-MOP to the Muskie "meetings with Russians" MOP in Fig. 9.15. This E-MOP includes the generalized information that was included in the Muskie E-MOP and in addition holds generalized information about the topics of these meetings and their locations. Thus, in addition to the generalization listed above, the Vance "meetings with Russians" MOP organizes the following two generalizations:

Meetings with Russians are about SALT.

Meetings with Russians are in Moscow.

The reason CYRUS can make the first generalization in the Vance data base and not in the Muskie one is that the events entered into the Vance memory have topic information. The generalizations that can be made depend on the amount of information available. As a result of the sparseness of its event descriptions, the Muskie data base has many fewer indices for each event and also makes fewer generalizations.

The reason CYRUS makes the second generalization in the Vance data base and not in the Muskie data base is because Vance's meetings with Russians happened in Russia, whereas Muskie's did not have location in common. Generalizations in the two data bases correspond to the differing similarities between the two men's experiences.

The following generalizations (paraphrased in English) are representative of those CYRUS has made about Vance's activities.

1. Meetings in the Middle East are about Arab-Israeli peace.

2. When Vance meets in the Middle East with Egyptians, he also meets with Israelis, and the topic is the Camp David Accords.

3. When Vance meets with Begin, the topic is the Camp David Accords.

4. When Vance goes to a conference concerning Egyptian concerns, the topic of the conference is the Camp David Accords.

5. When Vance negotiates with Egyptians, the topic is the Camp David Accords.

6. Trips to Russia are for the purpose of negotiating SALT.

7. When Vance attends a conference with Gromyko, the topic is SALT.

8. When Vance takes a trip to negotiate Arab-Israeli peace, the trip is to the Middle East.

Notice that while the first two generalizations both refer to "meetings in the Middle East," the topics they predict are different. This is because the first generalization is a generalization about "meetings in the Middle East" in general. It is associated with that E-MOP. The second is a generalization associated with "meetings in the Middle East with Egyptians," a sub-MOP of "meetings in the Middle East" and "meetings with Egyptians." In fact, "the Camp David Accords" is a specialization of "Arab-Israeli peace," and the two do not conflict.

8. SUMMARY

CYRUS searches and updates its memory as described in previous chapters. In addition, CYRUS' question-answering loop includes processes for parsing questions, resolving their pronominal references, extracting their target concepts, and after searching memory, formulating answers. CYRUS updates its memory when it receives a story summary. CYRUS can process story summaries coded by hand or by FRUMP (DeJong, 1979a, 1979b). FRUMP-coded stories generally contain less detail than hand-coded stories and must be pre-processed by CYRECV. CYRUS' Vance and Muskie data bases differ in level of detail and relative similarities between the events in the two data bases. Because the events in the Vance data base are more similar to each other, CYRUS has made more interesting generalizations concerning Vance's activities than it has made about Muskie's activities.

10 Discussion, Perspective, Conclusions

1. INTRODUCTION

This book has presented a theory of organization and processing in long-term event memory. The theory of reconstructive memory has been presented as a model of (1) conceptual memory, (2) long-term memory for events, (3) question answering, (4) data base organization for large amounts of interrelated facts, and (5) intelligent fact retrieval. As a model of event memory in people, CYRUS raises interesting issues in psychology. As a conceptual memory, it suggests what the memories in intelligent systems will have to look like. As a natural-language fact retrieval system, it has implications for information retrieval and data base management. Each of the areas of memory organization, retrieval from memory, and memory update addressed in this report has been studied individually in the past by researchers in computer science and psychology. This work is novel in addressing problems in each of these areas simultaneously. In this chapter, CYRUS' importance and relationship to the fields of psychology, artificial intelligence, and computer science are discussed, and conclusions that can be drawn from the research are presented. Related work in each field is also examined.

2. HOW CYRUS FITS IN WITH OTHER RESEARCH

Because CYRUS addresses so many areas, there is a vast amount of work related to it. In this section, the most closely related research in psychology, artificial intelligence, and computer science are presented.

2.1. Retrieval from Very Long-term Memory

This research is certainly not the first research to claim that human long-term memory is reconstructive. Psychologists as far back as Bartlett (1932) have described memory as reconstructive. Psychologists, however, have presented very little in the way of an overall theory of long-term memory for episodes.

A number of recent experimental results illustrate the reconstructive nature of human memory. In asking people to name persons in their high-school classes, Williams (1978) found that his subjects recalled features of a person's name, such as its first letter, the number of syllables, and what it rhymed with, and used that information to come up with the name. When he asked people to recall whether a karate expert in a particular story had broken a block, Spiro (1979) found that they used their knowledge about karate experts in general to answer the question, rather than retrieving actual story details. In both of these cases, only partial information was retrieved from memory, and using generalized knowledge, "actual" items were reconstructed.

The recent work of Norman and Bobrow (1979) and Bobrow & Norman (1975) addresses some of the problems addressed in this research. They have proposed a theory of memory "descriptions" and constructive processes that operate on those descriptions. Their theory of reconstructive memory states that in order to find something in memory, its description must first be constructed. They have described reconstruction as a process comprised of (1) specification of a retrieval description, (2) search for that description, (3) evaluation of the memory record retrieved, and (4) failure diagnosis of that evaluation resulting in a new retrieval specification.

Although the reconstructive process they have described is similar in nature to that described in this report and used by CYRUS, Norman and Bobrow have chosen to ignore the problem of memory organization, and thus have not addressed the problem of what kinds of information are included in "descriptions" and how they might be organized with respect to each other in memory. Nor do they address the problem of how any particular specified description is found. Rather, their concern is with very general processes that describe a retrieval mechanism independent of any particular organization.

Williams' (1978) work has drawn on the Norman and Bobrow theory of descriptions and is closest to that presented here. Williams (1978) has described the reconstructive process as a three-step retrieval process: find a context, search, verify. Each of those steps, he explains, is a reconstructive process with the same three steps. Williams has gone on to describe some of the strategies people use in constructing the "descriptions" (Bobrow & Norman, 1975; Norman & Bobrow, 1979) that are necessary for remembering people they have known.

Although Williams identified some of the strategies people used for that task, his emphasis was not on identifying strategies for retrieval or explaining a memory organization. Like Norman and Bobrow, his interest was in identifying and explaining very general memory phenomena independent of a specified underlying memory organization. As a result, he has uncovered many of the general reasoning processes people use in remembering and has explained some of the retrieval failures people have, but his explanations are on a very general level and do not explain how particular pieces of knowledge can guide reconstructive processing. He observes that contexts for search are chosen, for example, but does not describe how memory can guide that search.

In many ways, the work presented in this book is complementary to the work of Norman and Bobrow, and of Williams. While they have proposed general mechanisms for retrieval without worrying about underlying memory organization, we propose a memory organization that supports reconstructive processing, and well-specified processes for retrieval that depend on that underlying organization of information and knowledge in memory.

A theory in psychology that explains very low-level memory mechanisms is the "spreading activation" (Anderson, 1976, Anderson & Bower, 1973) theory, or theory of "associative memory." According to this theory, memory is seen as a network of nodes, or associations. When a description of something or a series of features are entered into memory, nodes representing those features are excited. This excitation is transferred to neighboring nodes, but not completely. In the simple model, excitation is additive. When paths of activation converge, their intersections will be more excited than the rest of memory. When the excitation of a node reaches a threshold, that node's contents emerge into conscious thought. This model has been used to describe many memory phenomena (e.g., Anderson, 1976; Anderson & Bower, 1973; Quillian, 1968).

Although this model seems to explain memory's organization, it does not attempt to explain what the nodes, links, or associations in the network look like. It is not a model of memory organization, then, but rather a model of very low-level memory processing. This theory, like that of Norman and Bobrow, is complementary to that presented here. It is an attempt to explain low-level traversal from node to node in memory. This book has presented a theory of the content of the nodes, their connections, and higher level processes guiding communication between the nodes.

Another effort CYRUS is reminiscent of is EPAM (Feigenbaum, 1963), an early AI endeavor that modeled human reconstructive memory phenomena observed in verbal learning experiments. EPAM's discrimination nets provided an organization, encoding strategy, and retrieval process for paired associate and serial list learning of nonsense syllables. CYRUS and EPAM have many similarities. Both place new items in their networks based on discriminating features and remember items by traversing their networks. Both reorganize their networks based on new inputs. Both explain forgetting and interference in terms of particular encoding and retrieval processes. There are a number of important differences between EPAM and CYRUS, however.

First we address memory organization and encoding. EPAM built a discrimination net in the course of its learning, and thus the structures it produced had all of the problems associated with discrimination nets (Barsalou & Bower, 1984).

Their arcs hold negative features rather than positive ones. As a result, there is no place to store generalized information. E-MOPs, on the other hand, store positive rather than negative information on their arcs, allowing them to be used for storing both instances and generalized information. In addition, only one discrimination is made at each level of EPAM's network, while in CYRUS multiple discriminations are made at each level.

There are a number of consequences for retrieval arising from this organization. In discrimination nets, search is set by the order in which items were initially added to memory. Thus, search is guided by the structure of the network rather than the structure of the target item. Questions with no bearing on a new input will be asked of it to decide where to place it in the network. Similarly, questions asked of a retrieval key may have no relevance to the key itself. An E-MOP's structure, on the other hand, allows retrieval and update to be directed by the target event or new item itself. Second, EPAM provides only one path to each item and only one entry point into its network. Because multiple discriminations are made at each level in CYRUS, there are multiple paths to each item in memory, allowing it to be retrieved through many different combinations of cues. CYRUS' E-MOPs provide multiple entry points into memory by providing multiple memory structures. CYRUS' context instantiation strategies provide ways of choosing entry points into memory during retrieval. CYRUS also provides context-driven strategies for elaborating and transforming given item descriptions, and for guiding search to parts of memory plausibly related to a target item when its traversal procedure fails.

Finally, it should be pointed out that the items CYRUS stores (events) are significantly more complex and detailed than those EPAM worked with (nonsense syllables). CYRUS and people have a great deal more contextual information available to use in remembering events than in remembering nonsense syllables. The use and organization of that knowledge was an important part of deriving CYRUS' structure and processes. While EPAM's organization and processes provide an explanation of people's behavior in verbal learning experiments, we have found that discrimination nets are not sufficient for describing the more complex phenomena we observe in examining retrieval of episodes from very long-term memory.

A fourth theory of long-term memory, developed concurrently with this one, and complementary to it, is Schank's (1980) theory of Memory Organization Packets (MOPs). Schank's MOPs are an attempt to explain how personal experiential memories can be organized in memory. He proposes that MOPs organize experiences according to their differences and also organize similarities between the events. This work has extended that theory by explaining processes for index selection, memory organization maintenance, and retrieval. The major differences between Schank's MOPs and the E-MOPs presented here are differences in emphasis. He was interested in explaining the interconnectedness of memory structures, while this work has been more concerned with storage and retrieval of individual episodes.

In his most recent work, Schank (1982) goes beyond the organizational framework presented previously, looking at the organization of episodes with respect to the goals they are derived from and their relationships to steps in achieving those goals. As part of that larger framework, CYRUS explains in detail one way events are organized in episodic memory and gives a set of procedures for traversing that part of the memory organization. Though CYRUS does not specify in detail how to search more goal-related structures, the memory principles and processes presented here should carry over to those structures. Indexing by differences remains the best way to index. New memory structures still need to be created based on similarities between events in memory. Retrieval strategies to choose contexts for search, to elaborate given event descriptions, and to direct search in alternate structures are still necessary to search memory. The knowledge those strategies and procedures use, however, becomes more diverse in considering goal-based structures, possibly creating the need for more control. Additional strategies particular to goal-based knowledge will also need to be derived.

2.2. Organization of Conceptual Memory

Unlike psychological research, which for the most part has not focused on memory organization, previous research in AI has addressed problems of organizing concepts in memory. The emphasis in previous AI research on conceptual memory, however, has been with conceptual structures used for understanding, and not with structures used for long-term storage of events. Thus, there has been no previous work done in AI on the organization of events in a long-term memory. The emphasis in natural-language research has been on text understanding and isolating the conceptual structures necessary for the understanding process, but not on storing the contexts of those texts for later retrieval or use in understanding. This research, on the other hand, has been concerned with how to organize the information extracted from texts in a long-term memory, and how to retrieve it from that organization. The model of long-term memory that has been presented is the logical next step in explaining what conceptual memory looks like and follows naturally from previous AI work on conceptual memory.

Previous text understanding systems have focused on the use of knowledge structures in understanding and controlling inference. SAM (Cullingford, 1978) and FRUMP (DeJong, 1979a, 1979b), for example, used scripts as knowledge structures that held the information necessary for understanding script-based stories. Charniak's (1977) frames hold the conceptual information necessary for understanding stories about painting. PAM (Wilensky, 1978) used goals and plan boxes as knowledge structures that held the information necessary for understanding stories about goals. The BORIS system (Dyer, 1983, Dyer & Lehnert, 1980) uses MOPs and TOPs to hold the generalized information needed to understand more complicated stories.

There are two important differences between those systems and CYRUS. The first difference is one of emphasis. Each of those endeavors isolated a particular type of knowledge necessary for understanding, represented that information in conceptual structures, and used that knowledge in understanding, but none of these programs remembered stories they had read after processing them. CYRUS, on the other hand, is designed to store facts extracted from news stories in long-term memory so that they can later be retrieved.

Another important difference between those systems and CYRUS, which follows from the first, is in the different ways conceptual structures are used. Understanding systems use conceptual structures as knowledge structures for organizing generalized information. By contrast, E-MOPs not only organize generalized information, but also act as conceptual categories to organize what has been processed.

There is an important implication of this dual functionality. Because E-MOPs organize both the generalized information used for processing and items that are processed, both are equally accessible upon retrieval of a particular E-MOP. In addition, as new items are added to memory, new generalized knowledge is acquired. This integrated memory organization suggests the possibility of an understanding system fully integrated with long-term memory. Because generalized and episodic knowledge are equally accessible, both can be used during the understanding process.

IPP (Lebowitz, 1980), which has been developed concurrently with CYRUS, is an integrated understanding system. It uses MOPs to hold generalized information about international terrorism and also to organize terrorism episodes it has read about. As it reads stories, it adds them to memory, creating new sub-MOPs and building up generalized information similarly to the way CYRUS does. It uses the generalized information it builds up to make inferences while understanding subsequent stories. For example, after IPP has read a number of stories about kidnapping in Italy in which businessmen are kidnapped and held for ransom, it makes the generalization that "when there is a kidnapping in Italy, the victim is usually a businessman." Upon reading a later story about a kidnapping in Italy, if the victim's occupation is not mentioned, IPP will use that knowledge to make the inference that the victim was probably a businessman. In previous understanding systems that did not remember what they had read and that did not update their generalized information, an inference such as the one above could not have been made.

Although the memory organization and generalization processes in IPP and CYRUS are similar, IPP's emphasis has been on using its generalized knowledge in later understanding, while CYRUS' has been on retrieval and reconstruction of episodes from memory.

2.3. Retrieval from Conceptual Memory

Because previous AI research into conceptual memory has centered on story understanding, approaches within AI to retrieval from conceptual memory have emphasized search of story representations or retrieval from specified conceptual structures, and not search of a large memory. These approaches have centered on question answering, as opposed to memory search. A context for search, in those systems, is always immediately available, and questions are answered by using that context. Thus, the problem of searching memory initially for a relevant context has, for the most part, not been addressed. What has been addressed is the problem of how to interpret what kind of information a question is asking for, and what kinds of processing have to be done to extract that information from a known context. Some of the people who have addressed these QA problems have been Lehnert (1978), Scragg (1975), and Woods et al. (1972).

Lehnert (1978) has defined 15 conceptual categories for questions. Each question category requires different processing for extraction of a good answer. "Causal antecedent" questions, for example, usually ask "why" and require backwards chaining through causal links in the appropriate event to find an answer. Thus, to answer "Why did the plane crash?" after a representation of a story has been formulated, the backwards causal connections from the event "the plane crashed" in the story representation would be searched. "Concept completion" questions, on the other hand, require only that a component (or slot filler) of the concept being asked about be retrieved from the memory representation of the appropriate event. Thus, to answer "Where did the plane crash," the same plane-crash event as above would be found in the story representation, and its place would be extracted from it.

Another problem addressed by Lehnert was the problem of inferential analysis of questions and giving the appropriate amount of information in an answer. When somebody asks a yes/no question, for example, they normally want more than just a yes or a no. They are looking for additional explanation of the answer. Thus, a more appropriate answer than "no" to "Is Edmund Muskie a senator?" would be "No, he is out of public office since Reagan became president." A more appropriate answer than "yes" to "Was Muskie secretary of state?" would be "Yes, under Carter after Vance resigned." By the same token, when somebody asks "Do you have the time?" they are not asking for a yes or no answer at all, but want to know what time it is. Lehnert's question answerer was implemented to answer questions about stories processed by the SAM program (Cullingford, 1978), which processed script-based stories (Schank & Abelson, 1977), and was later extended to answer questions about plan-based stories processed by PAM (Wilensky, 1978).

More recently, Dyer (Dyer, 1983; Dyer & Lehnert, 1980) has been working on retrieval of information from more complicated stories than were dealt with in SAM and PAM. He has defined sets of access functions for accessing available memory representations and story components, and has presented strategies for reconstructing parts of detailed narratives. His emphasis has been on detailed story representations and has not included looking into the problem of storing these representations in long-term memory and retrieving them from among other similar contexts in memory. Although he is dealing with retrieval as a memory search problem, he is dealing with search of a given context rather than search for appropriate contexts in long-term memory. A combination of the processes he defined with those described here may yield results interesting to both endeavors.

Some other question-answering work which relates to that presented here is Collins' (1978) plausible reasoning research. He has defined 30 types of plausibility inferences people make in answering questions. Many of those inference types have been implemented in the SCHOLAR system (Carbonell & Collins, 1973). Collins, however, has not tried to integrate his inference types into a full process model of retrieval. He has not defined strategies for controlling the inferences, nor has he defined a memory organization or memory search processes that support them. Some of the inferences he defines fit into the reconstructive model in obvious places. His "lack of knowledge" inference, for example, is used by the traversal/elaboration process to decide that a particular fact is not in memory. Other default reasoning rules he defines fit into the reconstructive model as instantiation rules.

2.4. Organizing Large Amounts of Knowledge in a Computer Memory

Within computer science, the fields of information retrieval and data base management have been concerned with organizing large amounts of information in the computer memory. In this section, approaches within computer science to memory organization and retrieval are presented.

2.4.1. Conceptual Memory and Information Retrieval

Although CYRUS has been presented as a model for an intelligent information retrieval system, it bears little resemblance to current information retrieval systems. Most research in information retrieval (IR) has been aimed toward document retrieval. Only recently have researchers in information retrieval begun to be interested in direct access to data (e.g., legal texts, [Larson & Williams, 1980] other tabular and textual values [O'Connor, 1980; Wangar & Landau, 1980], also [Oddy, Robertson, van Rigsbergen, & Williams, 1981; Salton, 1981]). Because the emphasis has been on systems that could be used immediately, the techniques that have been developed for information retrieval have been schemes that could be applied independently of the particular domain that documents in the system belonged to.

Nearly all systems are key-word based, with all the advantages and disadvantages of key words. Key-word schemes are easy to implement in a hurry, and seemingly simple for people to use. However, they have a number of problems. First, in organizing categories by key words, a diverse set of unrelated abstracts are often stored in the same category. A "memory" category might hold articles about different kinds of hardware memory, data base memory, memory in information retrieval systems, and memory in artificial intelligence systems, to name just a few. The only thing these articles would have in common is the word "memory," in their titles or abstracts.

As a result of this, a person inexperienced in querying one of these systems will specify search keys that are either too general or too specific. A search key that is too general will retrieve many documents unrelated to what is actually sought. When that happens, the user must wade through all of the unnecessary documents to find the relevant ones. A search key that is too specific will fail to retrieve relevant documents. As a result of this problem, such systems can really only be queried efficiently by somebody with intimate knowledge about their contents, key-word schemes, synonyms, and other idiosyncrasies—usually a technician specially trained for that purpose.

Other problems arise in classifying documents in the system. Traditionally, indexing terms have been assigned manually. More recently, automatic means of choosing indexing terms have been attempted (e.g., Cooper, 1978; Harter, 1978; Maron, 1979; Salton, Yang & Yu, 1974) with some success.

Another problem inherent in storage and retrieval systems is that of relating a request to the documents in the system. A number of strategies have been developed for taking user requests which are either too broad or too narrow and transforming them into usable retrieval keys. Some of these strategies include thesauri, phrase formation (Salton, 1975), term weighting, clustering, and feedback (see Williams, 1979, for more background).

While all of these improvements and augmentations serve to make systems more usable, almost all have a lexical and statistical basis—few consider the conceptual content (i.e., meaning) of documents or of questions being asked. Though some allow natural-language description of a retrieval request (e.g., Doszkocs & Rapp, 1979), the subtleties and ambiguities inherent in the natural language of documents and questions are not taken into account.

Of course, some of the problems in storing large amounts of information are the same, whether key-word schemes or conceptual categories are used. In particular, a major problem that has been addressed both here and in information retrieval has been the problem of how to retrieve items without enumerating large categories. Indexing methods should be general enough to provide good recall, but specific enough so that not too many irrelevant items are retrieved (Borko & Bernier, 1978; Salton, 1975).

Techniques for non-enumeration in IR involve both category reorganization techniques during update and elaboration during retrieval. In IR systems, categories are divided by applying statistical methods to the key words in the stored documents (Heaps, 1978). The groups of key words that divide a category into usefully sized pieces are used. When a category is divided, each document is stored in only one of the new categories (Heaps, 1978). Elaboration in IR systems involves use of synonym lists, word truncation, universal symbols, and associated indices—all key-word schemes (Salton, 1975).

Our approach to good recall and specificity has involved both organizational and retrieval strategies. Organizational strategies are used during memory update to index and sub-divide memory categories. In CYRUS, indices are based on salient features of a conceptual category, rather than on lexical items, and are knowledge based. The goal of good recall (i.e., accessibility) is provided by defining salient features for a category and indexing on those features. The goal of specificity, or not retrieving irrelevant items, is provided by the elaboration processes, which use knowledge about conceptual categories and knowledge-based correspondences of components to infer relevant indices and search for alternate contexts.

2.4.2. Data Base Management

Research in data base management has had two major aims: producing tools for storage and retrieval of tabular types of information; and developing mathematical models to prove that those systems are complete, sufficient, and secure. The relational model (Codd, 1979) lends itself to storage of tabular information and is the model most often used for those sorts of proofs.

One of the primary principles of data base management has been the decoupling of data base semantics from the content of a data base (Wiederhold, 1977). Semantics, in data base systems, refers to the meanings of the data base's relations, and their relationships to each other. Thus, a data base model, such as the relational model, provides a formalism for storage and manipulation of tabular information without having to specify exactly what the relations should be for any domain. The reason data base semantics and content have been decoupled is to ensure that the same data base manipulations could be performed regardless of the data base content.

Decoupling data base semantics from the data, however, makes it hard to query the data base about the kinds of data it holds. It also makes it hard to automatically reorganize the data on command. It became clear with the call for better interfaces to data bases that this separation was more of a detriment than an advantage. People designing natural language front ends for those data bases had to develop their own semantic models of the data base contents (Hemphill & Rhyne, 1978).

One data base researcher who has been interested in extending the semantics of the relational data base model so that it can be used for intelligent fact retrieval is Codd (1979). He has been attempting to define an extension to the relational model that is capable of capturing more of the meaning of data in the data base while preserving the independence of the implementation. In other words, he is interested in designing a system capable of more sophisticated storage and retrieval than has previously been the case with the relational model, which will be applicable independent of the domain of information being stored.

In his extensions to relational data base model, Codd (1979) has proposed hierarchical relationships between memory categories and time relationships between events in a data base. Thus, he has begun to address the problem of episodic organization in a relational data base. Codd, however, does not go far enough in his data base extensions. Events, for example, can be related through causality and containment; his addition addresses only their time relationships. The additions Codd proposes to the relational algebra in order to support hierarchical organizations of categories support only strict hierarchies, and do not support specification of the relationship between the parent and child categories. Thus, a category can be specified as a generalization of another category without specifying which feature(s) of the child category it is generalized from. It also does not address the fact that some categories in a hierarchy might not inherit all properties from their parent categories. Although a category ''meetings'' might specify that the location of meetings is conference rooms, its subcategory ''meetings with members of secret organizations'' might specify that their locations are usually forests.

He does not address the problem of associating generalized information with categories directly in the data base, and he mentions as a problem but does not address the issue of automatic data base reorganization.

3. CONCLUSIONS

This book has presented a theory of reconstructive memory processing. The organization of such a memory, strategies for maintaining its organization, and strategies for retrieval have been presented. The memory organization described is one where items are arranged in memory in conceptual categories, and differentiated within those categories according to their differences. Retrieval is a process of construction and elaboration of contexts for search. In this section, conclusions are presented.

3.1. Forgetting

Perhaps the most important observation to make about the reconstructive retrieval process described is that it is fallible. There is always the chance that the right memory will not be remembered. This is true for two reasons. First, the traversal algorithm requires that indices be specified before they are traversed. Thus an item cannot be retrieved unless a suitable discriminating feature can be generated for it. Strategies geared toward specifying plausible features cannot be used to generate deviant features. Thus, items whose features are different, but related to the norms, will be easier to find than those whose features deviate excessively. The best example of this comes from examining one of CYRUS' mistakes. During memory update, CYRUS had incorrectly generalized that ''diplomatic meetings are about Arab-Israeli peace.'' That generalization (in the content frame of ''diplomatic meetings'') had the following effect on retrieval:

When asked to enumerate the diplomatic meetings Vance had attended, it used its knowledge about the topics of diplomatic meetings as a constraint on the elaboration it was doing. Thus, it searched for the meetings with features that would have been plausible if the topic were "Arab-Israeli peace," but didn't recall other meetings (e.g., meetings about SALT). Its retrieval strategies were working correctly at that point. The knowledge in memory which constrained their application to only relevant features also kept CYRUS from remembering items with deviant features (in this case, an alternate topic). Memory's constraints, then, can cause forgetting.

In addition, the information available in a retrieval specification constrains retrieval. Strategies are dependent on the information or cues available at the time of retrieval. This includes cues available from previous context and those present in a question. In choosing a context for search, for example, the proper context can only be chosen if some aspect of the retrieval specification refers to that context. If a person were answering "who is the most famous person you've ever met?" for example, we would not be surprised if he failed to remember meeting a famous person in a museum, since there is no obvious cue to initiate retrieval of museum experiences. On the other hand, if the person were prompted with "how about in a museum?" or if previous conversation had concerned museum experiences, there would be a better chance of his retrieving that experience.

The same problem appears in alternate context search. If, during processing, an executive strategy that would yield an answer is neglected, episodes that would have been found by that strategy might not be found. In addition, alternate context search allows retrieval of only standard types of related episodes. CYRUS is fallible in this regard in trying to recall ceremonies. Because a ceremony commemorating the opening of air-traffic routes by flying between the two airports is not a standard type of ceremony, alternate context search is not sufficient for CYRUS to recall that ceremony.

Forgetting can also happen because a question incorrectly specifies the details of an event to be retrieved. In that case, it may be impossible to get to the correct parts of memory. More interesting, a memory may be recalled but then rejected because its details don't match that of the incorrectly specified retrieval key. For example, a question could ask about an event that happened in the spring, when in fact the event happened in the summer, or it could ask for a meeting in Jerusalem that actually took place in Tel Aviv. As people, sometimes such problems cause forgetting, but we are often able to recognize and point out another person's mistaken presuppositions and retrieve what was "really" requested. Our model is overly sensitive to incorrectly specified cues, and this is one area that still needs to be worked out.

3.2. Directed Retrieval

Why, if there is a possibility of forgetting, is reconstructive retrieval advantageous? The major advantage of reconstructive retrieval is that it is a way of directing search only to relevant places in memory. Component-to-context instantiation strategies, for example, constrain search only to relevant memory categories—in CYRUS' case, relevant E-MOPs. The traversal/elaboration process, along with the indexing scheme, restricts search within memory categories or E-MOPs. If an E-MOP had hundreds or thousands of indices organizing tens of thousands of events, only those directly related to the targeted event would be traversed. Extra effort is put forth in directing search so that the search itself is highly constrained.

3.3. Non-Enumeration / Maintaining Accessibility

There are other conclusions to be drawn from this research, the most important of which is the following:

> **A few powerful strategies for search, combined with rich conceptual indexing, allow retrieval without category enumeration.**

Two types of retrieval strategies have been presented: instantiation strategies, which construct and elaborate contexts for search, and executive strategies, which guide search for and within alternate contexts. In addition, strategy application depends on three types of knowledge being present in memory:

1. context-to-context relationships
2. component-to-component relationships
3. relationships between types of components and contexts for search

In order to retrieve events from a category, memory's organization must provide *discriminability* between events. In a memory with that organization, specification of a unique set of features will allow an item to be retrieved. Thus, although retrieval does not involve category enumeration, a series of similar events can be found in a directed way, by reconstructing possible details, and searching for events with those details or by searching for an alternate context that might refer to a target event.

The potential problem in a richly indexed system is that indexing takes up space and can get out of hand. In CYRUS, that problem was handled by the notions of *salience, predictability,* and *generalization.* Indices are created only for salient features of a context. After a number of events with the same feature are indexed, that feature is maintained as an index only if it proves to have *predictive power.* As events are indexed in sub-MOPs, relevant similarities between the events in those sub-MOPs are computed and stored on each sub-MOP as generalized information about the E-MOP. Features common to events in an E-MOP are not indexed.

In order to maintain retrievability as memory grows, new memory categories must be created, and generalized knowledge must be associated with them.

Because new categories are created when multiple events are indexed in the same way, the same generalization process that controls index creation also constrains the creation of new categories. Generalized knowledge is built up by extracting the salient similarities between items in a subcategory. Newly created generalized knowledge aids the retrieval process and constrains subsequent indexing within the subcategory.

3.4. Organizing and Retrieving Generalized Information

Another feature of this retrieval algorithm and memory organization is that generalized information is organized and retrieved in exactly the same way as individual items. Generalized knowledge is integrated into memory by associating it with the items it is generalized from. When a category is encountered during memory traversal, its indices and its generalized information are equally available. Additional search outside a data base for ''meta-level'' information is not necessary to retrieve the generalized information needed for further processing. It is available at the same level as the indices to the items themselves. In addition, associating generalized knowledge with items it is built up from allows it to be refined and updated as new examples are entered into memory. This organization of generalized knowledge has an important processing implication:

> **Associating generalized information with the items it is generalized from makes retrieval of generalized information the same as retrieval of actual items.**

In the model described, memory categories organize similar items and also have generalized information associated with them describing the similarities between those items. Generalized knowledge is organized in the same hierarchical, interconnected structures that organize the items themselves. Retrieval of a category requires the same reconstructive processing as retrieval of an event from a category. In terms of the human model, this supports the theory that *there is no distinction between episodic and generic memory*. Both types of information are integrated into the same memory structures, and retrieval of both is the same.

It also has implications in the design of computer systems. In a computer system that makes retrieval of generalized information the same process as retrieval of actual items, a user can retrieve information about the nature of the data base, and not only data items themselves. Using the retrieval strategies for retrieving actual items from memory, and using the CYRUS data base, answering questions such as the following would be a trivial extension to the system.

(Q1): When Vance goes on diplomatic trips, where does he usually stay?

(Q2): Do welcoming ceremonies for Vance usually include parades?

(Q3): What kinds of things does Vance discuss at diplomatic meetings?

Instead of retrieving actual events that correspond to the target event in each of these cases, E-MOPs that correspond will be retrieved, and their generalized information will be consulted.

In a retrieval system that does not allow queries about the nature of the data, a user must request all or many instances of the kinds of events he is interested in and draw his own conclusions. Retrieving individual items requires elaboration by the system or a series of questions by the user. Either way, it is less efficient.

3.5. Retrieval Failures and Ease of Retrieval

The theory presented makes the following psychologically relevant prediction:

> **The closer a retrieval cue is to the encoding of an item at the time of retrieval, the easier retrieval of that item should be.**

An item can be retrieved only by specifying features on which it was discriminated during processing. When an event specification refers to features that have not been discriminated, retrieval can only occur if the specified features can be transformed into features that have been discriminated. Psychologists have called this phenomenon *encoding specificity* (Tulving, 1972). According to that theory, the ease with which an item can be recalled from memory depends on the nearness of the retrieval specification to the description initially encoded in memory for the item.

Memory, however, is constantly reorganizing itself over time. Thus, the indices for an event at the time of retrieval must be taken into account in judging the retrievability of an item. Any time a retrieval specification refers to features of events that have not been discriminated, it will be necessary to elaborate or reconstruct aspects of the retrieval specification to correspond to features that are discriminated in the conceptual category.

Ease of retrieval depends on ease of finding unique indices: Retrieval failure occurs if necessary cues are not available for construction of an appropriate retrieval context. Because reconstructive retrieval processes are knowledge-based, if the knowledge necessary to construct or elaborate a context appropriately is not available at the time of reconstruction, then retrieval will fail.

3.6. Recall and Recognition

Psychologists have often noted that there are many items in memory that can be recognized but cannot be recalled. The CYRUS retrieval processes can be used to explain this. We assume that recognition probes have many more features of an event specified than do recall probes. Because a lot of information is given, there are multiple ways of searching memory without the need for extensive elaboration. Recall probes, on the other hand, provide fewer ways to search memory, and elaboration will be needed. Free recall will require more extensive elaboration than cued recall. Recognition is easier for two reasons: First, it offers more ways to search memory. Second, it allows more directed search of memory without the need to generate features to help direct the search.

3.7. Is CYRUS a Good Model of People?

In previous sections, we have discussed CYRUS' successes as a human model. In evaluating CYRUS' generalizability to human memory, we must also consider features of human memory that CYRUS does not directly address.

First, CYRUS depends on rich indexing of events in memory. Currently, in the implementation, each event is indexed by approximately ten features. Most real-life events that we experience have many hundreds or thousands of features. Thus, we must consider what would happen in a CYRUS-like memory that had to consider that many event features. Would the indexing get out of hand? What is needed to answer that question is a theory of "important feature selection." In part, CYRUS has such a theory. Because individual events are indexed in many different conceptual structures in memory (e.g., a particular party may be both a political event and a social event), only those features which are domain-related are used as indices in each structure. Second, because indices are only as good as the content-frame of the E-MOP they index, only those features that can make predictions about the probable values of other features make good indices. Thus, we may never have to worry about too many indices. Experimentation based on this model to find out how people index events will shed light on this problem.

Another consideration in deciding if CYRUS is a good model of people is the way it forgets. While CYRUS' errors of omission are obvious, its errors of commission are not. CYRUS never really comes up with a wrong answer. In principle, it should be able to. In implementation, there is no mechanism for it. This is because CYRUS' algorithm combines what is usually thought of as reconstruction (i.e., coming up with an event description) with verification of that description. If it cannot verify a memory, it will not produce it as an answer. CYRUS considers many plausible but wrong memories as it searches memory, but suppresses all of them. It needs a way of judging the veracity of a plausible memory without explicitly "finding" it.

There are a number of features of human memory that we did not consider in developing CYRUS. First, people seem to know what they know and do not know. CYRUS does not. Thus, a person can answer a silly question quickly, make judgments about whether he has remembered all instances of a type of event, make judgments as to whether further memory search will help, and so forth. CYRUS cannot do any of these things, not out of principle, but because they were not considered in developing the model. Second, CYRUS cannot make recency and frequency judgments. Again, this is a problem we did not consider in developing our framework, but is an important consideration for furthering the theory. Similarly, we did not consider the role of practice in memory. Nor did we consider how incorrect information in a cue effects the retrieval process.

Development of CYRUS was an iterative process of observing people, coming up with a model to explain some behavior, evaluating that model through implementation on the computer, adding features to the model or changing it, then going back and looking at people, and so on. Our initial aim was to address the broad problem of reconstructive retrieval from very long-term memory and to design a mechanism to explain it. CYRUS is the result. We have been able to provide an algorithm for reconstructive retrieval. Some aspects of memory that we did not initially consider we got for free from that algorithm—forgetting, generalization, and the combination of episodic and generic memory, to name a few. Other aspects of memory, such as those addressed above, did not come out of the model for free. Now is the time in the iterative process to consider those problems. We test CYRUS as a model of human memory by running experiments on people to see if its predictions hold and by seeing if additional aspects of human memory can be made to fit *naturally* into the already-existing framework.

3.8. Psychological Issues Raised by the Model[9]

Since CYRUS has been presented as a model of human information processing, our conclusions would not be complete without a discussion of the psychological issues raised by CYRUS. The first set of issues is raised by CYRUS' retrieval and updating processes. One aspect of the model that has received some empirical investigation is reconstructive retrieval strategies (Norman & Bobrow, 1979; Williams & Hollan, 1981). People appear to elaborate upon requests to remember in many of the ways CYRUS does. Nevertheless, many issues remain untouched or at least require further attention. How does the organization of a set of events constrain the manner in which people elaborate on retrieval cues? Do people employ all the elaboration strategies used by CYRUS? Do they use others? What strategies are used most often, in what order, and for what reason? To what extent is elaboration affected by immediately previous searches for other events? for the same event? Given retrieval failure while searching an organized set of events, how do people select new parts of the organization for search? How does a retrieval access change organization? How sensitive is retrieval to incorrectly specified cues? Is the model too dependent on correctness of cues?

We can ask similar questions about the strategies CYRUS employs in adding new items to memory. Are these strategies consistent with people's strategies? How, for example, do people choose features to discriminate and subsequently

[9]Many of the issues raised in this section stem from work done jointly with Prof. Larry Barsalou, Dept. of Psychology, Emory University, Atlanta, GA.

index two similar episodes? There may be numerous features that distinguish two events, but CYRUS predicts that only those that will be useful in the later evolution of generic knowledge should be chosen for indexing. How can such features be chosen? And how many and which of those features are actually used in organization? Are new generalizations (i.e., new E-MOPs) constructed every time someone is reminded of an old event by a current one?

A second set of psychological issues is raised by CYRUS' organizational assumptions, namely that E-MOPs are the central organizing units for events in memory. Is this the way events are organized in human memory? Are E-MOPs the fundamental units of organization for events? Or do people prefer to use other organizational principles? And how does this organization change over time?

CYRUS assumes that generic events (e.g., going to a restaurant, diplomatic meetings, giving a speech) are the fundamental organizing units for events in memory. All of the processes proposed are based on this underlying assumption. From a processing point of view, this seems reasonable. There is very convincing evidence from AI models of natural-language understanding (Lebowitz, 1980; Schank & Abelson, 1977) and from observations of people remembering (Schank, 1980) that this is true. However, it has never been tested in a formal way. If we were to find that people's memories of events were organized primarily in some other way, then it might require rethinking previous theories of natural-language understanding and memory organization. If we found that people's memories do conform to the E-MOP hypothesis, then it would lend support to the understanding and memory processes that have been proposed.

Another important organizational issue stems from the fact that MOPs and their sub-MOPs in CYRUS form hierarchies in which common properties are stored once at the highest possible point in the hierarchy. This economy of storage parallels what psychologists have called "cognitive economy" (Collins & Quillian, 1969). To date, it appears that the organization of semantic memory (i.e., lexical meaning) violates cognitive economy (Conrad, 1972). But to what extent is this violation true of other types of generic knowledge? Does human organization of events (i.e., episodic memory) reflect cognitive economy? Or do people have much looser, less integrated and non-inclusive organizations for events?

An important implication of E-MOP structure is that they combine "episodic" and "generic" memories. This implies that episodic and generic memory are not separate entities but are intimately connected. If so, what exactly is the connection? When does episodic information (e.g., E-MOP indices) become generic (e.g., E-MOP norms or frame information)? When and how does generic information become confused with episodic information to generate confusions? In E-MOPs, both happen as generalizations are refined and corrected.

Another interesting organizational issue concerns the role of similarity among events and its relationship to retrievability and forgetting. Similarity can facilitate people's memory performance on some occasions (e.g., clustering in recall) and interfere with it on others (e.g., false alarms in recognition). Indexing events within E-MOPs directly reflects similarity among the events. An event similar to the norms of an E-MOP will not have many indices differentiating it from other events. This may make it harder to discriminate in recognition, but facilitate clustering in recall. On the other hand, an unusual event is likely to have more indices differentating it from other events. This may make it easy to discriminate on a recognition test, but hard to recall if those indices are unusual and therefore difficult to generate during elaboration of the recall cues.

There are a number of issues relevant to long-term memory for events that are not explicitly stated as part of the CYRUS model. One such issue concerns the definition of generic event types. Although the CYRUS model and Schank's MOPs (1980) consider generic events to be central to memory organization, no systematic means has been devised for determining which sets of features define these entities. How many and which types of features are necessary to define an event category? And which combinations, if any, typically occur together?

Another important issue concerns automatic versus conscious processes. CYRUS does not differentiate between such processes. In people, however, observations have been made that temporal, spatial, and frequency information seem to be automatically acquired without conscious attention (Hasher & Zacks, 1979), whereas retention of other content information requires attention. How do these two types of processes interact in storing events in memory? Conscious attention may be responsible for the construction, organization, and reorganization of generic structure, whereas automatic processes may be responsible for strengthening that knowledge and for coding information about location and time.

Another interesting issue is the relationship of CYRUS, a first-person memory model, to third-person memory. The two types may be qualitatively similar and differ only in level of detail (since one generally knows more about oneself than about someone else). Social psychologists have discovered some interesting differences, however, in how people attribute causes of behavior to themselves versus others. It is possible, then, that organization of one's own experiences and those of other people could be fundamentally different.

A final issue concerns analogy. CYRUS does not address the migration of generic information from old E-MOPs to new ones. Generic knowledge associated with a particular E-MOP might be useful, however, in creating a new related E-MOP or in understanding something in a similar E-MOP. To what extent does "generic" structure generalize from one set of events to another? Must a completely new structure be built for each new set or does transfer occur? What procedures transfer the structure of an old E-MOP to a new one? How can knowledge in one E-MOP (e.g., for Vance) be used to understand something about a related referent (e.g., Haig)?

3.9. More Unanswered Questions

Work on CYRUS addressed many important problems associated with long-term memory organization and retrieval. It provided algorithms and memory structures that provide the capability of doing reconstructive retrieval and that explain many of the memory phenomenon we observe in people. Just as importantly, it has pointed out a number of areas that still need attention.

In the current CYRUS model, events are retrieved reconstructively. Little has been said, however, about the control of retrieval strategies. In a fully reconstructive memory, not only should retrieval of events be reconstructive, but control and retrieval of the strategies themselves should also be reconstructive. Choosing the kinds of indices to elaborate during retrieval, for example, may be guided by choosing a prototypical event from a memory category and choosing from among its salient features. If this is reasonable, then how can a prototypical event be chosen, and how can its salient features be enumerated in a well-structured way?

In the current model, memory organization happens as new events are added to memory. A possible extension to that is reorganization because of retrieval access. If a particular kind of information is requested often, for example, memory should reorganize itself to make that information available. Furthermore, organizational strategies should be automatically refined so that as new items are added to memory, their most relevant information is made available. Recently accessed and rehearsed information is easier for people to retrieve than unrehearsed information (Bjork & Whitten, 1974). What this suggests is that each time memory is accessed, whether for retrieval or update, it is reorganized taking recency information into account.

In CYRUS, this has been partially realized through maintenance of a dialog context, and by keeping track of the most recent event added to an E-MOP. Information available from the context of a previous answer is easier to retrieve than other information. A most recent experience is easier to retrieve than other experiences like it. Recency has not been addressed in the general case, however. When an event is no longer the most recent of its type, or no longer in the immediate conversational context, its recency has no effect on its ease of retrieval.

Similarly, frequency judgments are something people tend to be able to make, yet CYRUS cannot make them. As a first pass, CYRUS keeps track of E-MOP size until six events are added to a MOP. But this doesn't explain how frequency judgments such as "about a dozen times," "hundreds of times," or "two or three times" can be made.

This, of course, is just part of the general problem of knowing what's in memory. How can we make CYRUS know that it doesn't know something (e.g., Abe Lincoln's telephone number) without searching memory to try to find an answer? Perhaps some consistency judgments need to be made before search ever begins. If so, what constitutes such judgments and by what process are they made?

Another area which needs more attention is the definition of additional retrieval and organizational strategies. Strategies associated with time, for example, would be quite useful. As in indexing other aspects of events in E-MOPs, it is the predictive features of time specifications that should be used as indices. Besides indexing events in E-MOPs, they can also be organized according to time. The "era" was developed for CYRUS to organize events by time, but has not been explored fully. An era breaks a time line into reasonably sized chunks, providing conceptual categories for storing generalized information about a time period. Strategies that would use time for retrieval would use the generalized information associated with eras, the relationships of eras to each other, as well as the placement of landmark events in eras (Kolodner, 1978).

Other questions that remain concern the representation of complex events in memory, maintaining and building up knowledge about concepts other than generic events, controlling indexing better, extending CYRUS' strategies to better reconstruct individual events in detail, and refining strategies over time.

Development of a memory model is an incremental process. The current CYRUS model covers the issues we have considered so far. Study of these and other issues related to conceptual memory will contribute to a more thorough analysis of CYRUS. If answers can be derived within the framework of reconstructive memory that has been presented, then it will lend credence to the model. If not, then study of these and the psychological issues will tell us how the model has to be changed.

4. WHERE DO WE GO FROM HERE?

Long-term memory and its associated reasoning processes play a major role in all of our interactions as humans. In terms of creating intelligence in computers, there are many areas where long-term memory is not only useful, but necessary. Among those are (1) intelligent fact retrieval, (2) expert systems, (3) dialog and control of conversation, and (4) machine learning. In this section, we briefly show how CYRUS is a step toward the development of such systems.

4.1. Information and Fact Retrieval

Although the techniques have been different, the goals of information retrieval are very close to the goals of the research presented here: to store and retrieve large amounts of relatively unconstrained information using a computer. Ultimately, this requires developing systems which can (1) understand the contents of documents and automatically organize them in the computer memory, and (2) retrieve the facts found in the documents when queried in natural language.

Although this research does not resemble current information retrieval (Heaps, 1978), we hope it can provide a framework for future research in intelligent fact retrieval (Kolodner, 1983a; Schank et al., 1981).

One ideal information retrieval system that we can imagine is a system that could read the newspaper, understanding articles about world events and storing those events. It would allow a user to query it in English to find out what was going on in the world. A current events data base with the capabilities described in this report is a step toward building such a system. A fact retrieval system with the capabilities mentioned would have to be able to (1) organize its memory for easy access, (2) understand the input document, (3) automatically integrate new facts into memory, (4) create search keys from natural-language queries, and (5) access its data base for retrieval (Schank, Kolodner & DeJong, 1981). This research addresses each of those issues except the second, and thus deals with many of the hard problems facing a person who wants to design an information retrieval system for events.

CYRUS, as an expert on Cyrus Vance, is the first step in designing an expert on current events. In order to make CYRUS into a current events expert, there are a number of additions that would have to be made. First, its domains of expertise would have to be expanded. Second, it would have to be able to access multiple data bases about numerous people. Third, its organizational structures would have to be extended to handle information about countries and political entities, in addition to handling information about people. It would also need to have a better notion of time than has been implemented in CYRUS.

Although this might seem like a lot of additions to be made to the implementation, the theory behind it would have to be changed very little. The retrieval and organizational strategies presented here would form the core of its memory processing. The same notions of salience, predictability, and generalization that are necessary to differentiate day-to-day events are necessary to differentiate world events.

4.2. Expert Systems

Another possible application for an episodic memory is in the design of expert systems. Research in expert systems has focused on rule application (Davis, Buchanan, & Shortliffe, 1977; Feigenbaum, 1977) and has not addressed the relationship between previous experience and expertise. Episodic memory organization and strategies for search can provide a basis for addressing that problem. Organizational structures in the system would correspond to situations from the expert domain. In particular, such a system would handle exceptions to rules very nicely. The general case would be stored at the category level, with exceptions indexed off it. In any but the exceptional cases, the general procedures would be retrieved. If a new case referenced a previous exception, knowledge about the previous exception would be used to suggest a procedure. When a procedure was successful a number of times for a particular exception, it would be generalized as the treatment for that exception. The general rule would not have to change unless an exception became the generalized case. Just as generalized information about episodes changes with experience, the norms for recognition and treatment of particular types of situations would have to change with experience. Applying the rules for memory reorganization presented in chapter 8 would allow that to happen.

Expert domains that require a decision to be made are different from the domain presented here in an important way. The decision that is made should be correct. Thus, a system based on experience must be given the capability of refining its procedures based upon its successes and failures. Feedback about its performance must thus be provided to such a system. Cause and effect are very important. A problem must be recognized and then treated. If the treatment doesn't work, it must be determined why not, and generalized information must be updated. Thus, in addition to the strategies and organization presented in CYRUS, failure-based memory reorganization (Kolodner, 1983b; Schank, 1982) and learning processes, as well as a theory of explanation, have to be developed.

4.3. Dialog

Past experience plays a major role in our conversations with other people. One of the goals of AI research is to make the computer accessible to computer novices. One way of doing this is to provide computers with the capability of carrying on a natural dialog in the course of performing its designated task. In carrying on a conversation with a person, the computer will have to be able to access enormous amounts of information in its memory. Memory must be organized efficiently in order for that to happen. It is also quite possible that memory's organization can direct the course of conversation by "reminding" (Schank, 1980) the conversant of appropriate things to say. A prerequisite to exploration of the relationship between reminding and conversation is a model of memory's organization and access methods.

One task where this is particularly important is computer-aided instruction or explanation. A computerized teacher must be able to guide instruction in a natural way, explaining problems at an appropriate level, and always giving the right amount of information. Strategies for directing search and extracting implicit information are important to that task.

4.4. Machine Learning

The processes of automatic indexing, category creation, and strategy refinement that have been proposed are examples of learning processes. An understanding of what "learning" is has been a primary goal of AI research (e.g., Lenat, 1976; Soloway, 1977; Winston, 1972). One of the differentiating features of this research and previous learning research is that the learning presented here is a natural consequence of another cognitive process—integration of new information into memory. In this way, it is similar to Lebowitz' (1980) research on generalization. Of course, it only begins to scratch the surface of the learning that goes on in the natural course of performing cognitive tasks. In addition to adding new facts and generalizations to memory, new strategies for both memory organization and retrieval should be learned as a natural consequence of understanding and remembering. As a natural consequence of performing both expert and everyday tasks, procedures must be refined, based on feedback from the environment. CYRUS provides a framework for pursuing such research by specifying ways of keeping track of the similarities and differences between items in memory.

5. SUMMARY

The theory of reconstructive memory that has been presented is meant to be a model both of human retrieval processes and of intelligent fact retrieval. As a fact retrieval system, it provides a framework for the construction of intelligent computer memories, necessary for any intelligent task. In terms of psychology, this research can be thought of as complementary to psychological research into reconstructive memory. It provides a memory organization and particular retrieval processes that help explain human behavior and make predictions about human memory organization.

The task of remembering that we want the computer to do is a task that comes naturally to people, yet it is one that psychologists do not fully understand. Numerous psychologists have proposed that memory is a reconstructive process (Bartlett, 1932; Norman & Bobrow, 1979; Spiro, 1979; Williams, 1978), but none have been willing to specify exactly what those reconstructive processes look like. They have also been unwilling or unable to speculate on a memory organization underlying those reconstructive processes. Using the computer as a tool has allowed us to define and implement reasonable processes for reconstructive retrieval. In finding out the requirements on memory in order to perform reconstructive retrieval, we predict what human memory organization might be like. In defining particular processes for memory update and search, we explain some of the behavior people exhibit in remembering. These predictions can be tested by controlled psychological experiments.

REFERENCES

Anderson, J. R. (1974). Retrieval of propositional information from a long term memory. *Cognitive Psychology,* Vol. 5, pp. 451–474.

Anderson, J. R. (1976). *Language, memory, and thought.* Hillsdale, NJ: Lawrence Erlbaum Associates.

Anderson, J. R., & Bower, G. (1973). *Human associative memory.* Washington, DC: Winston-Wiley.

Anderson, J. R., & Ross, B. H. (1980). Evidence against the semantic-episodic distinction. *Journal of Experimental Psychology: Human Learning and Memory* Vol. 6, pp. 441–466.

Barsalou, L. W., & Bower, G. H. (1984). Discrimination nets as psychological models. *Cognitive Science,* Vol. 8, No. 1.

Bartlett, R. (1932). *Remembering: A study in experimental and social psychology.* London: Cambridge University Press.

Birnbaum, L., & Selfridge, M. (1981). Conceptual analysis of natural language. In R. C. Schank & C. K. Riesbeck, (Eds.), *Inside computer understanding: Five programs plus miniatures.* Hillsdale, NJ: Lawrence Erlbaum Associates.

Bjork, R. A., & Whitten, W. B. (1974). Recency-sensitive retrieval processes in long-term free recall. *Cognitive Psychology,* Vol. 6, pp. 173–189.

Bobrow, D. G., & Norman, D. A. (1975). Some principles of memory schemata. In D. G. Bobrow & A. Collins, (Eds.), *Representation and understanding.* New York: Academic Press.

Borko, H., & Bernier, C. L. (1978). *Indexing concepts and methods.* New York: Academic Press.

Bower, G. H., Black, J. B., & Turner, T. J. (1979). Scripts in text comprehension and memory. *Cognitive Psychology,* Vol. 1, pp. 177–220.

Carbonell, J. R., & Collins, A. (1973). Natural semantics in artificial intelligence. *Proceedings of Third International Joint Conference on Artificial Intelligence,* pp. 344–351.

Charniak, E. (1977). A framed painting: The representation of a common sense knowledge fragment. *Cognitive Science,* Vol. 1, pp. 355–394.

Codd, E. F. (1979). Extending the database relational model to capture more meaning. *ACM Transactions on Database Systems,* Vol. 4, No. 4, pp. 397–434.

Collins, A. (1978). *Studies of plausible reasoning, final report* (Vol. I): *Human plausible reasoning.* BBN Report 3810, Bolt Beranek & Newman, Inc., Cambridge, Mass.

Collins, A. M., & Quillian, M. R. (1969). Retrieval time from semantic memory. *Journal of Verbal Learning and Verbal Behavior,* Vol. 8, pp. 240–247.

Collins, A., Warnock, E. H., Aiello, N., & Miller, M. L. (1975). Reasoning from incomplete knowledge. In D. G. Bobrow, & A. Collins, (Eds.), *Representation and understanding.* New York: Academic Press.

Conrad, C. (1972). Cognitive economy in semantic memory. *Journal of Experimental Psychology,* Vol. 92, pp. 149–154.

Cooper, W. S. (1978). Indexing documents by gedanken experimentation. *Journal of the American Society for Information Science,* Vol. 29, pp. 107–119.

Crowder, R. G. (1976). *Principles of learning and memory.* Hillsdale, NJ: Lawrence Erlbaum Associates.

Cullingford, R. (1978). *Script application: Computer understanding of newspaper stories* (Ph.D. thesis. Research Report #116). Department of Computer Science, Yale University, New Haven, CT.

Davis, R., Buchanan, B. G., & Shortliffe, E. H. (1977). Production rules as a representation for a knowledge-based consultation program. *Artificial Intelligence,* Vol. 8, pp. 15–45.

DeJong, G. F. (1979a). *Skimming stories in real time: An experiment in integrated understanding* (Research Report #158). Department of Computer Science, Yale University, New Haven, CT.

DeJong, G. F. (1979b). Prediction and substantiation: A new approach to natural language processing. *Cognitive Science,* Vol. 3, pp. 251–273.

Doszkocs, T. E. & Rapp, B. A. (1979). Searching MEDLINE in English: A prototype user interface with natural language query, ranked output, and relevance feedback. In R. D. Tally, & R. R. Deultgen, (Eds.), *Proceedings of the ASIS Annual Meeting,* Vol. 16, pp. 131–139.

Dyer, M.G. (1983). *In depth understanding: A computer model of integrated processing for narrative comprehension.* Cambridge, Mass: MIT Press.

Dyer, M. G., & Lehnert, W. G. (1980). *Organization and search processes for narratives* (Research Report #175). Department of Computer Science, Yale University, New Haven, CT.

Feigenbaum, E. A. (1963). The simulation of natural learning behavior. In E. A. Feigenbaum & J. Feldman, (Eds.), *Computers and thought.* New York: McGraw-Hill.

Feigenbaum, E. A. (1977). The art of artificial intelligence: Themes and studies of knowledge engineering. *Proceedings of the Fifth International Joint Conference on Artificial Intelligence.*

Gibbs, R. W., & Tenney, Y. J. (1980). The concept of scripts in understanding stories. *Journal of Psycholinguistic Research.* Vol. 9, pp. 275–284.

Harter, S. P. (1978). Statistical approaches to automatic indexing. *Drexel Library Quarterly,* Vol. 14, pp. 57–74.

Hasher, L., & Zacks, R. T. (1979). Automatic and effortful processes in memory. *Journal of Experimental Psychology: General,* Vol. 108, pp. 356–388.

Heaps, H. S. (1978). *Information retrieval: Computational and theoretical aspects.* New York: Academic Press.

Hemphill, L., & Rhyne, J. (1978). *A model for knowledge representation in natural language query systems.* IBM Research Report RJ2304(31046).

Kolodner, J. L. (1978). *Memory organization for natural language database inquiry* (Research Report #142). Department of Computer Science, Yale University, New Haven, CT.

Kolodner, J. L. (1981). Organization and retrieval in a conceptual memory for events. *Proceedings of the Seventh International Joint Conference on Artificial Intelligence,* pp. 227–233.

Kolodner, J. L. (1983a). Indexing and retrieval strategies for natural language fact retrieval. *ACM Transactions on Database Systems,* Vol. 8, pp. 434–464.

Kolodner, J. L. (1983b). Towards an understanding of the role of experience in the evolution from novice to expert. *International Journal of Man-Machine Systems.*

Kolodner, J. L., & Barsalou, L. W. (1982). Psychological Issues Raised by an AI Model of Reconstructive Memory. *Proceedings of the Fourth Annual Conference on Cognitive Science.*

Larson, S., & Williams, M. E. (1980). Computer assisted legal research. In M. E. Williams, (Ed.), *Annual review of information science and technology* (Vol. 15, pp. 251–286). White Plains, NY: Knowledge Industry Publications.

Lebowitz, M. (1980). *Generalization and memory in an integrated understanding system* (Ph.D. Thesis, Research Report #186). Department of Computer Science. Yale University, New Haven, CT.

Lehnert, W. G. (1978). *The process of question answering.* Hillsdale, NJ: Lawrence Erlbaum Associates.

Lenat, D. B. (1976). *AM: An artificial intelligence approach to discovery in mathematics as heuristic search.* Stanford Artificial Intelligence Laboratory Memo AIM-286. Computer Science Department, Stanford University, Stanford, CA.

Maron, M. E. (1979). Depth of indexing. *Journal of the American Society for Information Science,* Vol. 30, pp. 224–228.

McGuire, R. (1980). *Political primaries and words of pain.* Unpublished manuscript. Department of Computer Science. Yale University, New Haven, CT.

McKoon, G., & Ratcliff, R. (1979). Priming in episodic and semantic memory. *Journal of Verbal Learning and Verbal Behavior,* Vol. 18, pp. 463–480.

Minsky, M. (1975). A framework for representing knowledge. In P. H. Winston (Ed.), *The psychology of computer vision.* New York: McGraw-Hill.

Newell, A. (1973). Artificial intelligence and the concept of mind. In R. C. Schank & K. M. Colby, (Eds.), *Computer models of thought and language.* San Francisco: Freeman.

Norman, D. (1973). Memory, knowledge, and the answering of questions. In R. L. Solso (Ed.), *Contemporary issues in cognitive psychology: The Loyola Symposium.* Washington, DC: Winston.

Norman, D. A., & Bobrow, D. G. (1979). Descriptions: An intermediate stage in memory retrieval. *Cognitive Psychology,* Vol. 11, pp. 107–123.

Norman, D. A., & Rumelhart, D. E., (Eds.) (1975). *Explorations in cognition.* San Francisco: Freeman.

O'Connor, J. (1980). Answer passage retrieval by text searching. *Journal of the American Society for Information Science,* Vol. 31, pp. 227–239.

Oddy, R. N., Robertson, S. E., van Rigsbergen, C. J., & Williams, P. W. (Eds.) (1981). *Information Retrieval Research.* London: Butterworth. (Proceedings of Conference on Research and Development in Information Retrieval, St. John's College, Cambridge, England, June, 1980.)

Owens, J., Bower, G. H., & Black, J. B. (1979). The "soap opera" effect in story recall. *Memory and Cognition,* Vol. 7, pp. 185–191.

Quillian, M. R. (1968). Semantic memory. In M. Minsky (Ed.), *Semantic information processing.* Cambridge, MA: MIT Press.

Reder, L. M. & Anderson, J. R. (1980). A partial resolution of the paradox of interference: The role of integrating knowledge. *Cognitive Psychology,* Vol. 12, pp. 447–472.

Reiser, B. J., Black, J. B., & Abelson, R. P. (1982). Retrieving memories of personal experiences. *Proceedings of the Fourth Annual Conference of the Cognitive Science Society,* pp. 109–111.

Rieger, C. J. (1975a). Conceptual memory and inference. In R. C. Schank (Ed.), *Conceptual information processing.* New York: American Elsevier.

Rieger, C. J. (1975b). The commonsense algorithm as a basis for computer models of human memory, inference, belief, and contextual language comprehension. In R. Schank & B. Webber (Eds.) *Proceedings of the Conference on Theoretical Issues in Natural Language Processing.* Association for Computational Linguistics.

Riesbeck, C. K. (1975). Conceptual analysis. In R. C. Schank (Ed.), *Conceptual information processing.* New York: American Elsevier.

Salton, G. (1975). *Dynamic information and library processing.* Englewood Cliffs, NJ: Prentice-Hall.

Salton, G. (1981). Chairman's message. *ACM Special Interest Group on Information Retrieval,* Vol. 15, No. 4.

Salton, G., Yang, C. S., & Yu, C. T. (1974). Contributions to the theory of indexing. In *Information Processing 74,* Amsterdam: North Holland.

Schank, R. (1972). Conceptual dependency: A theory of natural language understanding. *Cognitive Psychology,* Vol. 3, No. 4, pp. 552–631.

Schank, R. C. (1975). The structure of episodes in memory. In D. G. Bobrow & A. Collins, (Ed.), *Representation and understanding.* New York: Academic Press.

Schank, R. C. (1975). *Conceptual information processing.* New York: American Elsevier.

Schank, R. C. (1980). Language and memory. *Cognitive Science,* Vol. 4, pp. 243–284.

Schank, R. C. (1982). *Dynamic memory: A theory of learning in people and computers.* London: Cambridge University Press.

Schank, R. C., & Abelson, R. P. (1977). *Scripts, plans, goals, and understanding.* Hillsdale, NJ: Lawrence Erlbaum Associates.

Schank, R. C., & Kolodner, J. L. (1979). *Retrieving information from an episodic memory* (Research Report #159). Department of Computer Science, Yale University. Short version in *Proceedings of the Sixth International Joint Conference on Artificial Intelligence,* Tokyo.

Schank, R. C., Kolodner, J. L., & DeJong, G. F. (1981). Conceptual information retrieval. In R. N. Oddy, S. E. Robertson, C. J. van Rijsbergen, and P. W. Williams (Eds.), *Information retrieval research.* London: Butterworth.

Schank, R. C. & Riesbeck, C. K. (1981). *Inside computer understanding: Five programs plus miniatures.* Hillsdale, NJ: Lawrence Erlbaum Associates.

Scragg, G. W. (1975). Answering questions about processes. In D. A. Norman & D. E. Rumelhart (Eds.), *Explorations in Cognition.* San Francisco: Freeman.

Smith, E. E., Adams, N., & Schorr, D. (1978). Fact retrieval and the paradox of interference. *Cognitive Psychology,* Vol. 10. pp. 438–464.

Soloway, E. (1977). *Knowledge-directed learning* (COINS Technical Report #77–6). University of Massachusetts, Amherst, MA.

Spiro, R. J. (1979). *Prior knowledge and story processing: Integration, selection, and variation* (Technical Report #138). Center for the Study of Reading. Champaign, Illinois.

Tulving, E. (1972). Episodic and semantic memory. In E. Tulving & W. Donaldson (Eds.), *Organization of memory.* New York: Academic Press.

Wanger, J., & Landau, R. N. (1980). Nonbibliographic on-line data base services. *Journal of the American Society for Information Science,* Vol. 31, pp. 171–180.

Weiderhold, G. (1977). *Database design.* New York: McGraw-Hill.

Wilensky, R. (1978). *Understanding goal-based stories* (Ph.D. Thesis. Research Report #140). Department of Computer Science, Yale University, New Haven, CT.

Williams, M. D. (1978). *The process of retrieval from very long term memory.* Center for Human Information Processing Memo CHIP-75, La Jolla, California.

Williams, M. D., & Hollan, J. D. (1981). The process of retrieval from very long-term memory. *Cognitive Science,* Vol. 5, pp. 87–119.

Williams, M. E., (Ed.) (1979). *Computer readable data bases: A directory and data source book.* White Plains, NY: Knowledge Industry Publications.

Winston, P. H. (1972). Learning structural descriptions from examples. In P. H. Winston (Ed.), *The psychology of computer vision.* New York: McGraw-Hill.

Woods, W., Kaplan, R., & Nash-Webber, B. (1972). *The LUNAR sciences natural language information system: Final report.* Bolt, Beranek and Newman Report No. #2378, Cambridge, MA.

AUTHOR INDEX

Numbers in *italics* denote pages with complete bibliographic information.

A

Abelson, R. P., 23, 24, 28, 37, 43, 83, 103, 121, 130, 138, 233, 244, *253*, *254*
Adams, N., 18, 137, *254*
Aiello, N., 70, *252*
Anderson, J. R., 18, 26, 229, *251*, *253*

B

Barsalou, L. W., 24, 229, 243, *251*, *252*
Bartlett, R., 228, 250, *251*
Bernier, C. L., 235, *251*
Birnbaum, L., 31, 200, *251*
Bjork, R. A., 246, *251*
Black, J. B., 24, 190, *251*, *253*
Bobrow, D. G., 228, 229, 243, 250, *251*, *253*
Borko, H., 235, *251*
Bower, G. H., 28, 190, 229, *251*, *253*
Buchanan, B. G., 248, *252*

C

Carbonell, J. R., 234, *251*
Charniak, E., 28, 138, 231, *251*
Codd, E. F., 236, *251*
Collins, A. M., 28, 70, 71, 234, 244, *251*, *252*
Conrad, C., 244, *252*
Cooper, W. S., 235, *252*
Crowder, R. G., 190, *252*
Cullingford, R., 28, 196, 231, 233, *252*

D

Davis, R., 248, *252*
DeJong, G. F., 20, 28, 31, 194, 207, 226, 231, 248, *252*, *254*
Doszkocs, T. E., 235, *252*
Dyer, M. G., 231, 233, *252*

F

Feigenbaum, E. A., 229, 248, *252*

G

Gibbs, R. W., 190, *252*

H

Harter, S. P., 235, *252*
Hasher, L., 245, *252*
Heaps, H. S., 235, 248, *252*
Hemphill, L., 236, *252*
Hollan, J. D., 133, 243, *254*

K

Kaplan, R., 233, *254*
Kolodner, J. L., 19, 24, 83, 103, 247, 248, 249, *252, 254*
Korsin, M., 200

L

Landau, R. N., 234, *254*
Larson, S., 234, *253*
Lebowitz, M., 28, 29, 31, 38, 232, 244, 250, *253*
Lehnert, W. G., 49, 50, 198, 206, 231, 233, *252, 253*
Lenat, D. B., 249, *253*

M

Maron, M. E., 235, *253*
McGuire, R., 207, *253*
McKoon, G., 26, *253*
Miller, M. L., 70, *252*
Minsky, M., 28, 138, *253*

N

Nash-Webber, B., 233, *254*
Newell, A., 76, *253*
Norman, D. A., 28, 71, 228, 229, 243, 250, *251, 253*

O

O'Connor, J., 234, *253*
Oddy, R. N., 234, *253*
Owens, J., 190, *253*

Q

Quillian, M. R., 28, 229, 244, *252, 253*

R

Rapp, B. A., 235, *252*
Ratcliff, R., 26, *253*
Reder, L. M., 18, *253*
Reiser, B. J., 24, *253*
Rhyne, J., 236, *252*
Rieger, C. J., 28, *253*
Riesbeck, C. K., 28, *253, 254*
Robertson, S. E., 234, *253*
Ross, B. H., 26, *251*
Rumelhart, D. E., 28, *253*

S

Salton, G., 234, 235, *253, 254*
Schank, R. C., 19, 23, 28, 29, 31, 33, 36, 37, 38, 39; 43, 67, 83, 103, 121, 130, 138, 167, 182, 195, 230, 231, 233, 244, 245, 248, 249, *254*
Schorr, D., 18, 137, *254*
Scragg, G. W., 233, *254*
Selfridge, M., 31, 200, *251*
Shortliffe, E. H., 248, *252*
Smith, E. E., 18, 137, *254*
Soloway, E., 249, *254*
Spiro, R. J., 228, 250, *254*

T

Tenney, Y. J., 190, *252*
Tulving, E., 241, *254*
Turner, T. J., 190, *251*

V

van Rigsbergen, C. J., 234, *253*

W

Wanger, J., 234, *254*
Warnock, E. H., 70, *252*
Weiderhold, G., 236, *254*
Whitten, W. B., 246, *251*
Wilensky, R., 231, 233, *254*
Williams, M. D., 7, 84, 133, 228, 229, 243, 250, *254*
Williams, M. E., 234, 235, *253, 254*
Williams, P. W., 234, *253*
Winston, P. H., 249, *254*
Woods, W., 233, *254*

Y

Yang, C. S., 235, *254*
Yu, C. T., 235, *254*

Z

Zacks, R. T., 245, *252*

SUBJECT INDEX

A

Alternate context search, 16–18, 52, 53, 76, 111, 238
  circumstances for, 130
  in people, 131
Analogy, 245
Analysis of text, 28
ATRANS, 34, 36
ATTEND, 35
Automatic reorganization, 138
Automatic vs. conscious processes, 245

B

BORIS, 231
Breadth-first search, 58

C

CA, 31, 200
CD (*see* conceptual dependency)
CP, 35
CANCAUSE, 36
Canonical representation, 33, 37
Category for retrieval, 13
  specification of, 12–14
  selection of, 12–14
  choice of, 14
Categories
  conceptual, 18
    indexing in, 19
  hierarchical organization of, 191
Causal chains, 36
Causal chain construction, 50
Causal link, 44
Causal syntax, 36, 37
Characteristic events, 83
Charts (*see* maps)
Choosing indices, 150–153
  algorithm for, 151
  memory support for, 151–152
Classifying documents, 235
Clustering, 235
  in information retrieval, 235
Cognitive economy, 244
Collapsing sub-MOPs, 177, 191
  problems with, 178
Combinatorial explosion
  control of, 153
Component instantiation, 200
Component instantiation strategies, 61, 75, 84, 94
  input and output, 77
  sources of guidance, 76
Component-to-context instantiation strategies, 14, 96, 239
  choice of, 97

Computer science, 24
Conceptual categories, 12, 30, 33
Conceptual dependency, 31, 33, 34, 36, 50, 195
Conceptual memory, 29
  organization of, 30, 31, 231
  retrieval from, 232–234
Conceptual primitives, 37
Conceptual representation, 30
Conceptual structures
  varying uses, 232
Consistency judgements, 246
Constraints
  hierarchy of, 78
  on indexing, 39
  provided by people, 25
Content frame, 39
  refinement of, 41
Context construction (*see also* alternate-context search), 52, 95
  based on previous context, 203
  implications of, 108
  in people, 107
  memory support for, 103
Context for search, 52, 95, 96
  choice of, 52
Context instantiation strategies, 230
  inference types, 89
  steps of, 88
Context-to-context instantiation strategies, 61, 75, 85–94
Context specification, 55
Conversation, 51, 247, 249
Cross indexing, 43, 142
Cues, 52, 109, 238
CyFr, 194, 207, 208, 209, 211
CYRECV, 207, 208–212, 226
CYRUS, 4, 5, 19, 20, 23, 26, 27, 29, 33, 40, 43, 46, 50, 80, 81, 85, 96, 98, 99, 102, 116, 117, 119, 121, 123, 124, 131, 133, 134, 166, 169, 172, 175, 180, 182–190, 194–226, 231, 234, 236, 240, 243, 248
  an iterative process, 243
  answer formulation, 206–207
  as a framework for learning, 250
  as a model of people, 242–243
  as a tool, 22, 24
  component instantiation, 199
  context construction, 199
  creating indexes, 215
  creating new E-MOPs, 215, 219
  differences in two memories, 221
  E-MOPs, 194–198, 199
  E-MOP classifications, 196
  elaboration, 200
  evolution of memory, 182–190
  executive search strategies, 200
  failure of, 120
  generalizations, 224–226
  generalization refinement, 216
  implications of overgeneralization, 187
  integrating new events, 212–213
  memory update, 207–221
  modes of input, 207
  overgeneralization, 185
  parsing questions, 200
  predictive power, 188
  psychological issues, 243
  QA, 217, 220
  question categories, 206
  recognizing if an event is in memory, 212–213
  recovery from overgeneralization, 188
  reference resolution, 201–202
  reminding, 215, 218, 219
  relationship to psychology, 228–231
  retrieval in question answering, 198–207
  time as a retrieval context, 205
  traversal/elaboration, 199
  using previous context, 203–205

D

Data base, 13, 23, 24, 25, 31, 109, 227, 248
  retrieval, 49
  management, 236–237
Default information, 89
Deriving features, 14, 63
Descriptions, 228
Dialog (*see also* conversation), 249
Dialog context, 246
Differences, 20
Differentiation, 19, 26
  of similar concepts, 10, 15
Differentiating features, 11, 12
Directed retrieval, 39, 55, 69, 238, 239
Directing memory search, 14
Discriminability, 142, 143, 239
Discrimination nets, 229, 230
Domain relevant criteria, 38

E

E-MOPs (*see also* MOPs), 11, 18, 20, 37, 38, 39, 40, 43, 230, 244, 245
  classifications of, 153–163
  components, 46
  in CYRUS, 194–198
  monitoring norms, 177
  relationships of features to, 165
  relationships to other E-MOPs, 44–47
  representing events in, 71
E-MOP categories, 154
E-MOP creation, 167–171
E-MOP refinement, 171
Ease of retrieval, 241
Economy of storage, 74
Elaboration, 14, 16, 18, 19, 27, 52, 53, 59, 60, 74, 87, 183, 188, 190, 230, 243
  appropriate application of, 62
  direction of, 64
  faulty, 190
  in IR, 235
  in people, 67
  of event components, 76
  types of, 65
Elaboration/traversal (*see also* traversal/elaboration)
  dialog between, 64
ENABLE, 36
Enabling events, 92
Encoding, 25
Encoding specificity, 241
Enumeration, 7, 9, 19, 23, 25, 43
  strategies, 83–85
  well-ordered, 67
EPAM, 229, 230
Episodes
  internal structure of, 189
Episodic context, 203
  reconstruction of, 113
  search of, 203
Episodic memory, 244
  organization, 248
  structures, 23
Episodic Memory Organization Packets (*see also* E-MOPs), 38
Episodic and generic memory, 240, 243, 244
Era, 83, 247
Errors, 6
  suppression of, 27
Event components, 60
Event containment, 90–92
Event contexts, 60
Exceptions to rules, 248
Executive search strategies, 17, 52, 112, 132, 135, 238
  implications of, 132
  steps of, 113
  the need for them, 180
EXPEL, 35
Experts, 137
Expert systems, 247, 248–249
Expertise
  relationship to previous experience, 240
Explanation, 249

F

Fact retrieval, 247–248
  intelligent, 3, 19, 23, 27, 227, 247, 250
Failure-based memory, 249
False data, 25
False generalization (*see also* generalization), 173, 191
False recall, 6, 190
False starts, 9, 10
Features
  enumeration of, 66
  generalization of, 63
  inference of, 66
  specialization of, 63
  specification of, 66
  types of, 64
  values of, 64
Feedback, 249, 250
Feeling of knowing, 71
Find-from-Enabled-Events, 129
Find-from-Enablements, 128
Find-from-Following-Events, 129
Find-from-IMOP, 121, 199
Find-from-Larger-Episodes, 114, 121, 122, 199
Find-from-Preceding-Events, 127
Find-from-Preconditions, 127
Find-from-Reasons, 126
Find-from-Results, 128
Find-from-Seq-of-Events, 115, 199
Find-from-Standardizations, 118, 132, 199
First-person memory, 245
Focusing, 7

Forgetting, 9, 25, 48, 68, 109, 132, 187, 188, 189–190, 229, 237–238, 241, 242, 243, 244
in CYRUS, 187
Frames, 28, 138, 231
Frequency, 23, 246
FRUMP, 20, 28, 31, 194, 207, 208, 213, 218, 223, 226, 231
FRUMP-CYRUS hookup, 207, 208–212

G

Generalization, 19, 29, 138, 173, 191, 239, 243
arguments for, 180–182
control of, 138
direction of, 139
in CYRUS, 172
in prediction, 171
incomplete, 173
initial, 172, 173–174
recovery from false or bad ones, 139, 178, 179
refinement of, 171, 172, 173, 175–182
role of, 139
Generalized episodes, 38
Generalized knowledge, 17, 18, 19, 25, 33, 39, 47, 71, 87
derivation of, 139
dynamic nature of, 139
retrieval of, 69
organization of, 240
Generate and test, 76
Generating default answers, 181
Generic events, 244, 245
Generic memory, 26
Goals, 23, 231
Goal related knowledge structures, 231
GRASP, 35

H

Hierarchy, 20, 41
conceptual, 104
functional, 106
MOP/sub-MOP, 40
Human protocols, 5, 7, 9, 13, 15, 16, 24, 67, 75, 107, 110, 130, 131
context construction in, 107
elaboration in, 67

I

IM, 35
IMOP, 43, 121, 195
Implicit information
retrieval of, 31
Important feature selection, 242
Incorrect cues, 243
Incorrectly specified questions, 68
Index fitting, 15, 62, 63, 74
Index selection, 55, 56, 165
uses for, 141
Indexing
by differences in E-MOPs, 38
constraints on, 19
control of, 181, 191
controlling combinatorial explosion, 139
functions of, 139
in E-MOPs, 11, 41
initial, 166
monitoring of, 177
roles of, 142
Indices
creation of, 166
E-MOP, 11
monitoring of, 173
nature of, 65
selection of, 55, 56, 165
Infer-Country, 61
Infer-from-Location, 102
Infer-from-Participants, 97, 98, 99
as used by people, 107–108
Infer-from-Time-Specifications, 103
Infer-from-Topic, 97, 100
Inference, 25, 28, 29, 30, 31, 32, 33, 70
storage of, 33
Inferring plausible features, 190
Inferential analysis, 233
Inferential knowledge, 13
Information retrieval, 234–236, 247–248
INGEST, 34
Inheritance, 8, 28, 104
INITIATE, 36
IPP, 31, 232
INSTANCE-OF, 8
Instantiate-Enabled-Events, 93
Instantiate-Enablements, 92
Instantiate-Following-Events, 93, 126, 127, 128
Instantiate-Larger-Episodes, 86, 90, 92, 115, 122

Instantiate-Preceding-Events, 128, 129
Instantiate-Preconditions, 92
Instantiate-Results, 93
Instantiate-Seq-of-Events, 90, 91, 121, 122
Instantiate-Standardizations, 94, 118
Instantiation strategies, 15, 52, 60, 75, 135
 for location, 78
 for participants, 80
 for time, 82
 functions of, 76
Integrated approach, 25–26
Integration of events into memory, 19, 25
Intentional MOP (*see also* IMOPs), 43
Interference, 9, 229
ISA hierarchy, 8

K

Key words, 31, 234
Key word systems, 30
Knowledge structures, 28, 29, 138

L

Lack of knowledge inference, 70, 234
LEADTO, 36
Learning, 29, 37, 38, 137, 247, 249–250
Lexical organization, 30
Locations
 used in context construction, 101

M

MAINCON, 196
Maintaining accessibility, 239–240
Maps, 83–85
 application of, 67
MBUILD, 35, 36
Memory
 as a process, 25
 as a store, 25
 associative, 229
 computer, 14
 conceptual, 227
 controlling growth of, 19
 episodic, 23, 48
 episodic vs. semantic, 47–48
 factual, 23
 generic and episodic, 26
 human vs. computer, 23–25
 long term, 19, 35, 50, 227, 233, 246, 247
 organization of, 26
  maintenance of, 137
 reconstructive, 5–6, 22, 23, 227, 228, 229
 reorganization of, 20
 rote, 23
 search of (*see also* retrieval), 50
 semantic, 23, 48
Memory Organization Packets (*see also* MOPs and E-MOPs), 230
Memory update, 138
 and understanding, 138
Meta-level information, 240
Mistaken presuppositions, 68
MOPs (*see also* E-MOPs), 38, 39, 230, 231, 232
Most general description of a feature, 148
MOVE, 35
Ms. Malaprop, 28
MTRANS, 35, 210

N

Narrowing concept, 9
Natural language query, 13, 30
Networks
 conceptual, 9
 locked conceptual, 11
 semantic, 8
New subcategories
 creation of, 139
Norms
 used in recognizing differences, 144–146
 used in noticing similarities, 138

O

Obscure event, 130
Occupational activities, 159
Organization
 conceptual, 4, 8
 memory, 4, 5, 18–19, 20, 26, 33
  supporting reconstructive retrieval, 6–12
Overgeneralization (*see also* generalization), 173

P

Paired associate learning, 229
PAM, 231, 233
Partial matching, 68
Participant specifications
 used in context construction, 97

Personal relationships
  used in context construction, 99
Phantom event, 25
PHLUENT, 207
Phrase formation, 235
Plan, 233
Plan boxes, 231
Plausible description, 9
Plausible-index generation, 15, 62, 74
Plausible reasoning, 234
Plausible scenarios, 71
Political activities, 156
Potential generalizations, 175
Potential predictive power, 149
Potential predictiveness of features, 150
Practice, 243
Preceding events, 92
Preconditions, 92
Predictability, 239
Prediction, 76, 138
  context-related, 150
Predictive power, 239
  as criterion for choosing indices, 163
  monitoring of, 173
  of features and indices, 148
Predictive power judgements
  maintenance of, 180
Primitives, 33, 34
Process model, 24, 25
PROPEL, 34
Protocol (*see* human protocols)
Psychology, 24, 250
  issues in, 227
Psychological literature, 24
Psychological issues, 243–245
Psychological model, 25
Psychologists, 26, 29
PTRANS, 34, 210

Q

QA, 20
Question answering, 29, 48–50, 198, 227, 233
Question concept (*see also* target event), 49, 198
Question category, 50

R

REASON, 36
Recall, 242
  clustering in, 245
Recall intrusion, 190
Recall and recognition, 241–242
Recency, 23, 246
Recency and frequency judgements, 242
Recognition, 241
  false alarms in, 245
Recognition confusion, 190
Reconstruction, 7, 9, 11, 72, 76, 113, 188, 190, 233, 242
  control of, 9
  of enabling events, 125
  of larger episodes, 120
  of preceding events, 125
  of resulting events, 128
  of sequence of events, 115
Reconstructive memory, 23, 227, 228, 229
  in people, 5–6, 22
Reconstructive retrieval, 237, 238, 241, 243, 246, 250
Reconstructive search, 20
Rehearsal, 246
Relational data base model, 236, 237
Remembering, 138, 250
Reminding, 3, 167, 168, 249
  and generalization, 169
Representations of meaning, 30
RESULT, 36
Retrieval, 25
  confusion in, 6
  directed, 11, 12
  failure of, 25, 243
  from an E-MOP, 55–58
  in people, 250
  interferences, 190
  strategies for, 52
    application of, 239
    control of, 246
  the process, 53, 96, 112
Role themes, 83
Rule application, 248

S

Salience, 239
SAM, 28, 231, 233
Schemata, 26
  change over time, 26
  in organizing individual items with respect to each other, 26
  organizing, 26
SCHOLAR, 233

Scripts, 23, 28, 37, 38, 43, 50, 195, 196, 200, 231, 233
Search, 18
  sequential, 9
Search strategies (*see* executive strategies)
Semantic memory, 244
Similarity, 30, 31, 48, 74
  as basis for generalization, 168–171
  as constraint, 19
  coincidental, 175
  recognition of, 33
  role of, 244
Simple MOPs (*see also* sMOPs), 43, 195
Simulating intelligence, 24
Specifying details, 7
Sketchy script, 208
S-MOP (*see also* simple MOPs), 38, 121
Social activities, 161
Social protocol, 37
SPEAK, 35
Specialization, 170
Spreading activation, 229
Standard methods, 93
Stereotypic situations (*see* scripts)
Storage, 25
Subindexing, 142

T

Target concept (*see* target event)
Target event, 50, 55, 57, 198
Term weighting, 235
Themes, 23
Third-person memory, 245
Time
  used in context construction, 102
Topic specifications
  used in context construction, 100
TOPs, 231
Transformation of features, 63
Traversal, 8, 10, 11, 53, 55–58, 74, 96, 230, 237
  as a recursive process, 58
  directed, 11
  downward, 14
  failure of, 59, 62
  lateral, 17
  parallel, 58
Traversal/elaboration, 65, 199, 234, 239
  failure of, 111
  implications of, 68
  in people, 68

U

Undergeneralization, 173
Understanding, 3, 23, 30, 37, 39, 48, 138, 182
  integrated, 232
  natural language, 23, 28, 50, 244
  story, 231
Uniqueness
  of features and indices, 147
UPI, 20

V

Vance activities, 158
Verbal learning, 229
Verification, 27, 242

W

Well-structured concepts, 7

Printed in the USA/Agawam, MA
April 28, 2014
588515.005